BLESSED ARE THE PEACEMAKERS:

A THEOLOGICAL ANALYSIS OF THE THOUGHT OF HOWARD THURMAN AND MARTIN LUTHER KING, JR.

C. Anthony Hunt

BLESSED ARE THE PEACEMAKERS:
A THEOLOGICAL ANALYSIS OF THE
THOUGHT OF HOWARD THURMAN
AND MARTIN LUTHER KING, JR.
by C. Anthony Hunt
The Rhodes-Fulbright Library series

ISBN: 978-1-55605-381-8

Library of Congress Control Number: 2005927337

WYNDHAM HALL PRESS
Lima, Ohio 45806
www.wyndhamhallpress.com

Printed in The United States of America

Table of Contents

ACKNOWLEDGEMENTS

This book is the result of more than twelve years of advanced formal theological studies and research at Wesley Theological Seminary, St. Mary's Seminary and University, and the Graduate Theological Foundation.

I offer words of profound appreciation to Dr. Cecil Gray of Gettysburg College, my ordinarius for this Doctor of Philosophy dissertation, and to Dr. John Richardson, advisor for my Doctor of Ministry project at the Graduate Theological Foundation. Dr. Gray offered invaluable intellectual and spiritual guidance, insight and encouragement at the more difficult junctures of this project while in its dissertation phase. Many of the ideas developed herein were conceived in discussions with Dr. Richardson regarding the historic nature, current state, and future prospects of the Christian church – with particular focus on the need for a heightened understanding of the spirituality incumbent in the church.

I also offer words of gratitude to the late Dr. Mancur Olson, former Distinguished Professor of Economics at the University of Maryland, College Park, and Dr. James C. Logan, E. Stanley Jones Professor of Evangelism and Theology, emeritus, at Wesley Theological Seminary, Washington, DC, both of whom graciously allowed me to serve as a graduate teaching assistant. My gratitude is also extended to Dr. Calvin Morris, my pastor, mentor and teacher at Gibbons United Methodist Church in Brandywine, Maryland, and the former executive director of the Martin Luther King, Jr. Center for Nonviolent Social Change in Atlanta, Georgia.

I owe a debt of gratitude for the collegiality of the faculty, students and staff of the Ecumenical Institute of Theology, St. Mary's Seminary and University in Baltimore, Maryland where I am privileged to teach, and the place where many of the ideas contained in this project were presented in one form or another.

To faculty, students and staff colleagues at Wesley Theological Seminary, Goucher College, American University, the McKendree College of Religion and Africa University (Zimbabwe) where I have also been privileged to teach and serve over the past several years, I am thankful.

I am grateful for the collegiality of those who are a part of the Multi-Ethnic Center for Ministry of the United Methodist Church, where I served as executive director for six years, and the Baltimore Harford District of the United Methodist Church where I am currently privileged to serve in ministry, and where we are challenged daily to live out the ideals of "peaceful community" contained in this project.

And to colleagues at the Graduate Theological Foundation, and Princeton's Center of Theological Inquiry, I am indebted for how our interaction in various seminars has served to challenge and deepen my thinking with regard to the opportunity for peace in the church and society.

To my wife, Lisa, and our children – Marcus, Kristen and Brian, for your unconditional love, prayers, patience, support, and understanding during the many hours I have had to be alone while researching and writing this project – words cannot convey the depth and breadth of my love and appreciation. And to my parents and grandparents, my siblings, and extended family, I offer thanks to each of you for continuing to teach me the ways of peace.

Finally, I offer praise to God who is constantly leading me toward new, and more exciting and challenging avenues of peace and community in my daily living.

INTRODUCTION

In this dissertation, I have attempted to accomplish the following:
A. to offer a biblical and theological analysis of conceptions of peaceful community;
B. to provide an historical overview of the spiritual and intellectual development of Howard Thurman and Martin Luther King, Jr.;
C. to analyze the development of the conceptions of peaceful community in the thinking of Thurman and King;
D. to determine the impact of the thinking and action of Mohandas Gandhi on the development of Thurman's and King's thought;
E. to analyze, through comparison and contrast, the conceptualities and nuancing of peaceful community in the thinking of Thurman and King; and
F. to identify and develop ten principles which serve as the theoretical framework for a contemporary model and orthopraxis for developing peaceful community in the church and society in the new millennium.

I. Statement of Problem

Howard Thurman and Martin Luther King Jr. were two of the seminal Christian religious figures of the twentieth century. The ministries and thinking of Thurman and King transcended various categories and characterizations of religious and public life, and their work continues to impact the entirety of the Christian community and the broader society into the 21st century. Thurman and King were both men of peace. As peacemakers, they sought – through their words and actions – to invite persons to live out the teachings of Christ who, in the Sermon on the Mount, offered a promise for those who would choose the road of peacefulness: "Blessed are the peacemakers, for they will be called children of God." (Matthew 5:9)

The prophetic voices of King and Thurman regarding the need for peace, and the Christian imperative to develop peaceful community, offer insights into new possibilities of community-building for the church and society in the new millennium. In a world in which religion often sponsors hatred and violence, it is important to revisit Thurman and King. Their message of love – as embodied in their unique visions of peaceful community - has a timeless and universal significance that is brought to light clearly in these times, as society seeks to forge alternatives to war in the conflict between nations, and the violence that afflicts so many communities, as seen in the ongoing proliferation of domestic, racial, class and ethnic conflicts.

Howard Thurman and Martin Luther King, Jr. were Christian ministers and social prophets who made significant contributions to religious and social life, in both the North American and global context. The search for peaceful community was a life-long quest for both men, and served to form the foundation of their respective ministries.

Although Howard Thurman is the lesser known of the two, his life and ministry have influenced many highly visible individuals – including King – in American society and the global community at-large.[1]

The contributions made by Howard Thurman and Martin Luther King, Jr. toward the development of peaceful community in human affairs is related to the concept of what theologians James Cone, Olin Moyd and Gustavo Gutierrez - among others - have referred to as "orthopraxis." Orthopraxis is a principle of thought and belief leading to action. In orthopraxis, right belief is inextricably related to right action. Thus, nonviolent social resistance, as a philosophical construct and means toward community-building, is militantly aggressive while remaining nonviolent.

James Cone (Union Theological Seminary), in his book *For My People: Black Theology and the Black Church,* offers insight on the matter of orthopraxis:

We do not begin our theology with a reflection on divine revelation as if the God of our faith is separate from the suffering of our people. We do not believe that revelation is a depository of fixed doctrines or an objective word of God that is then applied to the human situation. On the contrary, we contend that there is no truth outside or beyond the concrete historical events in which persons are engaged as agents. Truth is found in the histories, cultures, and religions of our people. Our focus on social and religio-cultural analyses separates our theological enterprise from the progressive and abstract theologies of Europe and North America. It also illuminates the reasons why *orthoproaxis* in contrast to *orthodoxy* has become for many of us the criterion of theology.[2]

Olin Moyd (St. Mary's Seminary and University), in *Sacred Art: Preaching and Theology in the African-American Tradition,* offers additional analysis on orthopraxis as a methodological concern in doing theology:

> Practical theology is a theology put together on the assembly line of existence in the experience of a pilgrim people. Its genesis, its beginning and development, was in orthopraxis rather than in orthodoxy. Orthodoxy is concerned with right beliefs and right doctrines, while orthopraxis is concerned with right action and right involvement in God's plan of redemption.[3]

Gustavo Gutierrez, in *A Theology of Liberation*, offers perspectives on the purpose of orthopraxis as it relates to doing theology:

> The intention... is not to deny the meaning of *orthodoxy,* understood as a proclamation of and reflection on statements considered to be true. Rather the goal is to balance and even to reject the primacy and almost exclusiveness which doctrine has enjoyed in Christian life and above all to modify the emphasis, often obsessive, upon the attainment of an orthodoxy which is nothing more than fidelity to an obsolete tradition or a debatable interpretation. In a more positive vein, the intention is to recognize the work and importance of concrete behavior, or deeds, or action, or praxis in the Christian life.[4]

This study will offer an analysis of the contributions of Thurman and King to Christian thought, conflict resolution and community-building through their orthopragmatic appropriation of non-violent social action.

Peter Paris, in *The Social Teaching of the Black Churches*, suggests that the black churches, under the norm of the black Christian tradition, are characterized by their common quest for human freedom and justice – that is the equality of all persons under God.[5] Martin Luther King, Jr. offered that "true peace is not merely the absence of tension, but it is the presence of justice."[6] Both Thurman and King epitomized the quest for freedom and justice, and sought to bring to bear the spiritual, social and political resources of the church and society upon the incumbent problems of injustice in ways which constructively addressed the divisiveness extant in religion and culture, thus moving toward the fulfillment of the vision of equality for all persons.   This quest for freedom and justice – germane to the black church out of which both Howard Thurman and Martin Luther King, Jr. came – will be a principle that underlies this study.

II. Review of Sources of Information

The primary sources of information utilized throughout this study are the numerous writings, speeches, sermons and discussions of Howard Thurman and Martin Luther King, Jr. in which the concept of peaceful community is addressed. The public ministry and life of both Thurman and King reflected a persistent yearning for a peaceful society. Their prophetic and passionate plea for peace was embodied in their work. Both were prolific writers and public speakers. Howard Thurman was the author of twenty-two books, and more than forty-five published articles. This, according to Luther E. Smith, Jr. (Emory University), has distinguished him as the most prolific black writer on religion.[7]   Much of Thurman's work dealt with the mystical nature of religious life, and yet, his was a constant attempt to link spirituality from mystical perspective, with prophetic witness and the imperative for social justice and unity among persons of all races, creeds, and labels. Historian Lerone Bennett, Jr. suggests that Thurman's book, *Jesus and the Disinherited,* is perhaps the best systematic exposition of the philosophy of non-violence in a Christian context[8].

Martin Luther King, Jr. was the author of at least six full-length published texts, which served to expound upon his ethical paradigm of Christian love, non-violence and community in the 1950s and 1960s. King was also a regular contributor to periodicals such as *The Christian Century and Ebony Magazine.* Some of King's most prominent work is found in his sermons and public speeches, which have been compiled in many published forms since his assassination. Perhaps his seminal work is *Strength to Love,* a compilation of sermons, in which King focuses on many of the nuances and dimensions of the Christian love-ethic. Also of note and of particular relevance to this project is *Stride Toward Freedom*, written in 1958, in which King outlines the six principles and characteristics which serve as the foundation of his philosophy of non-violent resistance and the practice of community-building.

III. Review of the Work of Other Investigators

Numerous works have been produced by writers and scholars who address, both directly and indirectly, their understanding of the search and calling of Howard Thurman and Martin Luther King, Jr. for nonviolence, peace and community. Of specific note with regard to this project is the work of Luther E. Smith, Jr., the author of *Howard Thurman: The Mystic as Prophet.* Smith considers the life of Thurman and analyzes the dual attributes of his mystical nature and prophetic witness. *A Strange Freedom: The Best of Howard Thurman On Religious Experience and Public Life,* edited by Walter Earl Fluker (Morehouse College) and Catherine Tumber (Harvard University), offers a comprehensive explication of the thinking of Thurman with regard to the nexus of Christian spirituality and social witness. Alton Pollard in *Mysticism and Social Change: The Social Witness of Howard Thurman,* offers an analysis of the thinking of Thurman by placing his work within the context of "mystic-activism." According to Pollard, Thurman serves as an archetype of the potential of mysticism as a discomforting, yet compelling and principled, call to action. Finally, in *Good News for the Disinherited: Howard Thurman on Jesus of Nazareth and Human Liberation,* Alonzo Johnson – with Thurman's seminal work,

Jesus and the Disinherited as the backdrop - offers an analysis of Thurman's Christology in light of the black religious experience. Kenneth L. Smith (Crozier Theologial Seminary) and Ira G. Zepp (Western Maryland College), in *Search for the Beloved Community: The Thinking of Martin Luther King, Jr. (*1974*),* examine the thought of Martin Luther King, Jr. and the influences that shaped his thinking. Zepp wrote his doctoral dissertation on the intellectual sources of King's thought. Smith was one of King's seminary professors and, along with Zepp, offers detailed analysis of the intellectual sources found in King's doctoral dissertation ("A Comparison of the Conceptions of God in the Thinking of Paul Tillich and Henry Nelson Wieman," Boston University, 1955), with particular emphasis on the influence of Mohandas Gandhi. Robert E. Franklin (Interdenominational Theological Center), in *Liberating Visions: Human Fulfillment and Social Justice in African American Thought,* places King in conversation with three other seminal black figures, Booker T. Washington, W. E. B. Dubois, and Malcolm X, and offers significant insight into King's moral vision as rooted in the sources of his spiritual and intellectual development, resulting in his development and actualization of the notion of the *integrative person.* Noel Leo Erskine (Emory University) in *King Among the Theologians* presents a thoroughly researched analysis of the major influences on King's theology, which resulted in a synthesis of various ideologies into a pragmatic philosophical/theological/ethical framework. Erskine places King in conversation with some of the 20th Century's most prominent theologians – Paul Tillich, Karl Barth, and James Cone. Furthermore, Erskine posits that womanist theology provides an insightful contemporary critique of King's thought and helps supply a critical missing element in King's vision – the explicit acknowledgment of the place of women in the *Beloved Community.* Finally, the three-volume compilation, *The Papers of Martin Luther King, Jr.,* edited by Clayborne Carson, offers – through writings of and about King – an exhaustive view of King's life - from his birth in Atlanta, Georgia in 1929 to his assassination in Memphis, Tennessee in 1968.

In seeking to arrive at a synthesis of the thinking of Thurman and King with regard to the development of peaceful community, several works related to the thinking of Mohandas Gandhi will be cited throughout. Included among these are the following: *The Conquest of Violence: The Gandhian Philosophy of Conflict* (Joan V. Bondurant), *The Way to God* (Mohandas K. Gandhi), *Raising Up a Prophet: The African American Encounter with Gandhi* (Sudarshan Kapur), *Gandhi: Portrayal of a Friend* (E. Stanley Jones), and *Gandhi's Truth: On the Origins of Militant Nonviolence* (Erik H. Erikson).

Walter Earl Fluker in *They Looked for a City: A Comparative Analysis of the Ideal of Community in the Thought of Howard Thurman and Martin Luther King, Jr.* (1989), offers a comprehensive historical analysis of the general conceptuality of "community" in the thought of Thurman and King. While focusing on the ideal of community as "the defining motif in the lives and thoughts of Thurman and King,"[9] Fluker's work does not offer specific theological or sociological analysis of "peaceful community." That particular analysis is the proposition and province of this dissertation. Furthermore, in light of the scholarship that has heretofore offered a comparative analysis of the work of Thurman and King, this dissertation, while offering historical perspective, will seek to provide contemporary insights as to implications and applications of Thuman and King's work for the future of the church and society in the 21st century.

IV. Methodological Approach

The overall epistemological concern of this study involves engaging approaches to rationalizing knowledge about the contemporary Christian church within the context of society in general. Through an historical analysis of the life and works of Howard Thurman and Martin Luther King, Jr., new insights emerge as to ways of comprehending and appropriating peaceful community in a postmodern context.

There are essentially three elements of the methodology that will be employed in engaging in an historical and theological analysis of the thinking of Thurman and King. First, the approach will be expository. By unpacking and examining pertinent information from primary works of Thurman and King, along with select secondary works that have been written about them over the past forty-five years, a sense of their respective conceptions of peaceful community will be extracted. The exposited information will reflect the breadth of the lives and work of Thurman and King - from childhood to death – with particular focus on the development of their respective conceptions of peaceful community. Secondly, the approach will be comparative. This analysis will compare and contrast how Thurman and King came to understand the notion of peaceful community within the context of religious and secular American life. The comparative analysis will seek to provide co-herency not only with regard to the conception of peaceful commu-nity, but relative to their respective approaches to appropriating these perspectives into a workable orthopraxis.   Finally, a dialectical/ critical approach will be employed throughout this study. While this work is essentially an historical and theological analysis of the thinking of Thurman and King, numerous other disciplines will be drawn on throughout. At various points, the project will engage - in an integrative, praxeological and synthetic manner – the disciplines of sociology, anthropology, philosophy, history, and literature.

The dialectical/critical approach will seek to integrate and synthe-size historical data on the lives and work of Thurman and King by overlaying this information with interdisciplinary analysis, offering constructive critique and contemporary perspective with the objec-tive of arriving at a framework/model that can be useful in develop-ing peaceful community in the 21st century.   This approach will also engage various theological perspectives relative to the work of Thurman and King. Reflection on black theology, liberation theol-ogy, spiritual theology, womanist and feminist perspectives, neo-pentecostalism and neo-evangelicalism help to ascertain how these various religio-spiritual perspectives may lead to a convergence of thought with regard to developing peaceful community from a Chris-tian perspective in the 21st century.

Relative to methodology, three overarching and interrelated questions arise: (1) What, in the individual and combined conceptualities and nuances in the thinking of Thurman and King, can be useful for the church and society today? (2) In what ways might their work be strengthened and/or re-appropriated? (3) What adjustments might be suggested to make their respective conceptions of peaceful community relevant orthopraxis in the postmodern reality of the 21st century?

As Thurman and King were products of African-American life, culture and religion, several general distinctives can be identified. First, African-American life, culture and religion is *organic* – alive and interrelated in simple-and-complex ways. Rather than being linear in perspective, African-American metaphysics – rooted in African cosmology - is essentially dynamic, with individual, family and community life intricately related.[10] In this perspective, in as much as God is transcendent, God is also immanent – integral to all that is life and living. Second, African-American life, culture and religion is *holistic*. Several scholars have offered that there can be very little that is distinguishable between the secular and the sacred in black life. Thus, spirituality is understood not only within the context of the church building or organized religion, but also as an "invisible institution" – often manifest in the rhythms, beats and life-patterns of the broader community. With regard to the matter of the holistic integration of the 'sacred' and the 'secular' in the black perspective, Newell S. Booth, Jr., in an article entitled "An Approach to African Religion," offers the following perspective:

> It also appears that the description of religion in terms of a "sacred" reality which is opposed to the "profane" is based on non-African ways of thinking. If an important characteristic of African religion is its pervasive quality, then there are few phenomena that can be identified as distinctively sacred in the sense that they are separated from the rest of life. The whole of life is sacred…"[11]

Black life, culture and religion is also holistic in that it seeks to dynamically address a plethora of life matters for black individuals, families, communities, and extant institutions. While being concerned with issues related to mercy and compassion, the spirituality of black persons is simultaneously concerned with matters of justice and righteousness; and while being pietistic (and individualistic) in perspective, African American life, culture and religion is at the same time corporate (communal).

In this study, several foundational principles emerge and will be explicated and utilized throughout. These principles are significant – even pivotal – as they shed light on the distinctiveness of African-American life, culture and religion, as the same relate to the search for peaceful community in the thinking of Thurman and King. The first principle is Howard Thurman's perspective and praxis of *multicultural community* - what he termed the "search for common ground." While, today, the term "multicultural" has become popularized, and in many respects politicized, Thurman viewed multiculturalism as a way of life – essentially a "means of grace" - for the church and society. For Thurman, multiculturalism was not a societal option – among the many ways that society might be shaped; it was necessary for the actualization of authentic community. The second principle explicated throughout is Martin Luther King, Jr.'s yearning for *beloved community.* Much like Thurman's perspectives on multicultural community, King viewed the beloved community as essential to the realization of authentic community through overcoming the various barriers that served to separate persons in the church and society.

A third principle, closely related to Thurman's construct and praxis of multiculturalism and King's notion of beloved community, is *satyagraha* (truth-force), which emerged in the thinking of Mohandas Gandhi and served to provide the philosophical foundation for Gandhi's approach to nonviolent social resistance in India's struggle for freedom in the early 20th century. As both Thurman and King had the opportunity to encounter and engage Gandhi's thinking with regard to *satyagraha*, each would affirm Gandhi's impact in helping to codify and synthesize their respective approaches to community-building.

The fourth principle related to African-American life, culture and religion, with regard to the search for peaceful community, is the African (Egyptian) concept-and reality, *MAAT*. In "Toward a Sociology of MAATIAN Ethics," Maulana Karenga (California State University, Long Beach) points out that *MAAT* is expressed in the seven cardinal virtues of righteousness, truth, justice, peace, balance, reciprocity, and order. It can be understood as both a standard and an invitation. *MAAT* is a standard for living – a lifestyle and path of righteousness, and is an invitation into a right relationship with God, self and community. In addition to being a right way for living (in an ethical sense), in ancient Egyptian society (circa 2750 through 2180 B.C.E.), *MAAT* was understood as embodying a sense of being - the cosmic, natural, and social order established by God at the time of creation. *MAAT* is actualized in the fulfillment of human relationships. It is the recognition and pursuit of shared commitment to all creation in the cognitive and affective sense. *MAAT* is the basis for the existential unity between God and humanity. It is essentially seen in the context of Ptah-Hotep's urging that humans would strive for (practical and spiritual) excellence in all endeavors.[12]

MAAT is embodied implicitly in the thinking of both Howard Thurman and Martin Luther King, Jr. *MAATIAN* principles – especially peace and justice – are integral to the development of the respective ethical frameworks for peaceful community of Thurman and King. This matter will be revisited – as a point of synthesis - at various junctures throughout this project.

A principle that is closely related to *MAAT*, and which helps to place human connectedness – oneness, unity, globality and diversity - into context is the African concept, *UBUNTU*. It simply means "the quality of being human." *UBUNTU* manifests itself through various (humane) human acts, clearly visible in social, political and economic situations.

According to sociolinguist Buntu Mfenyana, "it runs through the veins of all Africans."[13] Lente-Louise Louw, in *Valuing Diversity,* elaborates on *UBUNTU* and states that the quality of being human for Africans is embodied in the oft-repeated proverb, "A person is a person through other people."[14] Louw continues:

> While this African proverb reveals a world view – a metaphysics - that we owe our self-hood to others, that we are first and foremost social beings, that, if you will, "no man is an island," or as the African might state, "One finger cannot pick up a grain" – *UBUNTU* is at the same time, a deeply personal philosophy that calls us to mirror our humanity for each other. To the observer, *UBUNTU* can be seen and felt in the spirit of willing participation, unquestioning cooperation, warmth, openness, and personal dignity demonstrated by the indigenous black population. From the cradle, every black child inculcates these qualities so that by the time adulthood is reached; the *UBUNTU*

philosophy has become a way of being.[15]

South African Anglican Archbishop and Nobel Peace Prize recipient Desmond Tutu emphasizes the criticality of *UBUNTU* when he states, "You might have much of the world's riches, and might have a portion of authority, but if you have no *UBUNTU,* you do not have much." Ultimately, *UBUNTU* involves conceiving ways in which persons who are "strangers" in socio-cultural, political and religious contexts might discover the essence of the meaning of living in peaceful community.[16]

Though it seems that Howard Thurman and Martin Luther King, Jr. were not consciously or formally familiar with the African concepts-realities and values of *MAAT* and *UBUNTU,* these were nonetheless subconsciously and functionally at the core of the thinking and praxis of Thurman and King as they searched for peaceful community.   The ten principles for peaceful community that will be developed in Chapter Six of this project will be based on these concepts-realities and values, and will serve as a means of synthesis of the thinking of Thurman and King with regard to peaceful community.   The proposition is that the said ten principles might serve as the foundation of the model for developing peaceful community for the church and society in the new millennium.   The principles will be informed by several sources, including the following: (1) an historical and theological analysis of the conceptions and work of Thurman and King with regard to peaceful community; (2) analysis of the work of other investigators into the work of Thurman and King; and (3) analysis of various methods and models employed both within the Christian church and in the broader society in the search for peaceful community.

NOTES

[1] Walter Fluker, *They Looked For a City: A Comparative Analysis of the Ideal of Community in the Thought of Howard Thurman and Martin Luther King, Jr.* (New York: University Press of America, 1989), xi.

[2] James Cone, *For My People: Black Theology and the*

Black Church (Maryknoll, NY: Orbis, 1984), 148.

[3] Olin Moyd, *Sacred Art: Preaching and Theology in the African-American Tradition* (Valley Forge, PA: Judson Press, 1995), 35.

[4] Gustavo Gutierrez, *A Theology of Liberation* (Maryknoll, NY: Orbis Books, 1971), 8.

[5] Peter Paris, *The Social Teaching of the Black Churches* (Philadelphia, PA, Fortress Press, 1985), 15.

[6] Martin Luther King, Jr., quoted in the speech, "True Peace," Atlanta, July 5, 1962.

[7] Luther Smith, *Howard Thurman: The Mystic as Prophet* (Richmond, Indiana: Friends United Press, 1991), 13.

[8] Lerone Bennett, Jr., "Eulogy of Howard Thurman: Tributes to Genius," in *The African-American Pulpit* (Valley Forge, PA: Judson, Winter 2000-2001), 63.

[9] Fluker, 155.

[10] Peter Paris, *The Spirituality of African Peoples* (Minneapolis: Fortress, 1995), 25f. Paris offers an analysis of the interrelationships and interconnectedness of individual, family, community, and spiritual life in the African experience. Also see John Mbiti, *African Religions and Philosophy* (New York: Anchor Books, 1970).

[11] Newell S. Booth, "An Approach to African Religion," *African Religions: A Symposium*, ed. Newell S. Booth (New York: NOK Publishers, 1977), 16.

[12] Maulana Karenga, "Toward a Sociology of Maatian Ethics: Literature and Context," *Egypt Revisited,* ed. Ivan Van Sertima (New Bunswick: Transaction, 1989), pp. 373, 383.

[13] Lewis Brown Griggs and Lente-Louise Louw, *Valuing Diversity: New Tools for a New Reality* (New York: McGraw Hill, 1995), 159.

[14] Ibid.

[15] Ibid.

[16] Ibid.

CHAPTER ONE

BIBLICAL AND THEOLOGICAL
CONCEPTIONS OF PEACEFUL COMMUNITY

I. Biblical Origins of Peaceful Community

Humanity's longing for peace has its origins in the biblical narrative, which begins the book of Genesis. The first two chapters of Genesis describe a world created in peace and harmony, a unified world perfectly ordered according to the plan of God, a world with everything in right relationship, wholesome and good.

In Genesis 1:31, it is recorded: "God looked at everything God had made and found it very good." This primordial peace was soon fractured, however, and conflict began. In the course of time Cain brought an offering to the Lord from the fruit of the soil, while his brother Abel, for his part, brought one of the best firstlings of his flock. The Lord looked with favor on Abel and his offering, but on Cain and his offering God did not. Cain greatly resented this and was crestfallen...Cain said to Abel, "Let us go out in the field." When they were in the field, Cain attacked his brother Abel and killed him. (Genesis 4:3-5, 8)

The quest for peace, for a return to the uninjured wholeness of creation, is one of the deepest longings of humanity. It is a search for the essence and synthesis of human life, the harmony of all life's energies, and is based on the fundamental recognition that the divine intention is true; the world is indeed intended to be very good. Commitment to peace, then is not just one task among the many that humans are to engage. It is integral to the life of the world. The Psalmist clearly articulates the task of humanity: "Seek peace and pursue it." (Psalm 34:14) This is a theme that goes to the very heart of the identity of people of faith.   It is a commitment inspired by scriptural witness and vision, and not only guides daily lives but challenges persons to do more in the search for community. It is a vision that gives meaning to everything persons do as individuals.

II. Shalom: Peaceful Community in the Hebrew Tradition

Peace is a central theme of the biblical writings. The basic significance of *shalom* as faring well, prospering, goes far beyond the so-called negative concept of peace common to us, which means the absence of the open and collective use of violence; in thought under Greek influence, peace is simply the opposite of war.[1]

The biblical concept of peace (*shalom, eirene*) is an amazingly comprehensive term. It includes salvation, wholeness, integrity and healing. Healthy relationships – interpersonal, cultural, economic, social and environmental are implied. It is undivided integrity and oneness with God, inner peacefulness, and harmony in family, neighborhood, society and nations. Peace is the antithesis of disruption, alienation, separation and segregation. To wish someone *shalom* is to wish them perfect happiness (Isaiah 26:3), well-being, health and joy, as well as perfect relationships with God, neighbor and self. It is an all-embracing term expressing the original harmony of creation intended by God. (Genesis 1-2)[2]

With regard to understanding community, biblical theologian Walter Brueggemann shares that the central vision of world history in the Bible is that all of creation is one, every creature in community with every other, living in harmony and security toward the joy and well-being of every other creature.[3] Brueggemann continues by pointing out that s*halom* – the Hebrew concept of peace, salvation and wholeness – is the substance of the biblical vision of one community embracing all creation. Shalom refers to all those resources and factors that make communal harmony joyous and effective.

The term *shalom*, frequently rendered as peace, is one of the most common yet complex words of the Hebrew language. In its most elementary form, *shalom* is a salutation, a greeting that expresses a wish of peace and completeness for the other person. Another prevalent understanding of the word is that *shalom* is the total absence of strife or warfare. These are the most familiar usages, but they hardly exhaust the many nuances of the word. Derived from the Hebrew root SH-L-M, the word connotes not only the absence of war, but the conditions necessary for the state of peace and the feelings experienced when peace is actually attained.

In the Bible, the root SH-L-M appears to convey several meanings. In Genesis 33:18 when Jacob arrives in the city of Shechem, Scripture depicts him having arrived *shalem,* or safely. In Genesis 34:21, *shalem* with another individual (sh'lay-mim in plural form) implies a state of well-being in relationship. In this particular instance it is the sound relationship that comes from being an ally. Yet caution must be exercised, for those derived translations are not simply synonyms that can be freely interchanged. One can be "safe" even in the absence of peace, while the state of peace does not necessarily guarantee a person's *shalem,* safety or well-being.[4]

Shalom can also carry with it the implication of equity. Zechariah 8:16 says, "Speak the truth to each other, administer true and sound justice in the city gates." True and sound justice is not peace *per se,* particularly since a nation at war can still preserve a system of true and sound justice, but *misphat shalom* is certainly a prerequisite for the result of a society infused with shalom.[5]

In the Hebrew scriptures, peace is much more than the absence of war. It is a positive term signifying well-being and balance. For the Bible, peace is synonymous with prosperity. Psalm 122:7 offers a sense of the active presence of peace in the lives of people: "Peace within your walls, prosperity within your buildings." Peace means security; and for that reason, shalom is a component in the very name of the holy city *yeru' shalom, Jerusalem (peaceful city).* As a positive all-embracing reality, peace is synonymous with good (*tov*). The author of the Book of Genesis describes the order and harmony of creation. So, too, the psalmist wrote a masterful parallelism of Hebrew structure, "Turn away from evil and do good; seek peace and pursue it." (Psalm 34:14) Here the rejection of evil (*mera*) and the practice of good (*tov*) are related to peace (*shalom*) and the pursuit of peace.

Peace, in its biblical and theological context, is essentially to be viewed as a gift of God. "I will give peace in the land, and you shall lie down, and none shall make you afraid." (Leviticus 26:5-6) Peace is at the heart of God's promises and is the fruit of divine love for all creation. Although peace is human action, it remains, in its most foundational sense, a gift of God. Because peace is such a comprehensive reality, it is inextricably bound to other human values, i.e., truth, justice, freedom and love. For the prophet Isaiah, peace was "the enterprise of justice." (Isaiah 32:17) There cannot be peace in a world ruled by deception, violence, hatred, oppression and injustice.

The peace of the Kingdom of God is a richer concept, which combines inner peace with social and external peace. Eating and health are as much part a of *shalom* as community and hope. In *shalom* not only is violence between human beings overcome, but also economic need and exploitation, the lack of political freedom and psychological anxiety. Some Jewish rabbis said that *shalom* is a name of God.[6]

At many points the Bible speaks of the longing of the people for peace, for the end of state violence and of the hope for the 'Prince of Peace' who rules in such a way that 'peace will have no end.' (Isaiah 9:6f.) The Hebrew Bible indicates that God wants peace, and not the rule of force by arms and war, by saying that God not only converts human hearts but also reforges or destroys the weapons of violence, because these instruments of the rule of force, which we so often see as 'neutral', have in fact long possessed human hearts.[7]

When confronting the reality of a fractured world, the Hebrew concept of peace reveals itself to be both gift and vision. As divine gift, it transcends all human concepts and abilities; and as vision, it challenges each individual of faith to strive toward the glorious realization of God's own peace. War and the threat of war, violence in all its forms, injustice and aggression, mistrust and fear are prevalent among people of the world today, thus leading to a paucity of peace as a societal possession. Peace, however, is an integral part of the eschatological vision of the Bible – a vision which looks to the future in hope, and which is both an ideal to emulate and a goal to achieve. It is the vision that foresees the time when there will be no need for instruments of war, when "nation shall not lift sword against another," (Isaiah 2:4, Micah 4:3) and where God will speak directly to the people and "righteousness and peace will embrace each other." (Psalm 85:10-11) Then all creation will once again be made whole. This biblical vision of peace exists within a world marked by violence. Faithful believers live with the tension this creates, and at the same time are challenged to bring about this vision in history. This requires of persons a firm faith in the saving and healing power of God who has given life and who sustains all in divine and creative power. It also requires that persons become critically aware of the irrationality of war and violence.[8]

This vision is in fact eutopia (*eu – topos:* "a good place" or "a real place") - a place that can be and is meant to be for this real world. God's plan for the world is both a gift to be admired and a goal to be pursued.

The biblical prophets announced a kingdom of peace. But peace presupposes the establishment of justice: "Righteousness shall yield peace and its fruit shall be quietness and confidence forever." (Isa. 32:17; cf. also Ps. 85) This insinuates the defense of the rights of the poor, punishment of the oppressors, a life free from the fear of being enslaved by others, the liberation of the oppressed. Peace, justice, love, and freedom are not private realities; they are not only internal attitudes. They are social realties, implying historical liberation. A poorly understood spiritualization has often made persons forget the human consequences of the eschatological promises and the power to transform unjust social structures, which they imply. The elimination of misery and exploitation is a sign of the coming of the Kingdom of God. This will become a reality, according to the Book of Isaiah, when there is happiness and rejoicing among the people because "men shall build houses and live to inhabit them, plant vineyards and eat their fruit; they shall not build for others to inhabit nor plant for others to eat... My chosen shall enjoy the fruit of their labor" (65:21-22) because the fruit of their labor will not be taken from them. The struggle for a just world in which there is no oppression, servitude, or alienated work will signify the coming of the Kingdom of God. The Kingdom and social injustice are incompatible (cf. Isa. 29:18-19 and Matt. 11:5; Lev. 25:10ff. and Luke 4:16-21). "The struggle for justice," rightly asserts Dom Antonio Fragoso, "is also the struggle for the Kingdom of God."[9]

In the book of Judges (6:24), Gideon dedicates an altar to God and calls it *Adonai-shalom*, the Eternal is peace. God is peace; during creation the various elements of the universe were united and made suitable for sustaining life. God made peace in the high places, by uniting fire and water, and causing them to dwell together in harmony. (Job 25:2)   As creatures of God, the ability to unify creation can be an integral part of the collective human endeavor. When exercising our humanity, we arduously labor to bring a sense of *shalom,* completeness and wholeness to our lives, to our community, even through selfless deeds to those we do not know. Peace is a constant ideal, vision and striving of the human community, and can be realized if we are diligent "to seek and pursue it."

With this understanding, it is easier to comprehend the exhortation to "seek peace and pursue it." (Psalm 34:14)   If in fact peace is a state that is definable and attainable, if we are able to successfully seek peace, we are also encouraged to pursue it once it has been identified. The wisdom of the Bible knows and asserts that life is not simply war or peace, good or evil. Life does not consist exclusively of absolutes such as love or hate. Were peace merely the opposite of war, the absence of war would bring peace. While *shalom* frequently connotes peace, which is usually understood to be the absence of war, the Hebrew concept enables us to appreciate realistically that there are degrees of peace; *shalom* is a balance and harmonization of forces that are sometimes contradictory and often beyond human control.

The people of Israel realized that they had not yet achieved wholeness. They were not fully what they ought to be. They believed that they *once* were whole. They also believed that they would *once again* be whole – but that time was *not yet.* They saw the full reality of *shalom* as God's gift in the beginning, and that which they persistently yearned to attain. They saw *shalom* as God's eschatological gift at the end. Thus, *shalom* was an elusive reality for them. That is why Isaiah could speak of beating swords into plowshares, and also of beating plowshares into swords. *Shalom was in the beginning. It will be in the end. But it is not yet realized.*[10]

What then is actually suggested in the Psalmist's exhortation to "Seek peace and pursue it?" (Psalm 34:14) To "seek" means to be receptive to opportunities for making peace. This is consonant with the first section of verse 14, which states in the imperative form, "Depart (turn away) from evil and do good." In seeking, we "depart" or "turn away from" areas of life that are devoid of shalom, and courageously pursue peace, not permitting apathy or the difficulty of such challenges to hinder or deter us. This interpretation appears satisfactory, but even as we "seek peace" in one area of life, we are commanded and challenged to "pursue" peace in the other realms and at future times, for life is continually in a state of change and peace is ephemeral. It can be lost easily, even if obtained only after much struggle and expenditure. As a result, we must not simply look for opportunities to attain peace and pursue them, but once having achieved peace, we must be ever conscious of forces that would eliminate safety (*shalem*). The imperative form, to "pursue" is a reminder that peace, and more importantly its preservation, continually requires recognition that life is a dynamic process, and not stagnant.

One gesture may temporarily bind the hearts of persons, but that peace will hardly be permanent. One worship service, one hour of seeking God through prayer or study may enable persons to achieve spiritual solace and a sense of communion and unity, but such efforts can hardly make such an accomplishment permanent. It is evident that one good deed, one act of charity, cannot in and of itself bring total peace and healing amidst the world's ills.

Shalom then is to be understood as a balance of often changing and conflicting interests. Often what has existed among nations and within a nation's political and social reality is not an absolute state of peace, but a balance, a compromise and harmony of conflicting interests and agendas that is workable and agreeable to the parties concerned. Each side is generally satisfied with the approach of the other not to resort to means that would drastically alter the existing arrangement. And even though there is a modicum of peace, or at least a temporary balance that is somewhat comfortable for the time being, there continues to be a need to "seek" the peace of every day balance, and "pursue" a higher degree of harmony in the areas that separate humanity. One human being is not exactly like the other, one nation is not exactly like another, but the imperative to "seek peace and pursue it" reminds us that it is God's ideal that persons live together united as one human family.

The same state of peace, of living together in unity with each other while balancing conflicting and competing loyalties is even possible for individuals. We as individuals are continually tempted by different forces that demand our allegiance. Individuals are like nations, which often compete with differing agendas. Therefore, the process of seeking *shalom* for the individual is actually the clarification of one's values and desires. Shalom is the balance that enables persons to live with a clear conscious, with the knowledge that they are giving their best in all aspects of life so that no aspect of the human experience goes wanting, and so that there is truly a state of *shalom.*

On a collective level, the discovery and retention of peace is dependent upon those who comprise a particular community. The quest for *shalom* with others is no easy task and frequently requires a balance between individual interests and the broader needs of those who comprise community. Such a goal of *shalom* is often elusive. Complete and rewarding personal relationships cannot exist outside "seeking" peace - being sensitized to the needs of others, and then "pursuing" it - addressing and acting upon those impulses with sincere and selfless efforts. But seeking and pursuing peace should not be limited to one occasion, for that will hardly yield a sound and solid relationship. Peace must be "sought" always, and a deeper relationship than presently exists must be "pursued." In this way *shalom* is created, and harmony between different people with different agendas is realized. We arrive at a relationship with others, where we are not necessarily one, but where we dwell together in unity (Psalm 133:1), cognizant always of the realistic balance between being self-concerned and other-concerned.

Surely no one person can heal the pain of society where so many people suffer. But peace can be sought by looking for small ways to make a difference; and peace can be pursued regardless of how inconsequential the act of peacemaking may appear. This recognizes that cumulative acts of peacemaking positively affect the common fate and well-being of all human beings.

One rabbinical teaching intimates a perspective on sharing in acts of peacemaking:

Iron is strong, but fire melts it
Fire is strong, but water quenches it
The water is strong, but sun evaporates it
The sun is strong, but clouds can cover it
Clouds are strong, but wind can drive clouds away

> Wind is strong, but man can shut it out
> Man is strong, but fears cast him down
> Fear is strong, but sleep overcomes it
> Sleep is strong, yet death is stronger
> But the strongest is the beautiful act,
> For that survives death.[11]

The ability to "seek peace and pursue it" is a divinely bestowed attribute. Just as God is eternal, we have been given the ability to live eternally through our acts of peace that can live on after us.

III. New Testament Perspectives:
Peaceful Community as an Aspect of the Messianic Promise in Lukan and Pauline Literature

The New Testament has little to say in explicitly sociopolitical terms on the subject of peace. Much has been written in recent years in an attempt to develop a "theology of peace," however, and these attempts have necessarily had to deduce a theological construct from wider contexts and from the biblical understanding of such topics as sanctity of life, call to discipleship, and reverence for creation. Victor P. Furnish, writing in an article entitled "War and Peace in the New Testament" concludes:

> War and peace conceived as social and political issues were not specifically topics of Jesus' teaching or concerns of his ministry. Rome was not at war, nor were the Jews at war with Rome, and Jesus' message concerned the sovereign justice, mercy, and love of God whose rule was at hand. It is also apparent, however, that his understanding of God, of God's claim, and of God's Kingdom precluded his advocacy of any military action against Rome – just as it gave impetus to his ministry to the impoverished, the oppressed, and the despised of his society and just as it led, finally and ironically to his arrest and execution as an insurrectionist.[12]

Therefore, it is clear that Christ's concern for peace among persons and various religious and social factions during his time, while not always explicitly stated, was evident in his concern for justice, mercy and love. Justice could not exist without peace, and conversely peace could not thrive without justice, mercy and love.

In this light, the question inevitably arises concerning precisely what content Christian biblical literature does present with respect to peace. In the New Testament, the adjective *eirenkos* (peaceful or peace-like) occurs twice (Hebrews 12:11 and James 3:17); and the verb *eireneuo* ("be at peace") occurs four times (Mark 9:50, Romans 12:18, 2 Corinthians 13:11, and 1 Thessalonians 5:13). Larry Myers of Concordia Seminary points out that there are over one hundred references to *eirene* in the New Testament, with most of them occurring in Lukan and Pauline literature. The classical Greek understanding of *eirene* is usually described as a "state" in contrast to an "attitude" or "relationship."[13] Specifically, *eirene* is the "state of peace" versus the "state of war" *(polemos)*.

When considering the topic of *eirene* in the New Testament, it is helpful to consider the Hebrew concept of *shalom.* Nowhere is the Rabbinic Hebrew understanding of *shalom* more evident than in the greetings and farewells of the New Testament.

In the Gospel of Luke, Jesus pronounces upon the sinful woman who anointed his feet, "your faith has made you whole, go in peace." (Luke 7:50) Likewise, Jesus instructs the seventy (or seventy-two) to offer a greeting of peace at each house they might enter. (Luke 10) The same farewell greeting in Luke 7:50 ("go in peace") occurs again in Luke 8:48. Somewhat surprisingly, even the jailkeeper in Philippi uses this greeting when dismissing Paul and Silas. (Acts 16:36) When the resurrected Lord appears to the disciples, again it is the *shalom* greeting that is used. (Luke 23:36) The full import of *shalom* is spelled out in the Gospel of John (20:19-23) in connection with the authority to forgive and retain sins.

William Shannon, in *Seeds of Peace,* speaks of the gift of *shalom* as offered in the coming of Jesus and explicated in the Gospel of Luke:

> Luke draws open the curtains on his narrative of the Jesus story with angelic choruses chanting: "Peace (*shalom*) to those on whom God's favor rests" (2:14) During Jesus'

public ministry, there were many times – some recorded, some not – when Jesus spoke to people with all sorts of afflictions these simple, powerful words: "Go in peace." (e.g., Mark 5:34; Luke 7:50) In Jesus' farewell discourse in John's Gospel, the atmosphere of the upper room is peace, and peace is the message. "Peace I leave with you, my peace I give you." (14:27) "I have said this to you, so that in me you may have peace." (16:33)[14]

Eirene is found as the opening greeting of every Pauline epistle, the precise form varying only in Thessalonians 1:1, and in the term *eleos* ("mercy") affixed in 1 Timothy 1:2 and 2 Timothy 1:2. A final greeting of peace in some fashion appears in the farewells of 2 Corinthians (12:11), Galatians (6:16), Ephesians (6:23), Philippians (4:9), 1 Thessalonians (5:23), and 2 Thessalonians (3:16).

The usages of *eirene* in Romans, which may, at first seem to convey varying concepts, are all related. "Peace with God" occurs only by, and also in, righteousness through faith in Christ. Peace in the community occurs as a result of having been declared righteous through faith, and as one lives by the Spirit. This relationship is also outlined by Paul in his letter to the Galatians, when he describes the fruits of the Spirit as consisting of "love, joy, peace, patience, kindness, goodness, faithfulness, gentleness and self-control." (Galatians 5:22-23)

In the minds of Luke and Paul, there seems to be no lasting "peace" apart for Christ as the "Prince of Peace." For both Luke and Paul, the primary use of *eirene* refers to salvation, reconciliation with God, achieved by the death and resurrection of Jesus, the Christ. *Eirene* as a concept referring to community relationships and socio-political conditions is derived out this primary usage. William Shannon offers a sense of the "inevitability of war" that might be connoted in *eirene*.

This sense of war's inevitability has made its way into the words we use for "peace". Our Western world is, in the main, a product of Greco-Roman civilization. It is instructive to note how the Greeks and the Romans spoke about peace. The Greek word for peace is *eirene*. *Eirene* describes an interlude of nonstruggle in the midst of what is the normal human condition: war. *Eirene*, therefore, has more the sense of truce between wars, not an end to war. *Eirene* is a "peace" that accepts the curse of the inevitability of war.[15]

The Latin word for peace, *pax,* has a slightly more positive meaning: it suggests a "pact," an "agreement" not to fight for the time being. It is a state more or less fragile that exists for a time in the midst of ongoing struggle and strife. It too accepts the belief that war is inevitable.

Shannon offers that the Hebrew word *shalom* is a word that refuses to accept the inevitability of war and conflict. *Shalom* gives a strongly positive content to peace and speaks to "wholeness," "completeness". Shannon writes:

> People – whether as nations or as individuals – are at peace when they achieve wholeness, when they realize their potential for goodness and love and truth and justice, when they become who they really are and who God intended them to be. When we become fully human, we must reject war and enmity and animosity, for all these things are dehumanizing. They make us less than human beings. War dehumanizes us. Enmity and animosity toward others dehumanizes others; and when they dehumanize us, they deprive us of peace.[16]

IV. Jesus, Shalom and the Messianic Promise

In the ninth chapter of the Book of Isaiah, the prophet spoke of the coming Messiah by declaring that he would be the "Prince of Peace," and the "governments would rest upon his shoulders." (Isaiah 9:6-7) In his prophetic vision, Isaiah continued by declaring, "there shall be endless peace, and he will uplift it with righteousness from this time onward and forevermore." An aspect of the messianic expectation and anticipation surrounding the birth of Christ was that his life and witness would inaugurate an era of peace among people. The angels heralded his coming by declaring this hope of peace: "Glory to God in the highest heaven and on earth peace and goodwill toward those he favors." (Luke 2:14)

It is in the New Testament that *shalom* becomes a reality

that is not only primordial and eschatological, but existential. The heart of the New Testament message is that the radical possibility of peace has entered the world in Jesus Christ. The incarnate Christ embodied *shalom*. In Ephesians, the apostle Paul offered a perspective on the early church's understanding of the relationship of Christ to peace:

> Christ Jesus is our peace; in his flesh he has made all groups into one and has broken down the dividing wall, that is, the hostility between us…and reconciles groups to God in one body through the cross. So then you are no longer strangers and aliens, but you are citizens with the saints and also members of the household of God, built upon the foundation of the apostles and prophets, with Christ Jesus himself as the cornerstone. In him the whole structure is joined together and grows into a holy temple in the Lord; in whom you also are built together spiritually into the dwelling place for God. (Ephesians 2:14-22)

Paul proclaimed that Jesus Christ *is* our peace. Christ has broken down the dividing wall, the hostilities that have separated persons, for he has made us into one. When Paul spoke of Christ making the two of us one, he spoke of the only world he knew; one divided into Jews and Gentiles. He could not have known the full import of his words. Jesus came to break down the barriers that separate all peoples…. He is the one who comes to reconcile the First World and the Second World and the Third World.[17]

The outcome of God's action in Christ is "to guide our feet into the path of peace." (Luke 1:79) "Salvation" and "peace" here are identified with each other. The peace which the coming Messiah offers persons is salvation itself…salvation through forgiveness of sins, and through the ministry of reconciliation that makes persons new creations in Christ. (2 Corinthians 5:17-19)

When Christ is presented in the temple on the appointed eighth day, Simeon requests dismissal "in peace" precisely because "my eyes have seen your salvation…" (Luke 2:29-32). When Jesus makes the triumphal entry into Jerusalem, he is greeted as the Messiah with words which include "peace in heaven…" (Luke 19:38). All of these references identify peace with that eschatological salvation that had been long awaited. Indeed, Jesus' weeping over Jerusalem and his declaration, "If you had only known on this day what would bring your peace…" (Luke 19:42), leave no uncertainty concerning the kind of peace that brings genuine political and societal harmony.

The eschatological promises are being fulfilled throughout history, but this does not mean that they can be identified clearly and completely with one or another social reality; their liberating effect goes far beyond the foreseeable and opens up new and unsuspected possibilities. The complete encounter with the Lord will mark an end to history. Thus, we must acknowledge historical events in all their concreteness and significance, but we are also led to a permanent detachment. The encounter is present even now, dynamizing humanity's process of becoming and projecting it beyond its hopes (1 Cor. 2:6-9); it will not be planned or predestined. This "ignorance" accounts for the active and committed hope for the gift: Christ is the 'Yes' pronounced upon God's promises, every one of them." (2 Cor. 1:20)[18]

This is the vision that Christ spoke of in the Sermon on the Mount: "Blessed are the peacemakers, for they shall be called children of God." (Matthews 5:9) Every Christian, according to this beatitude, is meant to be a peacemaker both in the community and in the church. It is clear throughout the teachings of Jesus, that we should never ourselves seek conflict and be responsible for it. On the contrary, we are called to peace, we are actively to 'pursue' peace; we are to 'strive for peace with all persons', and so far as it depends on us, we are to live peaceably with all. (Romans 12:18)[19]

V. Toward a Theology of Peaceful Community

Howard Thurman and Martin Luther King, Jr. sought to adopt and further develop theological perspectives of peaceful community that were rooted in the liberation motifs of the black church. Both were born and reared in the Southern Black Baptist religious tradition, which over the course of history has been called to speak to the injustices of race and class discrimination in America.

Henry Mitchell and Nicholas Cooper-Lewter, in *Soul The-*

ology: The Heart of Black Culture, assert that the most pervasive of all the divine attributes is the goodness of Creator and creation.[20] Yet the goodness of God has sounded too obvious to justify extended treatment in either spontaneous folk motif or formal theological writings. The notion of the goodness of God is rooted in the belief that the experience of creation and life itself must be ultimately beneficial or good. In this perspective, life is always worth more than death, and this attitude is at the very heart of emotional, spiritual and communal wholeness.[21]

This is the essence of *MAAT.* For African and African-American people, there has existed the certainty of the goodness of God. This certainty of the basic goodness of nature and of the human sojourn is essential to total well-being. Thus, the relatedness of the concepts *shalom, MAAT,* and *holism* can be seen. Although derived out of somewhat different social, cultural, spiritual and geographical contexts, each speaks to the concern for the well-being of persons and communities.

With regard to a conceptuality for a theology of peace, theologian Dorothee Solle asserts that peace within the context of the Kingdom of God has seldom become the object of systematic theological questioning. Apart from the historical peace churches - the Quakers, Mennonites and Brethren - the great churches have usually considered the theme of peace relevant only in social and ethical terms. It is completely absent from many of the outlines of Western theology and merely becomes the application of theological teaching, instead of being understood as the substance of God's action.[22]

In moving toward a relevant spiritual theology for peaceful community in the new millennium – or *theology of peace* - it is critical to comprehend that the theological task is essentially contextual and contemporary in its nature. While drawing upon various theological strands and perspectives in seeking to address the matter of peaceful community, the critical theological question is "What does God say to the church and society today?" Arising out of this foundational question is the ethical and moral concern, "What does this suggest to us about ourselves and our relationships with God and with each other?"

With regard to the theological task, James Cone states:

> Theology is not a universal language about God. Rather, it is human speech informed by historical and theological traditions, and written for particular times and places. Theology is *contextual* language – that is, defined by the human situation that gives birth to it. No one can write theology for all times, places, and persons.[23]

Cone offers the following definition of Christian theology:

> Christian theology is a theology of liberation. It is a *rational study of the being of God in the world in light of the existential situation of an oppressed community, relating the forces of liberation to the essence of the gospel, which is Jesus Christ.* This means that its sole reason for existence is to put into ordered speech the meaning of God's activity in the world, so that the community of the oppressed will recognize that its inner thrust for liberation is not only *consistent with* the gospel but *is* the gospel of Jesus Christ. There can be no Christian theology that is not identified unreservedly with those who are humiliated and abused. In fact, theology ceases to be a theology of the gospel when it fails to arise out of the community of the oppressed. For it is impossible to speak of the God of Israelite history, who is the God revealed in Jesus Christ, without recognizing that God is a God *of* and *for* those who labor and are heavy laden.[24]

Allen O. Miller, in his book, *Invitation to Theology: Resources for Christian Nature and Discipline,* gives a definition of "theology" and "theologian" which includes the concerns for vitality and religious experience – a definition which eliminates the "religion" (spirit) – "theology" (intellect) dichotomy. He says:

> ...Although theology means literally "a discourse about God," its content is more like a prayer of praise and thanksgiving than a scientific description of a matter of fact...the human response which the mystery of God evokes is primarily appreciation and intellectual satisfaction.
> ...Doctrinal beliefs are an important part of theology, but

they are not the heart of it. The heart of theology is like the heart of religion and of morality, a personal relationship. Moreover, all three express action. In fact, in our Christian understanding, theology, religion, and morality are all concerned with activity – the activity of God's holy love in human affairs.[25]

As the voice and presence of God has been evident in the past with regard to the need for peace, we seek to glean new theological insights as to the needs and opportunities for the development of peaceful community today.

VI. Socio-theological Perspectives of Community

Walter E. Fluker, in *They Looked For a City: A Comparative Analysis of the Ideal of Community in the Thought of Howard Thurman and Martin Luther King, Jr.*, suggests that there are a number of ways to understand community. Like most of our ordinary discourse, its meaning varies with context and usage. Among various settings and situations, there are different dimensions of meaning. Presupposed in such usage, however, is the idea that the word "community" denotes some determinate object, a particular type of social life and experience, e.g., a sense of belonging, a sense of place, a sense of identity and shared values.[26]

Such a common sense view of language, however, fails to address the problem of multidimensional levels and varieties of experiences covered in the broad terminology of community. In this sense, community, like love, covers a multitude of definitional and methodological sins.[27] Because of the highly complex and conflated usage of the term community, it is a futile enterprise to talk about it without first recognizing that empirical and evaluative dimensions in the idea are intertwined along with a host of other interrelated problems. Therefore, examining the notion of community necessarily involves careful attention to the socio-historical contexts from which the idea arises and how its normative character is understood within that framework. It would be extremely difficult, for instance, to talk intelligently about the notions of community in Plato and

Aristotle without some appreciation for the decline of the Athenian city-state. The two philosophers' politico-ethical construals of community are directly related to their respective socio-historical contexts.[28]

Community, Gustavo Gutierrez reminds us, draws us Christian men and women "out of solitude" and into connectedness. We are people in search of God in community.[29]

One of the major barriers to community is ethnocentrism.[30] Ethnocentrism is the assumption that the worldview of one's own culture is central to all reality. In ethnocentrism, there is the tendency to perceive and evaluate persons, things, and events according to one's own values, beliefs, and assumptions, often not knowing or accepting other worldviews as valid or important. When one is ethnocentric, one may react with denial to others who have a different cultural worldview, one may become defensive or judgmental, and one may minimize the differences as unimportant or nonexistent.

Milton J. Bennett's intercultural sensitivity model provides a framework relative to a person's response to cultural difference as an indicator of intercultural sensitivity within the context of community.[31] His theory is organized around six stages: (1) *Denial,* (2) *Defense,* (3) *Minimization,* (4) *Acceptance,* (5) *Adaptation,* and (6) *Integration,* as a means of describing how persons move through different states when interacting with a culture other than one's own. Self-examination and seeking to understand the dynamics incumbent in one's socio-cultural environment are critical to developing awareness with regard to intercultural sensitivity, and moving beyond ethnocentrism.

In developing a conception of community, one of the theological tasks therefore, is to examine the relationships between the socio-cultural and socio-historical contexts, and the politico-ethical claims associated with the search for peace in the work of Howard Thurman and Martin Luther King, Jr. Both Thurman and King sought to conceive and appropriate approaches to building authentic community. They viewed racism as perhaps the most pronounced form of ethnocentrism, and the greatest barrier to community-building and peace in America. Carlyle Fielding Stewart identifies racism as essentially an ontological problem. According to Stewart:

Ontology is the study of the science of being. The primary foundation of white racism is ontological, for it is the systematic discrimination and oppression of a people on the basis of race. Webster's *New Universal Unabridged Dictionary* defines racism as "the program or practice of racial discrimination, segregation, persecution and domination based on racialism." *Race* is thus an ontological category having to do with the physiognomy or the countenance of human beings. Accordingly, racism has profound theological implications as it relates to ontology, for it is difficult to condemn the created on the basis of race without condemning the Creator God who brought the various races into existence. The fact that God created different races of people confirms the capacity of God's creative imagination. Racism therefore is intrinsically antitheological and antiontological.[32]

Racism is to be understood in historical and contemporary context as a form of disunity, disintegration and non-community. By its very nature, it is antithetical to the realization of authentic community.

In seeking to move beyond ethnocentrism, and to arrive at an approach for the conceptualization of identity and otherness in the movement toward community, Miroslav Volf offers that several solutions – with regard to social arrangements - have been suggested along the following lines.[33] (1) *Universalist Option:* We should control the unchecked proliferation of differences, and support the spread of universal values – religious values or Enlightenment values – which alone can guarantee the peaceful co-existence of people; affirmation of differences without common values will lead to chaos and war rather than to rich and fruitful diversity. (2) *Communitarian Option:* We should celebrate communal distinctives and promote heterogeneity, placing ourselves on the side of the smaller armies of indigenous cultures; the spread of universal values will lead to oppression and boredom rather than peace and prosperity. (3) *Postmodern Option:* We should flee both universal values and particular identities and seek refuge from oppression in the radical autonomy of individuals; we should create spaces in which persons can keep creating "larger and freer selves" by acquiring new and losing old identities – wayward and erratic vagabonds, ambivalent and fragmented, always on the move and never doing much more than making moves.

M. Scott Peck points to three facets of community, which he asserts are interconnected and interrelated. No one can exist without the other. They create each other, make each other possible.[34] First, community is and must be *inclusive*. The great enemy of community is exclusivity. Groups that exclude others because they are poor or doubters or divorced or sinners or of some different race or nationality are not communities: they are cliques – actually defensive bastions against communities. Inclusiveness is not an absolute. Long-term communities must invariably struggle over the degree to which they are going to be inclusive. True communities are always reaching to extend themselves – to expand the "web of inclusion." The second characteristic of community is *commitment*. Commitment is the willingness to coexist. Exclusivity, the great enemy of community appears in two forms: excluding the other and excluding oneself. Sooner or later, somewhere along the line, the members of a group in some way must commit themselves to one another if they are to become or stay a community. The third characteristic of community is *consensus*. Consensus is closely related to transcendence where there is the willingness and ability within the group to move beyond individual agendas and interests for the good of the group. "Transcend" does not mean "obliterate" or "demolish." It literally means "to climb over." The achievement of community can be compared to the reaching of a mountaintop. Perhaps the most necessary key to this transcendence is the appreciation of difference. A community, in transcending individual differences, routinely goes beyond even democracy. Decisions in genuine transcendent community are arrived at through consensus.

VII. Peaceful Community and God's Love

The development of peaceful community involves spreading the love of God into the world. God demonstrated divine love for humanity and opened the door for the establishment of a humanistic understanding of love through the solitary act of sending Jesus Christ into the world. "For God so loved the world, that God gave His only begotten Son, so that whoever believes in Him will not perish, but have everlasting life." (John 3:16)

In Scripture, we are informed that "God is Love." (1 John 4:8) A loving and love-filled God created humanity out of divine love (*agape*). It was this same love out of which God sent Jesus into the world. Unconditional love is the essence of the Greek concept *agape*. Humans, according to Hebrew Scripture accounts of creation, have been created in God's image (*imago dei*). The love that is the very essence of God, as embodied in Christ, is the love that Christians are called to convey to the world. In seeking to create peaceful community, God's love must be translated into a love that demonstrates and perpetuates itself through acts of faithfulness toward other persons. Love within the context of peaceful community – when given the choice as to whether– in the words of Miroslav Volf - "to exclude or embrace" the other – will choose perpetually to embrace.[35]

Love, as lived out in peaceful community, seeks to embrace the other's culture, beliefs, perspectives, and ideologies. Love within the context of living into peaceful community means seeking to develop the capacity to love our enemies, in spite of, and perhaps even because of our differences.

With Jesus, peacemaking involved not merely a change of environment, but also a change of heart. This is shown in how Jesus dealt with an invitation to make peace by settling a dispute between two brothers who were quarreling over the division of their inheritance. But he dismissed the request with the pointed question, "Man, who made me a judge or a divider over you?" God's plan of making peace is not merely to bring about an outward settlement between (people) *but to create people of goodwill.*[36]

Christ states, "You have heard that it was said that you shall love your neighbor and hate your enemy. But I say to you, love your enemies and pray for those who persecute you, so that you may be children of your Father in heaven." (Matthew 5:43-45) Developing the capacity to love one's enemies is a difficult task – and involves perhaps the most radical form of love.

Howard Thurman in *Jesus and the Disinherited* points to

the need for reconciliation in loving one's enemy. Thurman says:

> To love such an enemy requires reconciliation, the will to
> re-establish a relationship. It involves confession of error
> and seeking to be restored to one's former place. Doubt-
> less it is this that Jesus had in mind in his charge: "If you
> bring your gift to the altar, and remember that your brother
> has sinned against you; leave your gift at the altar... and go
> be reconciled to your brother and then come and offer your
> gift."[37]

Martin Luther King, Jr. in *Strength to Love* points out that probably no admonition of Jesus has been more difficult to follow than the command to "love your enemies." With regard to the difficulty found here, King states:

> Some men have sincerely felt its actual practice is not pos-
> sible. It is easy, they say, to love those who love you, but
> how can one love those who openly and insidiously seek to
> defeat you? Others, like Nietzsche, contend that Jesus'
> exhortation to love one's enemies is testimony to the fact
> that the Christian ethic is designed for the weak and cow-
> ardly, and not for the strong and courageous. Jesus, they
> say, is an impractical idealist.[38]

King points out that loving one's enemies, or those with whom one might differ socially, politically, economically, or even morally, is indeed possible. First, King argues, we must develop and maintain the capacity for forgiveness. He who is devoid of the power to forgive is devoid of the power to love. Second, we must recognize that the evil deed of the enemy-neighbor, that thing that hurts, never quite expresses all that the person is. An element of goodness may be found even in our worst enemy. Third, we must not seek to defeat or humiliate the enemy, but to win his friendship and understanding. Every word and deed must contribute to an understanding with the enemy and release those vast reservoirs of goodwill which have been blocked by impenetrable walls of hate.[39]

It can be concluded that the result of *agape* is nonviolence. Howard Thurman observes: "The awareness that a man is a child of the God of religion, who is at one and the same time the God of life, creates a profound faith in life that nothing can destroy."[40] As one senses the love of God, that person is able to extend that same love to others (their enemies) despite the terrors and cruelties of forms of hatred that may be present. Regarding this, Thurman further states:

A man's conviction that he is God's child automatically tends to shift the basis of his relationship with his fellows. He recognizes at once that to fear a man, whatever may be that man's power over him, is a basic denial of the integrity of his very life. It lifts that mere man to a place of preeminence that belongs to God and to God alone. He who fears is literally delivered to destruction.[41]

Agape resulting in nonviolence seeks to address not only external violence, but what Robert McAfee Bown described as *structural violence*.[42] This form of violence includes psychological, emotional, and relational violence - violence that slowly destroys a person's self-esteem, value, and self-worth. Poverty is a form of structural violence, for while it is not as overt as physical violence, its devastation is just as ominous.[43]

Thus, the creation of peaceful community is intricately related to developing the capacity for *agape* – understanding, creative and redemptive goodwill for all persons, an overflowing and unconditional love which seeks nothing in return. *Agape* is love that allows persons in the church and society to move toward being in solidarity with the "other" – the actualization of community. It is love operative in the human heart. At this level, we love persons not necessarily because we like them – or their attitudes and actions – nor do we love others because they possess some virtue that is pleasing to us; we love others because God loves them.

VIII. Peaceful Community Amidst Human Diversity

At the dawn of the twenty-first century, one of the critical challenges for the church and society relates to how to most faithfully, effectively and compassionately address the complex social, economic and political dilemmas that exist in ways that will best facilitate peaceful community. Racism, classism, sexism, politicism, denominationalism and tribalism pervade society and serve to create and perpetuate tremendous barriers among people, and hindrances to true community.

At the heart of the search for peaceful community is how the church has in the past, and might in the future, be equipped to affirm both its universality (catholicity) and its inclusiveness (unity) in light of the diversity among people of the society. Though, in America, many Southern and Eastern European ethnic groups have assimilated into Anglo-American culture, they have done so at a great cost to themselves, in terms of a sense of personal identity and worth, and to society as a whole. Still, white Europeans could assimilate while non-white ethnic groups could not. At best, ethnic minority groups could only imitate the dominant culture, but never really merge into it. For this reason, "ethnicity" has come to refer to those ethnic groups which in reality are "unmeltable" – African Americans, Hispanic Americans, Native Americans, and Asian Americans. Indeed, the increasing "rediscovery" of ethnicity by whites of Southern and Eastern European ancestry has been spearheaded by efforts of the "unmeltable" ethnic groups to rediscover their identities. Also, it has been the so-called ethnic groups that have forced the growing realization among Anglo-Americans that they too are an ethnic group – one culture among many, rather than *the* culture.[44] The discovery of the diversity that comprises society, leading to community, is enhanced through honest and open dialogue with those of other cultures – with the constant realization that God is the creator of all peoples and cultures.

As the Body of Christ, the church is to serve as an integrative bridge for the many societal entities with which it relates. One way that this might be accomplished is by striving towards racial and cultural pluralism, which reflects the diversity among peoples. A comprehension and appropriation of pluralism is an important asset in the movement toward peaceful community.[45] The issue, therefore, remains how to discover common ground among persons from different cultural, socioeconomic, political, racial and even religious backgrounds.

The recognition and valuation of diversity entails several presumptions about God the creator, and the humanity that has been created by God. Christian ethicist J. Phillip Wogaman refers to this as the method of positive presumption.[46]   According to Wogaman, we presume: (1) *The goodness of created existence.*   God created humanity (all humans) in goodness and wholeness.   God's divine intention for created humanity is goodness and wholeness (shalom). (2) *The value of human life.* In each human being there is sacred and infinite worth as a result of humanity's creation in God's image (imago dei). (3) *The unity of the human family.* Humans have not been created to live in a vacuum, but in community with one another. Because of our creation by the same God, we are all interconnected and interrelated. (4) *The equality of all persons in God.* As God created all persons in the image of God, and as there is unity among humans in God, there is also equality among all human beings.

Amidst human diversity, there must be a comprehension and appropriation of the intrinsic equality of all persons. The apostle Paul stated, "There is neither Jew or Greek, there is neither bond or free, there is neither male or female; for you are all one in Christ Jesus." (Galatians 3:28)

Henry Mitchell and Nicholas Cooper-Lewter point out that equality is not merely political rhetoric; it involves God's justice expressed impartially.[47] With regard to equality, they further state:
> Either God regards all persons as intrinsically equal, or (God) is the unjust author of inequity, the very Creator of the oppressions suffered by persons and groups at the bottom of the social and economic system. As easy as it may be to practice inequality, the American dream will not permit it to be approved by the Creator…The founders of this nation attributed their egalitarian dogma to the very mind of God, and so Americans have believed ever since.

This equality is not to be mistaken for uniformity, however. Americans come in different sizes and shapes. They have various levels of giftedness, in a further diversified spectrum of specialties. They represent a fantastic variety of colors and cultures, from every corner of the earth, to say nothing of the profusion of personality patterns. Still, before the law, they are all equal in standing. Few affirmations have more sweeping consequences psychologically and spiritually, as well as legally, and few are so inadequately articulated, especially in America's circle of power. The pluralism of the dream is far better understood today than ever, but the drift toward the tyranny of single-group supremacy and enforced uniformity is always present.[48]

The familiar Negro spiritual speaks to the notion of the equality that intrinsically exists among persons:

> The fare is cheap, and all can ride,
> the rich and the poor are there.
> No second class aboard this train,
> no difference in the fare.
> Oh, get on board, little children,
> get on board, little children,
> Get on board, little children,
> there room for many a'more.[49]

IX. Peaceful Community and Culture

The search for peaceful community affirms the value of the diverse cultures of which persons are a part. Christian evangelist E. Stanley Jones, in his work with Mohandas Gandhi and the people of India, suggested that persons from diverse cultures could engage in authentic community-building.[50] The objective in cross-cultural context should not be to change persons' cultural orientation, or to impose one's own culture upon others, but to seek to understand and value other persons.

When the imposition of culture upon indigenous people has occurred, often in the name of religion, cultures have fallen apart. Noted Nigerian author Chinua Achebe refers to this as "things falling apart."[51] Cultures, communities, families and individuals are affected when there exists insensitivity and a lack of understanding and valuation of other cultures.

Jean Marc Ela, in *My Faith as An African,* speaks to the pervasive nature of culture, particularly in relation to the gospel of Christ. Ela points out that evangelizing people shaped by a certain culture must go hand in hand with their struggle for development in all aspects of their lives. The hope for a New World that is built in the framework of justice, peace and freedom is the heart of the Christian message.[52]   According to Ela, this is the starting point for a radical critique of all that is happening before us.

Any notion of Christ as Liberator, and a gospel that seeks to promote peace and to liberate those who find themselves in the bonds of injustice and oppression, operates from the ground up – at the existential point of cultural context – where persons currently find themselves.

According to cognitive theorists in cultural anthropology, culture is a knowledge system existing in people's minds that they use to govern behavior. It is not the behavior itself that governs culture, but the cognitive systems of ideas, values, and beliefs that people must know to generate behavior acceptable to the cultural group.[53]

Eric H.F. Law, in *The Bush Was Burning But Not Consumed,* defines culture as learned values, beliefs, perceptions, assumptions, patterns, and practices – both conscious and unconscious – that enable (persons and groups) to perceive, interpret, evaluate, and respond to life and the world. Culture... is not limited to race and ethnicity, even though for many (persons) race and ethnicity constitute the major parts of one's cultural (identity and makeup). Other components that contribute to a person's culture can include gender, age, physical ability, sexual orientation, economic status, religion, marital status, education, community, work, family structure, and individual interests and experiences.[54]

Culture can thus be seen as embodied in the language, symbols, music, dress, *mores,* customs and traditions that serve as the source of vitality and perpetuity for a group of people. In the valuation of cultures, the church and society are called to understand the contributions that existing cultures make to the whole body of Christ. In two lectures given at the Greenfield Center for Human Relations at the University of Pennsylvania in 1954, which was expanded into a volume entitled *Cultural Pluralism and the American Idea,* Horace Kallen offered what has become a classic analysis of culture:

> A living culture is a changing culture; and it is a changing culture, and not an auctioneer's storage house or an archaeological dump of fragments, fossils and ruins, because of the transactions wherewith living, altering individuals transform

old thoughts and things while laboring to preserve them and to produce new. Cultures live and grow in and through the individual, and their vitality is a function of individual diversities of interests and associations. Pluralism is the *sine qua non* of their persistence and prosperous growth. But not the absolutist pluralism which the concept of the unaltering and inalterable Monad discloses. On the contrary, the *sine qua non* is fluid, relational pluralism which the living individual encounters in the transactions wherewith he constructs his personal history moving out of groups and into groups, engaging in open or hidden communion with societies of his fellows, every one different from the others, and all teamed together, and struggling to provide and maintain the common means which nourish, assure, enhance, the different, and often competing, values they differently cherish.[55]

The valuation of and openness toward diverse cultures can be understood within the context of *inculturation* or *contextualization*. The implication is a renewed understanding of the church and the church's service within the world. It suggests "incarnation" and "insertion" and the impossibility of separating a people's culture and religious habits; and it does so precisely because it recognizes that wherever we go, our culture goes with us. The processes of inculturation and contextualization seek to move persons toward *interculturation* and *multiculturation*. This begins at the point of the ethnocentricity of individuals and communities who – through exposure to cultures other than their own - begin to gain an awareness of aspects of the other's culture within the context of their own ethnocentric perspective. Through this heightened awareness, persons begin to gain a more profound understanding of the differences and similarities of other cultures, which leads eventually to a sense of valuation. In valuation, one gains a respect for the importance of "other" cultures to their own spirituality and growth – thus resulting in the eventual selective adoption of some aspects of other cultures into one's own lifestyle.[56]

Movement toward an appropriation of peaceful community involves an understanding of the nuances of culture, which is rooted in self-awareness as well as the increasing awareness of, and sensitivity to, the "other" that becomes a part of one's reality over time. This process of interculturation/multiculturation is critical to the development of authentic community.

X. Peaceful Community and the Church's Mission and Ministry

The Christian church is the vehicle that continuously carries forth the ministry of Jesus Christ in the Kingdom of God. The church, through its various means of serving the world, is the bridge between God and all humanity. It is God working in and through persons, as God continues to reconcile the world unto Godself. (2 Corinthians 5:17-18)

The model of ministry as taught to the world by Christ is one of inclusive, universal service. Christ's ministry was directed particularly toward the marginalized: those persons with needs that various societal institutions had failed to address. By feeding the hungry, clothing the naked, and healing those who suffered, Christ demonstrated that the commonality of human strengths and weaknesses far transcends the many diversities that tend to divide persons.

Throughout his ministry, Jesus demonstrated that there is an ongoing relationship between the church and the world. The mission of the church is thus to be carried out in and with the world on behalf of God, from whom all ministry originated and to whom it belongs.

The church's active participation in the world can be translated as its mission. This mission has its origin in divine grace, which is ultimately witnessed to in the Christian community by God's unconditional love in sending Jesus into a troubled world. It is this mission, derived out of grace, that is the motivation, context, and content of the church's ministry in the world. The church exists to exemplify and embody God's grace even amidst the suffering and violence extant throughout the world. Even in brokenness, God's justice and mercy are intended to be evident in and through the church.

As the church engages in creating peaceful community, it

endeavors to model the ministry of Christ - a ministry of love, compassion, and reconciliation which sought to address the particular spiritual and social concerns of those with whom he came in contact. To engage in a ministry of peacemaking is to participate in the mission of God, and to live a life in radical service to Christ. As Christ offers peace with justice to the world, the church is likewise called to share in ministries of peace and justice.

XI. Peaceful Community as a Means and Ends of Social and Spiritual Transformation

Peaceful community as a vision of hope is ultimately a call to seek transformation of the world in which we live. As such, it is a forceful challenge to rise above ourselves – our personal differences - and live according to the plan of God. The Psalmist's exhortation to "seek peace and pursue it" has all the urgency and realism of the law of love and, as such, has the transforming power to take us beyond whatever we thought possible. Paul encouraged Christians in Rome to "Be not conformed to the world, but be transformed by the renewing of your minds." (Romans 12:1) To be transformed, we must first be attuned to our weaknesses.

The peacefulness that so characterizes our age has its roots in self-deception and in a neurosis stemming from repressed truth.[57] This manifests itself in our prejudices and misunderstandings, often unconscious, which become embedded in our language and patterns of thought.

Dorothee Solle speaks of the relationship of righteousness to peace and social transformation:

> The foundation of peace is righteousness, 'Grace and truth meet each other, righteousness and peace kiss each other.' (Psalm 85:10) The goal is the state in which God has destroyed the chariots and put an end to aggression. Without social justice, without righteousness, there is no peace. According to the prophets the criterion is the rights of those without rights – for example women and orphans, who have no male advocate. The lowest class is made the criterion for the prosperity of all: those who have been most deprived

of their rights, who have the least to say, who not only have no money but also no advocate, no connections, who cannot even go to the authorities because they do not know what they can claim – they are the criterion for what righteousness really is.[58]

At the heart of the prophet Amos' challenge and vision to "let justice roll down as waters, and righteousness as an ever-flowing stream," (Amos 5:24) is the hope of transformation of persons and communities. There can be no hopeful enterprise of peace if we do not become aware of the social distortions in our midst, and keep watch over our motives and intentions. We must be willing to critique the genuineness of our love. The hope of peace demands that we become critically conscious of the interests and motives that guide our actions. Unbridled pursuit of material achievement, coupled with a sense of self-righteousness and exaggerated self-interest, can make people blind to higher values and to the real needs of our neighbors. Such interests can lead to institutionalized injustice and violent conflict. Critical self-awareness will help us avoid blind utilitarianism, which confuses human values with materialism, and freedom with exploitation. The ultimate objective of making peace is the social transformation of persons and institutions. It therefore is not sufficient to simply maintain the present condition, plight or status quo. The objective is to effect positive and progressive change, to help persons experience the life-transforming, all-enveloping presence and love of God which will empower them to stretch beyond the comfort zones of human circumstances. The search is for a creative catalyst that will energize humanity's quest to transform and be transformed. As peace is discovered, lives and relationships are eventually changed to reflect the reality of *shalom* – the wholeness, well-being, and salvation that is the essence of authentic community.

NOTES

[1] Dorothee Solle, *Thinking About God: An Introduction to Theology* (Philadelphia: Trinity International Press, 1990), 154.

[2] Bernard Haring, *The Healing Power of Peace and Nonviolence* (New York: Paulist Press, 1986), 8.

[3] Walter Brueggemann, *Living Toward a Vision* (New York: United Press, 1976), 15.

[4] Samuel Weinstein, "SHALOM in the Jewish Tradition," *Military Chaplains' Review (*Washington, DC: U. S. Army Chaplaincy Services Support Agency, Summer 1988), 17.

[5] Ibid.

[6] Solle, 154.

[7] Ibid., 155.

[8] Haring, 34.

[9] Gustavo Gutierrez, *A Theology of Liberation,* 97.

[10] William H. Shannon, *Seeds of Peace: Contemplation and Non-Violence* (New York: Crossroad, 1995), 108.

[11] This is a paraphrase from the Jewish Talmud.

[12] Victor P. Furnish, "War and Peace in the New Testament," *Military Chaplains' Review,* 23.

[13] Forester, Werner. "Eirene," Theological Dictionary of the New Testament, ed. by Gerhard Kittel, trans. by Geoffrey W. Bromiley. (Grand Rapids; Eerdmans, 1964, no. 11), 400-417.

[14] Shannon, 119.

[15] Ibid., 107.

[16] Ibid., 108.

[17] Ibid., 109.

[18] Gutierrez, 97.

[19] John R.W. Stott, *The Message of the Sermon on the Mount* (Downers Grove, IL: Inter-Varsity Press, 1978), 50.

[20] Henry Mitchell and Nicholas Cooper-Lewter, *Soul Theol-*

ogy: The Heart of Black Culture (Nashville: Abingdon, 1986), 66.

[21] Ibid.

[22] Solle, 154.

[23] James Cone, *A Black Theology of Liberation* (New York: J. P. Lipppencott, 1970), xi.

[24] Ibid., 1.

[25] Luther Smith, *Howard Thurman: The Mystic as Prophet*, 47. Smith here cites Allen O. Miller, *Invitation to Theology: Resources for Christian Nature and Discipline.*

[26] Walter E. Fluker, *They Looked for a City,* xi, Here, Fluker refers to the concept of "community" as developed by Raymond Plant in *Community and Ideology: An Essay in Applied Philosophy.*

[27] Ibid.

[28] Ibid.

[29] Gustavo Gutierrez, *We Drink from Our Own Wells* (Maryknoll, NY: Orbis Books, 1984), 128.

[30] Eric H. F. Law, *The Bush Was Burning But Not Consumed* (St. Louis: Chalice Press, 1996), 46.

[31] See Milton J. Bennett, "A Developmental Approach to Training for Intercultural Sensitivity," in *Theories and Methods in Cross-Cultural Orientation,* ed. Judith N. Martin, International Journal of Intercultural Relations, Vol. 5, No. 2 (New York: Pergamon Press, 1986), 179-196, and Milton J. Bennett, "Towards Ethnorelativism: A Developmental Model of Intercultural Sensitivity," in *Cross-Cultural Orientation,* ed. R. Michele Paige (Lanham, MD: University Press of America, 1986), 27-69.

[32] Carlyle Fielding Stewart, III., *Soul Survivors* (Louisville, KY: Westminster John Knox, 1997), 35-36.

[33] Miroslav Volf, *Exclusion and Embrace: A Theological Exploration of Identity, Otherness, and Reconciliation* (Nashville: Abingdon, 1996), 20.

[34] M. Scott Peck, *The Different Drum: Community Making*

and Peace (New York: Touchstone, 1987), 61f.

[35] Miroslav Volf, in *Exclusion and Embrace,* Volf offers a comprehensive socio-theological exposition of the choice between "exclusion" and "embrace" in intercultural relations.

[36] Clarence Jordan, *Sermon on the Mount* (Valley Forge, PA: Judson Press, 1952), 20.

[37] Howard Thurman, *Jesus and the Disinherited* (Richmond, IN: Friends United Press, 1969), 92.

[38] Martin Luther King, Jr., *Strength to Love* (New York: Harper and Row, 1967), 41.

[39] Ibid., 42.

[40] Thurman, *Jesus and the Disinherited*, 56.

[41] Ibid., 51.

[42] Robert McAfee Brown, *Religion and Violence* (Philadelphia: Westminster Press, 1973), 34-38.

[43] Stewart, 30.

[44] Ibid.

[45] Ethnic Ministries, Board of Discipleship, *Ethnic Ministries in the United Methodist Church* (Nashville: Discipleship Resources, 1976), 1.

[46] J. Philip Wogaman, *Christian Moral Judgment (*Louisville: Westminster/John Knox Press, 1989), Wogaman discusses the method of positive presumption on pages 89-115.

[47] Mitchell and Lewter-Cooper, 95.

[48] Ibid., 96.

[49] Ibid.

[50] E. Stanley Jones, *Gandhi: Portrayal of a Friend* (Nashville: Abingdon, 1948), Based on his relationship with Mohandas Gandhi, Jones offers insight on how relationships can be built across cultures and religions, with particular reference to Christianity and Hinduism.

[51] Chinua Achebe, *Things Fall Apart* (New York: Anchor Books, 1959), Achebe offers a complete exposition of the

effect of western, Christian colonization upon Ibo (Nigerian) culture.

[52] Jean Marc Ela, *My Faith as an African* (New York: Maryknoll, NY: Orbis), 91.

[53] Carolyn C. Denard, "Retrieving and Reappropriating the Values of the Black Church Tradition through Written Narratives, in *The Stones that the Builders Rejected,* ed. Walter E. Fluker (Harrisburg, PA: Trinity Press International, 1998), 84.

[54] Law, *The Bush Was Burning But Not Consumed,* xi.

[55] Horace M. Kallen, *Cultural Pluralism and the American Idea* (Philadelphia: University of Pennsylvania Press, 1956), 55. William B. McClain in *Travelling Light* (New York: Friendship Press, 1981), pp. 99-101, offers an analysis of Kallen's thoughts on cultural pluralism.

[56] Jonamay Lambert and Selma Myers, *50 Activities for Diversity Training* (HRD Press, 1994) Lambert and Myers outline the process of interculturation/multiculturation in the "Path of Intercultural Learning."

[57] Haring, 3.

[58] Solle, 156.

CHAPTER TWO

THE SPIRITUAL AND INTELLECTUAL DEVELOPMENT OF HOWARD THURMAN

I. Early Development and Identity

The grandson of slaves, Howard Thurman came out of the black religious tradition with a message of hope and wholeness for all people. Born in segregated Daytona, Florida on November 18, 1900, Thurman stayed in that city until the absence of educational opportunities for Negroes forced him to go to Jacksonville, Florida for a high school education. He completed undergraduate studies at Morehouse College in Atlanta, Georgia in 1923, and his graduate studies in Theology at Rochester Divinity School in Rochester, New York in 1926.

Thurman's ministerial career formally began in Oberlin, Ohio where, from 1926 until 1928, he pastored an African-American Baptist congregation. From 1932-44, he served as Dean of Rankin Chapel and Professor of Theology at Howard University. In 1953, Thurman became the first African-American dean at a majority white university, the Dean of Marsh Chapel and Professor of Spiritual Resources and Disciplines at Boston University. During this same period, he formed the Howard Thurman Educational Trust, which disburses funds for various humanitarian endeavors, most notably scholarships for African-American students in the South. Prominent among his many involvements, however, was the San Francisco based church which he cofounded and copastored from 1944-53 – The Church for the Fellowship of All Peoples (Fellowship Church) – heralded as the first authentically inclusive model of institutional religion in the United States.[1]

Howard Thurman was a multidimensional person who lived on all levels of existence – physical, emotional, and spiritual. Describing his attributes is like constructing a bridge. The bridge, to be effective, must reach both sides, or the traveler will fall.[2] Vincent Harding captured the essence of Thurman as a "God-intoxicated" man when he wrote about Thurman in the introduction to *For the Inward Journey.* Harding observed that Howard Thurman was a person who was constantly moving toward the source of all human life and truth via the concrete beauty and terror of the black experience in the United States.[3]

Lerone Bennett, Jr. in his eulogy of Howard Thurman in 1981, pointed to Thurman's perspective on life, "A man cannot be at home everywhere, unless he is at home somewhere."[4] One has to know from whence he has come in order to understand how he is to operate within the context of present reality and future possibility. Thurman seemed to be at home with his roots in Southern black culture.

Luther E. Smith, in his seminal work on Howard Thurman, *The Mystic as Prophet,* places Thurman's life within the context of the dual attributes of his mystical nature and prophetic witness.[5] Several scholars have asserted that Thurman's primary identity was that of mystic.[6] Briefly defined, the mystic is one who believes that she or he has experienced a special angle of perception or encounter with ultimacy (however construed), which encounter departs from normative social constructions of what is "real."[7] Cheslyn Jones of Oxford University suggests that there seem to be four constants in mystical experience. First, the mystic is in touch with an 'object' which is invisible, intangible and inaccessible, beyond sensual contact. Second, the 'object' is inexhaustible, infinite, and incomprehensible (in the present sense cannot be captured or surrounded), and therefore is also inexpressible, beyond full description. Third, the contact is intuitive, 'immediate' (unmediated) and direct, even if after introduction by a third party or book. Fourth, even so, there is an inward affinity between the 'object' and the person, an attraction or fascination, even leading to mutual interpenetration or communion.[8]

Thurman was a mystic who recognized the necessity of social activism for enabling and responding to religious experience. This is evident when he says:

> Therefore, the mystic's concern with the imperative of social action is not merely to improve the condition of society. It is not merely to feed the hungry, not merely to relieve human suffering and human misery. If this were all,

in and of itself, it would be important surely. But this is not all. The basic consideration has to do with the removal of all that prevents God from coming to himself in the life of the individual. Whatever there is that blocks this, calls for action.[9]

Luther Smith asserts that when you study a prophet, you simultaneously study his people. The prophet's significance is the result of his relationship with his community.[10] Walter Brueggamann, in *The Prophetic Imagination,* offers that four characteristics emerge as indicators of prophetic ministry: (1) the establishment of an "alternative community" which is conscious of its unique identity and mission to others; (2) the prophetic insights are communicated in every activity of ministry, and they define sources of life and death for every context; (3) persons are helped in seeing the world as it really is, and to become fully sensitive to the hurt and pain experienced in life; (4) prophetic ministry seeks to penetrate despair so that new futures can be believed in and embraced by us.[11]

Thurman's ministry can be clearly viewed within the context of these four expressions of the prophetic. His constant yearning was toward a clearer personal and communal comprehension of what he often referred to as "the irreducible essence" of life. Activist Jesse L. Jackson recounts how Thurman would often challenge him to move toward this "irreducible essence." According to Jackson, Thurman's point was that if you ever developed a cultivated will, with spiritual discipline, the flame of freedom would never perish. The irreducible essence, developed through the cultivated will with spiritual discipline, would result in spiritual and social transformation.[12]

Howard Thurman's search for peaceful community is intricately connected to the yearning for this irreducible essence as rooted in his own search for a spirituality and sense of connectedness with God. This yearning for God-connectedness is evident in Thurman's prayer:

> Lord, I want to be more holy in my heart.
> Here is the citadel of all my desiring,
> where my hopes are born,

and all the deep resolutions of my spirit take wings.
In this center, my fears are nourished,
and all my hates are nurtured.
Here my loves are cherished,
all the deep hungers of my spirit are honored
without quivering and without shock.
In my heart, above all else,
let love and integrity envelop me
until my love is perfected and the last vestige
of my desiring is no longer in conflict with thy Spirit.
Lord, I want to be more holy in my heart.[13]

Thurman's desire to experience God is further articulated in another prayer:

O Holy God, open to me light for my darkness,
courage for my fear, hope for my despair.
O loving God, open for me wisdom for my confusion,
forgiveness for my sins, love for my hate.
O God of peace, open for me peace for my turmoil,
joy for my sorrow, strength for my weakness.
O generous God, open my heart
to receive all your gifts.

In his work, Howard Thurman sought to "utilize the raw materials of daily experience as the time and place for the encounter with God."[14]   He viewed nature as critical to helping persons understand the life of the spirit. At one point he compared life to a river. The river flows constantly seeking to connect with its source – the sea. In human life, persons perpetually seek to discover that which is the source of life – the source of being and the source of meaning. That being the divine source.[15]

In his reflection, "The Will to Live," Thurman described a personal encounter with nature that helped him experience existence at a deeper level. He wrote:

You have seen trees growing out of sheer rock; or roots, finding no soil below or being unable to penetrate the rocky substance of the earth, spread themselves, fan shape, on the surface, sending their tendrils into every crevice and cranny

where hidden moisture and soil fragments accumulate. You
have seen human beings with their bodies reduced to mere
skeletons and all the vestiges of health wiped out – yet for
interminable periods they continue breathing, as if to breathe
were life.[16]

While walking down a street in Georgia, Thurman observed
a tree that had broken through the concrete pavement. The pavement could not contain the tree's desire to live. In spreading itself
and breaking through, the tree demonstrated its determination to
live.

Howard Thurman's yearning for the fullness of life, and
for an appropriation of peaceful community was rooted in his own
spirituality. In *Meditations of the Heart,* he wrote:

Here is in every person an inward sea, and in that sea there
is an island and on that island there is an altar, and standing
before that altar is the "angel with the flaming sword."
Nothing can get by that angel to be placed upon that altar
unless it has the mark of the inner authority. Nothing passes
"the angel with the flaming sword" to be placed upon your
altar unless it is a part of "the fluid of your consent." This
is your crucial link to the Eternal.[17]

Thurman's intense belief in the personal, private experience of God has resulted in his being labeled an advocate of personal piety. This labeling is not completely accurate, according to
Luther Smith.[18] Although Thurman's insistence on self-awareness
and transformation can be cast within the pietistic tradition, he had
just as intense a commitment to community. His mystical experiences were the basis of this commitment to community. Thurman
writes:

It is in the moment of [mystical] vision that there is a sense
of community – a unity not only with God, but a unity with
all of life, particularly with human life. It is in the moment
of vision that the mystic discovers that (his) "private values
are undergirded and determined by a structure which far
transcends the limits of one's individual self."…The ascetic
impulse having as its purpose individual purification and

living brings the realistic mystic face to face with the society in which he functions as a person. He discovers that his is a person and a personality [which] in a profound sense can only be achieved in a milieu of human relations. Personality is something more than mere individuality – it is a fulfillment of the logic of individuality in community.[19]

In Segundo Galilea's article "Liberation as an Encounter with Politics and Contemplation," there is confirmation for Thurman's convictions about the process of moving from the autonomy of the mystic to the prophetic unity of community.[20]   Galilea writes:

Authentic Christian contemplation, passing through the desert, transforms contemplatives into prophets and heroes of commitment and militants into mystics. Christianity achieves the synthesis of the politician and the mystic, the militant and the contemplative, and abolishes the false antithesis between the religious-contemplative and the militantly committed. Authentic contemplation, through the encounter with the absolute of God, leads to the absolute of one's neighbor.[21]

Galilea then describes effective responses to contemplation, which make a better world (community). One response is political activity, which involves the contemplative in party politics. A second response, which describes Thurman's commitments and ministry, is what Galilea calls "the prophetic pastoral option." He characterizes the option in the following way:

In it [the prophetic pastoral option] charity, the source of contemplation, is channeled into the effective proclamation of the message of Christ about the liberation of the poor and the "least." The message becomes a *critical consciousness*, and is capable of inspiring the deepest and most decisive liberating transformation. In this sense it has social and political consequences.[22]

Alton Pollard employs the phrase "mystic-activism" as a description of Thurman's involvements. His was a form of mysticism – rooted in historic cenobitic perspective - which sought to constructively engage in the process of community-building. A designation of Thurman within the context of mystic-activism focuses attention on the real potential of mysticism as a discomforting yet compelling call to action.[23]

Mystic-activism is a praxis-orientation to the world that relies – at least in part – on the political and intellectual arguments and dictates of society. [24] For Thurman, transformed individuals are the first step in the remaking of the social order into a peaceful and just society. True peaceful community can only be established when transformed individuals act within and upon social structures, and become involved in social mechanisms. The movement toward peaceful community through social action (demonstrations, running for public office, critiquing social institutions and structures, community organizing and boycotts) is a natural consequence of personal piety.

II. Intellectual and Spiritual Influences

In assessing Howard Thurman's intellectual development, Mozella G. Mitchell makes the important observation that "for one reason or another ... perhaps for many reasons, one no doubt being the social limitations he faced as a Black American, Thurman chose a route of development different from the systematic. He chose to remain free of the restrictions of any exact discipline such as literature, theology, psychology, or philosophy.[25] Thurman never altered his ideas to conform either to the standard university or ecclesiastical life.

Luther Smith suggests that four persons stand out as having had a crucial impact upon the development of Howard Thurman's thought and spirituality: George Cross, Henry B. Robins, Rufus Jones, and Nancy Ambrose, Thurman's maternal grandmother.[26] These persons would serve as the major influencers for Thurman intellectually, as well as spiritually, and would help to shape his philosophy and practice of community-building.

A. George Cross

George Cross taught Howard Thurman systematic theology during his last year and a half of seminary education at Rochester Divinity School (1925-1926). Cross's influence on Thurman can be seen first in Cross's pursuit of an element which he could identify as the *essence* of the Christian faith. It is the basic, unchanging, unifying truth that characterizes and genuinely manifests the faith. This essential truth may be found in Christian doctrines, dogmas, creeds, and theologies, but it is never fully contained in them. This essential truth has the fundamental qualities common to all religions, yet it is distinctive within Christianity, according to Cross.[27]

The essence of Christianity is what Cross endeavored to define through his method for doing apologetics.[28] This essence is characterized in the following ways:

1. It is "a quality of spiritual life," where one acknowledges that one's ultimate interests and commitments must be with spiritual concerns.

2. The personality of Jesus Christ is the basis for understanding the essence. In Jesus, the Christian finds the perfect life. And through spiritual fellowship with this perfect life, its teachings and the meaning of its example, the Christian finds the way to "the higher life."

3. It has distinctive qualities that are similar to other religions. It takes the individual into a consciousness of the relation to God, which brings fulfillment to the heart like no other religion. Other religions are "Christianity in its beginning or lower stages."[29]

4. It is the practice of the most perfect fellowship, where the potentialities in every person are appreciated, developed, and made available to the needs of others.

5. It is "one and the same with true morality." Love and devotion to God mean love and devotion to the welfare of our fellow man and woman.

6. It has the power for moral redemption, such that it delivers humanity from the domination of evil.

7. It creates the experience of perfect peace for the believer. In the midst of suffering, fear and anxieties, this essence gives confidence and power to withstand and overcome.

The teleology of George Cross's conception of Christian essence is to lead the individual and community toward salvation. In his book, *Christian Salvation,* Cross defines salvation this way:

> ...to the modern Protestant it is the bringing of the man into such a fellowship with God as gives him a self-mastery and a self-devotion to the highest end of life. It is the entrance into an experience of conscious unity of life with one's fellowmen, a participation in the ministry of a universal good. It is to be endowed with that spirit of enterprise that enables him to turn the forces of the material world toward their true end, to make them angels of mercy sent forth to do service for the sake of them that shall inherit salvation.[30]

According to Cross, there must be individual salvation before a community can be saved. Christian salvation is ultimately the movement toward "perfect community" or "shalom." Perfect community for Cross is actualized at the place and time where persons are able to exercise their full potential and be in loving relationship with other individuals.

Howard Thurman's major disagreement with the liberalism espoused by George Cross was the fatuous positivism it displayed. Modernism's unmitigated belief in national destiny and world progress served to obscure the malignancy and pervasiveness of domestic evils, particularly as regards racism. For Thurman, a theological stance so readily given to ignoring hostilities directed at vast segments of the population (African Americans, women, various immigrant groups, etc.) was itself seriously impaired. He understood such optimism to be a critical if not fatal departure from social reality, utterly irreconcilable with his own experience as one of the dominated and disinherited.

Despite Thurman's attestation that Cross was the teacher who had a "greater influence on my mind than any other person who ever lived," he remained at variance with the idea of leisurely introspection as the means to human attainment. Thurman shared deeply in the concern of Cross and Henry Robins for the centrality of human personality, the universal life of the spirit, and other liberal motifs, but he had to express the "hunger of the spirit" which they encouraged inclusive of his own racial fact.[31]

B. Henry B. Robins

Henry B. Robins was professor of Religious Education and the History and Philosophy of Religion and Missions at Rochester Divinity School while Howard Thurman was a student there. Robins is credited with identifying for Thurman the *religious essence*, which is found in all expressions of religion. While George Cross's essence is the cohesive factor for Christian Apologetics, Robin's essence is the cohesiveness in Comparative Religion. For both Cross and Robins, Christianity is the culmination of the evolutionary process. Christianity, at its core, is universal in character. It has the ability to include and speak meaningfully to the religious aspirations of all the world's peoples. This universal quality makes it the greatest missionary religion.[32]

For Robins, the purpose of the essence is the "Kingdom of God," while Cross viewed purpose in the context of the "saved community." The Kingdom of God is the perfect human fellowship where redemptive love is fulfilled.[33]

While Cross was the one who commissioned Howard Thurman to garner all his energies to address the "hunger of the spirit," Thurman credited Robins as the teacher who "was as close to introducing me (Thurman) to the life of the spirit as any professor I had."[34] Cross raised the importance of spiritual matters. Robins gave definition to them, particularly their unifying and universal qualities. But most importantly, Robins led Thurman to an understanding of how he (Thurman) was to participate in the "spiritual adventure."

C. Rufus Jones

The liberal reconstruction of religion and the concern for social disorganization that emerged in the late nineteenth century was the inheritance of Rufus Jones. This orientation, combined with his deep roots in the mystical tradition of Quakerism, formed the framework for his thought. Thurman credited Jones along with George Cross as having most prominently "opened the way in my thinking." [35]   Jones's consuming interest in life was to interpret the validity of the mystical experience and the social role of the mystic. He was one of three leading interpreters of mysticism during his time, William James and Evelyn Underhill being the others. He rejected James' (psychological) and Underhill's near obsession with the substantive dimensions of mystical experience, as important as this was, for a more deliberate functional analysis. [36]

Howard Thurman became aware of Rufus Jones through his book, *Finding the Trail of Life*. Upon finishing the book, Thurman had a feeling of "instant kinship" with the author. He initiated correspondence with Jones, and for six months during 1929 became a "special student of Philosophy" in residence with this Quaker mystic at Haverford College. [37]

Rufus Jones gave Thurman his first extensive exposure to the historical, philosophical and experiential dimensions of mysticism. Though Thurman had remembered experiences of mystical consciousness since childhood, the internship brought definition, discipline, and perspective to the experiences. Jones boldly underscored Robin's emphasis that religion be an experience. More than any other teacher, Jones formed the nexus that religious experience, at its profoundest level, is mystical experience.

Jones, was deeply committed to a theology which claims issues of justice, freedom, and peace as inherent interests of the religious venture. Commitment to the spiritual life is a commitment to that power which is able to save the world. Spiritual issues are the very ground of all material concerns (e.g., politics, civil rights, poverty, crime).

Specifically, it was Jones who offered a linkage that gave Thurman the vision of how spiritual power could address the conditions that oppressed him as a black man in America. Howard Thurman confirms the significance of this linkage when he says:

> ...all my life I have been seeking to validate, beyond all ambivalence and frustrations, the integrity of the inner life... I have sought a way of life that could come under the influence of, and be informed by, the fruits of the inner life. The cruel vicissitudes of the social situation in which I have been forced to live in American society have made it vital for me to seek resources, or a resource, to which I could

have access as I sought means for sustaining the personal enterprise of my life beyond all the ravages inflicted upon it by the brutalities of the social order.[38]

According to Jones, the problem of race could be forcefully addressed through the ministry to the Spirit. Or more specifically, the race question could be understood as a spiritual matter.

D. Nancy Ambrose

While scholars like Cross, Robins and Jones significantly impacted Howard Thurman intellectually and spiritually in his later life, it was his maternal grandmother, Nancy Ambrose who cultivated his spirit and mind from an early age. Of his grandmother, Thurman says:

I learned more, for instance, about the genius of the religion of Jesus from my grandmother than from all the men who taught me all … the Greek and the rest of it. Because she moved inside the experience and lived out of that kind of center…[39]

Reared by his beloved Grandma Nancy, a former slave, young Thurman regularly read the Bible aloud to her as a child. From her he learned not only of the trials of slavery, but also of the slaves' deep religious faith, which profoundly shaped his vision of the transformative promise of Christianity. Nancy Ambrose appropriated a "religious essence" that was not just in dialogue with concern for the world but with the particular issue of what it means to be black in America. Howard Thurman was profoundly influenced by the views of his grandmother on religion and racism. Much of her thinking is captured in her views of Scripture. Thurman writes:

Two or three times a week I read the Bible aloud to her. I was deeply impressed by the fact that she was most particular about the choice of Scripture. For instance, I might read many of the more devotional Psalms, some of Isaiah, the Gospels again and again, but the Pauline epistles, never – except at long intervals, the thirteenth chapter of First Corinthians… With the feeling of great temerity, I asked her one day why it was that she would not let me read any of the Pauline letters. What she told me I shall never forget. "During the days of slavery," she said, "the master's minister would occasionally hold services for the slaves. Old man McGhee was so mean that he would not let a Negro minister preach to his slaves. Always the white minister used as his text: 'Slaves, be obedient to your master... as unto Christ.' Then he would go on to show how it was God's will that we were slaves and how, if we were good and happy slaves, God would bless us. I promised my Maker that if I ever learned to read and if freedom ever came, I would not read that part of the Bible."[40]

In contrast, she often told the story of the black preacher who had a different message for the slaves. In their gathering he would say: "You are not slaves, you are not niggers – you are God's children." As his grandmother finished her story with those lines, a kind of transformation took place in her. According to Thurman: "she would unconsciously straighten up, head high and chest out, and a faraway look would come on her face."[41]

Nancy Ambrose was not a scholar *per se,* but a sapient personality who understood the value of a cultivated mind. As a young girl living on a Florida plantation in the ante-bellum period no prospects for liberty existed, but early on she established the grounds for freedom. Liberty was conferred from without, but freedom, she discovered, was founded from within. She never received any formal education yet she was acutely aware of its importance. When the owner's daughter was punished for trying to teach her the rudiments of reading and counting, Nancy Ambrose knew "there must be some magic in knowing how to read and write."[42] Later, she would communicate to her grandson a fundamental reason for obtaining the "magic" of knowledge, sharing this message: "Your only chance is to get an education. The white man will destroy you if you don't."[43]

Nancy Ambrose was for Howard Thurman, a source of protection, hope and faith. Elizabeth Yates, Thurman's biographer, describes Nancy Ambrose's significance in his life as follows:
    She backed up her word with action and he knew he could

count on her. He boasted to his friends of her, saying she could kill a bear with her fist. No one disputed him, though no one felt a need for a test. There was not a person in the Negro community on the shore of the Halifax River who had not at a time of trouble felt anchored by her strength. She was a haven to them all. More than anyone else, she made Howard feel his significance, not only as a Negro boy but as a Child of God.[44]

The profound influence of Nancy Ambrose on Thurman and his understanding of Christian love and peaceful community is evident in a story from his childhood. After fighting another boy, he went home bruised and tattered. As he faced his grandmother the following exchange took place:

"No one ever wins a fight," were her only words as she looked at me. "But I beat him," I said. "Yes, but look at you. You beat him, but you will learn someday that nobody ever wins a fight." [45]

Throughout his lectures and writings, Thurman spoke of his grandmother in saintly, yet intimate tones. The prominence he gave to her ideas and example can be understood when one considers her meaning in the making of his personality. In a period of Thurman's life when his world seemed wrought with insecurity and death, she had attributes which translated into power. She acted as one who had inner authority. Rather than being controlled by her environment she exercised control over it. Nancy Ambrose became a role model for him. She was the exemplary mentor.[46]

It is not difficult to see the influence of Nancy Ambrose in Thurman's stress that the individual, rather than the institution or the group, is the key to social change. She was an individual who survived personal tragedy, challenged the church, influenced the local community, found integrity and worth in her racial identity, fearlessly confronted any aggressive action from their hostile environment, and who drew upon personal religious experience as the source of her life.[47]

III. The Development of a Conception of Peaceful Community in the Thinking of Howard Thurman

Grounded in and shaped by the vicissitudinous struggles of black America, Howard Thurman offered a perspective on the universal phenomenon of religiously-related social change among oppressed and exploited peoples that is at once accordant and distinctive. The capacity of African Americans to decry the debasements of the larger society through a plethora of means – often discernibly religious in promotion, both violent and non-violent in expression – is historic, deep-rooted and not without considerable documentation.[48]

It is a well-known fact that the condition of struggle is not restricted to the North American context, but has numerous counterparts wherever situations of cross-cultural contact – that is, Western forms of conquest and domination – have occurred in the modern world. A canvassing of literature in this area reveals a strong bond of commonality among these seemingly disparate movements, not infrequently reflected in their mystic-like envisagement or cognition of a regenerate and reordered society, where the value of all human life and the actualizing of human potential is ascendant. Thus, at least in their initial stages, a holisitc sense of re-creation and affirmation with respect to self, community, and culture is often found to inform and permeate movements in the "Two-Thirds World."[49]

Alton Pollard offers the concept "social regeneration" as the type of mystical action in which Howard Thurman engaged. Social regeneration discloses an ethical program working on three levels – synchronizing intra-individual (personal), inter-individual (communal) and inter-group (societal) orderliness. In Thurman's case, social regeneration denotes a holistic process that is generally critical of church and society, but not in a fundamentally hostile or negating sense. The impetus for social regeneration lies not so much in social structures as in the transformation of individuals, who alone are capable of generating a force fully vibrant and sufficient to break through oppressive structures. Social regeneration is increasingly effected as enough individuals experience the transforming "sense of wholeness" or ethical orderliness and will to implement its verity in society.   The aim of social regeneration, is not to perpetuate conflict in society simply because or whenever there is no abiding evidence of hope, but in order to facilitate and increase rapprochement between individuals and social groupings.   This is the *sine qua non* for Thurman's advancement of the concept of "community."[50]

Thurman further asserted that social regeneration would lead to social activism.   The unconditional seriousness of the religious experience itself impels social corroboration, causing one to engage "the powers of this world" with a strident social dimension. The knowledge accrued in this encounter is relational and transactional in character, ushering in a personally transformative system of values and a new, or at the very least, revitalized mode of interaction with others (community and society) and God.   The impetus for social regeneration occurs when an individual's ultimate allegiances – race, creed, gender, nationality, and socio-economic standing are transvalued to a less defensive, penultimate status.[51]

A. Pilgrimage to India

During his tenure at Howard University, Howard Thurman and his wife were asked to be members of a delegation on a "Pilgrimage of Friendship" to India, Ceylon and Burma.   Thurman's participation was considered important because "in a country divided by religious beliefs into Touchables and Untouchables, rich and poor, the testimony of representatives from another country's minority group might be far-reaching."[52]

Thurman and the delegation lectured and discussed issues at 45 academic centers in these three countries from October 1935 through the spring of 1936.   He was questioned continually about the compatibility of Christianity with black people's struggle for human dignity.   White Christians and churches had a history of being insensitive to black people's worth and freedom.   Thurman answered these queries by distinguishing Christianity from the religion of Jesus.   Despite this clarification, Thurman admits that:

> All answers had to be defensive because there was not a
> single instance known to me in which a local church had a

completely integrated membership. The color bar was honored in the practice of the Christian religion. From a 10,000-mile perspective, this monumental betrayal of the Christian ethic loomed large and forbidding.[53]

It was out of this background that he had a religious experience at Kyber Pass (between Afghanistan and West Pakistan) which excited a vision that would determine the thrust of his social witness for the rest of his life. Thurman writes:

> We saw clearly what we must do somehow when we returned to America. We knew that we must test whether a religious fellowship could be developed in America that was capable of cutting across all racial barriers, with a carryover into the common life, a fellowship that would alter the behavior patterns of those involved. It became imperative now to find out if experiences of spiritual unity among people could be more compelling than the experiences which divide them.[54]

In a sense, the trip to South Asia provided a crucial global context and served as a catalyst for Thurman's understanding of the relationship between what was for him authentic religion and human suffering. Here, he was confronted with the tension of political and social patterns of exclusiveness that rivaled racial discrimination in America. He discovered that the Hindu Untouchable and the African American alike were bound in their subordinate status. Equally unsettling was the fact that religion and culture had cojoined to legitimate and encourage this sordid quarantine. [55]

Thurman returned to Howard University convinced that a religious fellowship in America had to be conceived which would unite persons across social and creedal divisions. At Howard, he began to experiment with the arts, meditation, and innovative liturgies to create a worship experience which affirmed the unity within the audience, and which had religious, social, and philosophical diversity. These creative services were to evoke religious feelings that magnified the essence of religion, as opposed to religious dogmas and creeds that emphasized divisive differences. Members of the audience were not perceived as objects for theological discourse,

but as subjects of experience. A common religious experience had
the potential to transcend and diminish the meaning of all that separates.[56]

When the invitation came for Howard Thurman to help organize an interracial church in San Francisco, he saw it as an opportunity to realize his Kyber Pass vision.[57]   San Francisco, with its
cultural diversity, was not a controlled environment and could serve
as a true laboratory for Thurman's dream. It was an opportunity to
test the power of Christianity to overcome the separateness of discrimination, prejudice, and segregation – to test the ability of the
Church to be a loving interracial fellowship – to test, as Thurman
states, "the future of democracy."[58]

B. Church for the Fellowship of All Peoples

The opportunity to further explore his convictions about
the unifying nature of the religious experience came in 1944 when
Howard Thurman was invited by the Fellowship of Reconciliation
to join Alfred G. Fisk (a white Presbyterian minister and college
professor) as the co-pastor of a new interracial church in San Francisco. After prayerful consideration, Thurman left his tenured pro-
fessorship and position as Dean of Rankin Chapel at Howard University and ventured westward, excited about the challenges of an
interracial ministry:

> Here at last I could put to the test once more the major
> concern of my life. Is the worship of God the central and
> most significant act of the human spirit? Is it really true
> that in the presence of God there is neither male or female,
> child or adult, rich nor poor, nor any classification by which
> mankind defines itself in categories, however meaningful?[59]

The racial makeup of San Francisco in 1944 made it the
ideal location for the testing of this fundamental theological concern. Whites, Asian-Americans, Mexican-Americans, Native Americans and African Americans lived side by side during a time of
deep ethnic tension. Specifically, the steady arrival of black mi-
grants in search of jobs in the war industries; the white backlash to

increased racial diversity; and the relocation of Japanese-Americans to concentration camps, created a social climate that was a potential racial powderkeg.[60]

In this environment, Thurman wanted to prove that through authentic religious experience, people could transcend racial barriers and appreciate the interrelatedness of all humanity.[61] The Church for the Fellowship of All Peoples (officially organized in October 1944) developed a program and liturgy especially designed to foster unity in the midst of cultural and religious diversity. Both children and adults were regularly exposed to the contributions of different ethnic groups through worship experiences, forum discussions, lectures, games, recitals, art exhibits, and international dinners. As a result, "slowly there began to emerge a climate in which the fruits of culture could be appreciated, assimilated, and shared without patronage and condescension."[62]

Fellowship Church was the first church in American life that was intentionally interracial and intercultural in its membership and leadership. Black and white persons participated as equals in developing a Christian church that sought to model racial harmony. Thurman noted that until his departure from Fellowship Church in 1953, 60 percent of the membership was Caucasian, 35 percent were Negroes, and 5 percent were from other ethnic groups such as Mexican-American, Asian-American and Native American. There was also a broad range of educational levels in the congregation.[63] In addition to racial and cultural heterogeneity, the church represented a broad cross-section of the religious spectrum: Quaker, Baptist, Roman Catholic, Presbyterian, Jewish, Congregational, Methodist, and Episcopal, but also those who held no particular (religious) affinity.[64]

In his book, *Footprints of a Dream*, Thurman described the organizing, programming, worship and fellowship of the church. He stated that Fellowship Church's significance was not just in its ability to bring together separate groups, but in the quality of religious experience and the life-changing effect which that experience provided individuals. The church created, through its worship and fellowship, opportunities for persons to have a proper sense of self and the urge to establish community.[65]

In addition, Fellowship Church cultivated an openness to

religious truth beyond the confines of Judeo-Christian thought. The members expressed their ecumenical attitude in the spirit of Galatians 3:28:

> It is our faith that in the presence of God - with His dream of order – there is neither male nor female; white nor black, Gentile nor Jew; Protestant nor Catholic; Hindu nor Buddhist nor Moslem – but a human spirit, stripped to the literal substance of itself.[66]

Thurman's ecclesiology for social change was not to organize Fellowship Church as the base to spearhead a mass social movement. Instead, he placed importance on empowering the individual to live responsibly in whatever situations he or she works, socializes, recreates, or serves. For Thurman, Fellowship Church was a religious, and not merely a social experiment. This is evident in Thurman's statement, "The experience of worship became the keystone of the entire structure. My basic concern was the deepening of the spiritual life of the gathered people."[67]

Throughout the descriptions of his work at Fellowship Church, there is the emphasis on the development of the religious idiom that enabled people from various religious traditions to have a common experience of God's loving presence. Thurman's ecclesiology did not necessarily call for the involvement of Fellowship Church (as an institution) in the politics of society, but aimed to empower individuals to address economic, political and social needs as an outgrowth of religious experience. Thurman writes:

> The core of my preaching has always concerned itself with the development of the inner resources needed for the creation of a friendly world of friendly men... It was my conviction and determination that the church would be a resource for activists – a mission fundamentally perceived. To me it was important that individuals who were in the thick of the struggle for social change would be able to find renewal and fresh courage in the spiritual resources of the church.[68]

Fellowship Church received national acclaim for its example in race relations. The church became a model of possibility for churches nonplussed and paralyzed by social diversity. It became a model of Christian witness for a pluralistic society. Through Fellowship Church, Thurman proved the inclusive genius of Christianity. The church provided the empirical evidence he needed to confirm the insights from his own mystical consciousness about life's teleology toward community. The experiment of Fellowship Church verified the ability of Christianity and its institution to be a conduit that is capable of exposing and effectively addressing major contradictions of life, especially racism.

In the tradition of the Hebrew prophets and within the context of the prophetic pastoral option, Howard Thurman called America and the Christian church to recall the sources of their identity; for America the *Declaration of Independence and Constitution,* and for Christianity the inclusive love-ethic. The Church for the Fellowship of All Peoples sought to embody these resources.

C. The Christian Love-Ethic

Howard Thurman considered the terms "reconciliation" and "love" to be synonymous.[69] He defined love as "the intelligent, kindly but stern expression of kinship of one individual for another, having as its purpose the maintenance and furtherance of life at its highest level."[70]   Love responds to an individual's basic need of being cared for. It participates in the attempt to actualize potential, and therefore completes the fragmented and unfulfilled personality. But on a larger scale, it brings together separated lives. It makes apparent the significance of relationships by stressing how interdependence is inherent in all of life. Love creates community.[71]

Lerone Bennett asserts that Thurman was a pioneer of nonviolence in America and his book, *Jesus and the Disinherited,* offers perhaps the most comprehensive analysis of the Christian love-ethic.[72]   Bennett further suggests that Thurman had a great influence on Martin Luther King, Jr. and his thinking on the Christian love-ethic. When Bennett went to Montgomery, Alabama, shortly after the beginning of the Montgomery Bus Boycott, he was not at all surprised to find King reading not Mohandas Gandhi, but Howard Thurman.

Author and activist, Vincent Harding, recalls that Thurman's *Jesus and the Disinherited* was used by leaders in the civil rights movement as a theological foundation for their activism. They would regularly study and discuss the book together. It provided crucial instruction on nonviolence and the love-ethic as Christian means for overcoming social oppression. The leaders could better understand how to define and maintain their religious identity in the midst of political struggles. [73] Harding believes that this text defined the spiritual issues for social transformation, and that it inspired and emboldened leaders as they engaged in the struggle for justice.

Published in 1949, *Jesus and the Disinherited* gave a radical perspective of the mission, ministry and teachings of Jesus, as compared with the general view of the majority culture. Throughout, Thurman showed that Jesus' ministry in the world addressed the needs and aspirations of the disinherited. He pointed out that the concern of Jesus is still for the disinherited.[74]

For Thurman, there was no possibility of peaceful community without careful and constructive attention to the *disinherited*. He proclaimed that the mistreatment of America's *disinherited* and acceptance of "the will to segregate" are betrayals of American and Christian ideals of community-building.

Thurman's thoughts were rooted in his feelings of being personally victimized by racism. He was acutely aware that racism attacked his self-worth and freedom. It attacked the well-being of community. His mystical experiences, however, provided the assurance that he was a beloved child of God, and that harmonious relatedness is the underlying structure of reality. Racism denied the truth about God's intent for creation. It put the welfare of the community in crisis. The prophetic questions for Thurman became: How could he help shape a social reality that conformed to his religious beliefs? How could he speak to the crisis by restoring the community's (especially America's) sense of well-being?[75]

In *Jesus and the Disinherited*, Thurman wrote of the need to overcome hatred as a prerequisite for overcoming racism and building peaceful community.[76] Thurman's construct for understanding hatred begins in a situation where there is *contact without fellowship*. This is contact that is devoid of any of the primary overtures of warmth and fellow-feelings and genuineness. Secondly, Thurman points out that contacts without fellowship tend to express themselves in the kind of *understanding that is strikingly unsympathetic*. There is understanding of a kind, but it is without healing and reinforcement of personality. Thirdly, Thurman points out that unsympathetic understanding tends to express itself in the *active functioning of ill-will*.

To make his point, Thurman shared the story of once traveling from Chicago to Memphis, Tennessee.[77] He found his seat on the train across from an elderly lady, who took immediate cognizance of his presence. When the conductor came along for the tickets, she said to him, pointing in Thurman's direction, "What is *that* doing in this car?"

The conductor answered, with a touch of creative humor, "*That* has a ticket."

For the next fifty miles, this lady talked for five or ten minutes to all who were seated in that coach, setting forth her philosophy of human relationships and the basis of her objection to Thurman's presence in the car. Thurman says that he was able to see the atmosphere of the entire car shift from common indifference to active recognition of and, to some extent positive resentment of his presence in the car. He said, "An ill will spreading is like a contagious virus."

Fourth, Thurman suggests that active ill-will, when dramatized in a human being, becomes *hatred walking on earth*.

Thurman understood racism to be a contradiction of life.[78] Racism is inimical to the formation of identity. Neither blacks nor whites can attain a proper sense of self and give full expression to their potential in an environment of prejudice, segregation, and violence. Racism is also inimical to the formation of community. Systematic discrimination sabotages the function of community as a place of nurture and growth through cooperation. Destructive forces are released to rupture life's inter-relatedness.[79]

For Thurman, true community is the clearest manifestation of salvation. The essence of Christian life is to lead individuals and communities toward wholeness (*shalom*). Christian wholeness – according to Thurman – is ultimately the movement toward "perfect community."

Thurman's personal encounters with racism would serve to strengthen his resolve for peaceful community. He would share:

I know that the experiences of unity in human relations are more compelling than the concepts, the fears, the prejudices, which divide. Despite the tendency to feel my race superior, my nation the greatest nation, my faith the true faith, I must beat down the boundaries of my exclusiveness until my sense of separateness is completely enveloped in a sense of fellowship. There must be free and easy access by all, to all the rich resources accumulated by groups and individuals in years of living and experiencing.[80]

Amidst racism and other forms of hated, Thurman maintained that the religion of Jesus makes the love-ethic central. Regarding the love-ethic Thurman stated:

This is no ordinary achievement. It seems clear that Jesus started out with the simple teaching concerning love embodied in the timeless words of Israel: "Hear, O Israel: The Lord our God is one Lord: and thou shalt love the Lord thy God with all thy heart, and with all thy soul, and with all thy might," and "thy neighbor as thyself." Once the neighbor is defined, then one's moral obligation is clear.[81]

Thurman offered the story of the Good Samaritan as an example of how the love-ethic works:

In a memorable story Jesus defined the neighbor by telling of the Good Samaritan. With sure artistry and great power he depicted what happens when a man responds directly to human need across the barriers of class, race, and condition. Every man is potentially every other man's neighbor. Neighborliness is nonspatial, it is qualitative. A man must love his neighbor directly, clearly, permitting no barriers between.[82]

Thurman spoke of the difficulties faced by Jesus in attempting to teach and live out this love-ethic:

This was not an easy position for Jesus to take within his own community. Opposition to his teaching increased as the days passed. A twofold demand was made upon him at

all times: to love those of the household of Israel who became his enemies because they regarded him as a careless
perverter of the truths of God; to love those beyond the
household of Israel – the Samaritan and even the Roman.[83]

Regarding love of one's enemy, Thurman went on to state:
Love of the enemy means a fundamental attack must first
be made on the enemy status. How can this be done? Does
it mean ignoring the fact that he belongs to the enemy class?
Hardly. For lack of a better term, an "unscrambling" process is required. Obviously a situation has to be set up in
which it is possible for primary contacts to be multiplied.
By this I do not mean contacts that are determined by status
or by social distinctions. There are always primary contacts between the weak and the strong, the privileged and
the underprivileged, but they are generally contacts within
zones of agreement, which leave the status of the individual
intact. There is a great intimacy between whites and Negroes, but it is usually between servant and served, between
employer and employee. Once the status of each is frozen
or fixed, contacts are merely truces between enemies – a
kind of armistice for purposes of economic security.[84]

Clearly, Thurman's conception of Christian love was rooted
in the example of the unconditional love of Christ. The practice of
unconditional love is essential to the breaking down of social barriers such as racism.

Thurman suggests that nonviolent protests (i.e boycotts, non-
cooperation, demonstrations, sit-ins) are key means of providing
shock and transforming the social order. The development of a
philosophy of nonviolent protest in the black struggle is a foremost
achievement of his social witness. Here, Thurman makes a signal
contribution to providing a peaceful method for change in American race relations. Luther Smith argues that Thurman has done
more than any other person to articulate the ethical and spiritual
necessity for blacks' civil liberties struggle to be grounded in the
principles of nonviolence. As early as 1928 in his article, "Peace
Tactics and a Racial Minority," Thurman began to outline how a

"philosophy of pacifism" can begin to eliminate whites' will to control and blacks' will to hate. His primary concern was to call a truce to attitudes which promote separation.[85]

He began to outline more fully the basic principles of his philosophy of nonviolence in the early part of 1935 at the annual convocation on preaching at the School of Theology of Boston University. This material was later developed into the book *Jesus and the Disinherited.*[86]   He concluded that love is the force that creates full community, and nonviolent change is the best expression of love.   His *Disciplines of the Spirit* (1963) went further to explain the relationship of nonviolence to the spiritual quest for wholeness.[87]   Thurman stated:

> Since the will to segregate is a spiritual problem, only a spiritual answer which affirms the binding attributes of love will suffice. Violence is the act through which the nonexistence of the other person is willed, with hate as the dynamic. At the same time this is an act of self-affirmation, for hate becomes a man's way of saying that he is present. Ultimately, the human spirit cannot tolerate this because it denies the elemental truth of life that "men are made for each other." Violence is in opposition to the "fact of the underlying unity of life." Violence is in opposition to full community.[88]

The loving community of peace, justice and equality can only be attained by loving means. Community cannot be built on the tools of hatred. Nonviolence responds in a caring way to the perpetrator of violence. It announces that the well-being of the individuals involved is of ultimate concern. It moves the level of confrontation to a higher spiritual plane. Instead of merely defeating one's offender physically or psychologically, one begins to create the climate for love to be a force, which has to be dealt with within the context of relationship and fellowship. The presence of loving care introduces new possibilities for reconciliation. Only nonviolence permits love to enter conflict creatively and address the prevailing spiritual ills of separation, fear and hatred.

D. Fellowship

The concept behind Thurman's use of the term "fellow-ship" is explicated by Henry Nelson Wieman. Wieman distinguishes "sympathetic" and "instrumental" association from "organic" association. Sympathetic association is defined as "one in which the people associated share the same feelings, the same thoughts, the same aspirations, the same hopes and purposes."[89] Instrumental association is one in which persons work together in order to provide charitable services for others. It is organic association, however, which describes what Thurman means by "fellowship." [90]

In organic association, possessing the same feelings, thoughts, and purpose is *not* essential. Persons may differ significantly on issues, but through fellowship, members develop an appreciation of other perspectives while finding their own nurtured by the contact. Service is not excluded from organic association. Its purpose is to create the environment that makes organic interaction possible. Since, as Thurman believed, the universe is by nature organic, this type of fellowship is the only kind that produces harmonious living. Through organic fellowship inter-relatedness and reconciliation are discovered. Organic fellowship is synonymous with Thurman's concept of community.

Thurman criticized the Christian church as a supporter of a limited form of community, and a flawed sense of fellowship. He attributed this mainly to racial separation prevalent in church life, along with the church's zeal to identify the "saved" and the "damned." Separating and categorizing eventually lead certain groups of people to feel morally superior to others. When this mood infiltrates a group, conditions are set for a hostility which only works for limited community.[91] Thurman said:

It is to the utter condemnation of the church that large groups of believers all over the United States have stood, and, at present, stand on the side of a theory of inequality among men that causes the church to practice in its own body some of the most vicious forms of racial prejudice... The bitter truth is that the church has permitted the various hate-inspired groups in our common life to establish squatter's rights in the minds of believers because there has been no adequate teaching of the meaning of the faith in terms of human dignity and human worth.[92]

Thurman saw what he termed the "will to segregate" as the primary hindrance to the development of fellowship and authentic community in the church and society.[93]   The "will to segregate," Thurman said, "has taken the form of policy in business, in the church, in the state, in the school, in living zones." Thurman asserted that the church's task with regard to overcoming this "will to segregate" would be to engage in a radical reorganization of policy and structural change. Thurman said:

> I am realistic enough to know that this cannot be done overnight. My contention is that if the "will to segregate" is relaxed in the church, then the resources of mind and spirit and power that are already in the church can begin working formally and informally in the radical changes that are necessary if the church is to become Christian. This, of course, may not mean that there will be no congregations that are all Negro or that are all white, but freedom of choice, which is basically a sense of alternatives, will be available to any persons without regard to the faithful perpetuation of the pattern of segregation upon which the Christian church in America is constructed.[94]

For Howard Thurman, the Christian church has the potential for modeling authentic peaceful community. He believed that churches had too often been formed out of an ethos of exclusion. Churches typically excluded those who did not believe specific dogmas, and also excluded those who believed the accepted dogma, but who were of a certain socio-economic status or cultural background.[95]   Thurman believed that as long as the church operated on the principle of exclusion, it could not faithfully be the fully actualized trustee of religious experience and authentic, peaceful community-building.

Since community is ideally formed and nourished by the love-ethic, opportunities must be established for people to be in organic fellowship in order to express love and to be loved. Thurman asserted:

It is necessary, therefore, for the privileged and the under-privileged to work on the common environment for the purpose of providing normal experiences of fellowship. This is one very important reason for the insistence that segregation is a complete ethical and moral evil. Whatever it may do for those who dwell on either side of the wall, one thing is certain: it poisons all normal contacts for those persons involved. The first step toward love is a common sharing of a sense of mutual worth and value.[96]

In *The Search for Common Ground*, Thurman anticipated new opportunities to experience inclusive community when he wrote: It is time for assessing and reassessing resources in the light of the most ancient memory of the race concerning community, to hear again the clear voice of prophet and seer calling for harmony among all the children of men. At length there will begin to be talk of plans for the new city – that has never before existed on land or sea.[97]

Thurman continued to articulate his vision for organic fellowship by saying:

> One day there will stand up in their midst one who will tell of a new sickness among the children who in their delirium cry for their brothers whom they have never known and from whom they have been cut off behind the self-imposed barriers of their fathers. An alarm will spread throughout the community that it is being felt and slowly realized that community cannot feed for long on itself; it can only flourish where always the boundaries are giving way to the coming of others from beyond them – unknown and undiscovered brothers. [98]

E. The Vision of Peaceful Community

Howard Thurman identified community as the single most important quest of his life. It had occupied his thoughts and activities since childhood. Defining and appropriating community was the end purpose of Thurman's theology, with Christian love being the means – the instrument – for the realization of community. Establishing community was the commitment and labor of his ministry. [99]   The basic principle behind Howard Thurman's concept of community was that "the literal fact of the underlying unity of life seems to be established beyond doubt." He developed this principle in saying:

> If life has been fashioned out of a fundamental unity and ground, and if it has developed within a structure, then it is not to be wondered at that the interest in and concern for wholeness should be part of the conscious intent of life, more basic than any particular conscious tendency toward fragmentation… It (reconciliation) seeks to effect and further harmonize relations in a totally comprehensive climate.[100]

Thurman's book, *The Search for Common Ground,* is devoted to verifying this principle of the unity of life by examining the creation myths of culture, the life sciences, the philosophy behind utopias, and the social psychology of change in America as means of identifying and nurturing commonality among persons from diverse backgrounds. Thurman believed that the urge for and movement toward community, toward harmonious unity in life, could be found everywhere from the smallest cell to the whole universe.[101] This unity, as it relates to Thurman's concept of community, is characterized by its ability to allow persons (and nature) to actualize their potential. In actualizing potential, persons come to recognize and realize their worth and purpose in life.[102]

Thurman shaped his ministry out of the belief that all life is interrelated. He believed that nations, ethnic groups, and religious communities inhibit the realization of human community when they emphasize the differences that separate people instead of the common ties that bind them together.[103] Thurman captured the essence of his perspective on the interrelatedness of persons:

> To experience oneself as a human being is to feel life moving through one and claiming one as a part of it…It is not the experience of oneself as male or female, as black or white, as American or European. It is rather the experience

of oneself as being. It is at such a time that one can hear the sound of the genuine in other human beings.[104]

The formation of community is the teleology (essence) of life. The vision of community gives value, structure, and purpose to life; it saves life from meaninglessness, frustration, despair, boredom, anxiety, and chaos. Community is salvation; it is life at its highest level.[105] For Thurman, community (salvation) is not a beyond-this-world hope, but is a possibility for God's love to triumph in history. Jesus' message of salvation is eschatological in the sense that it pronounces the ability to experience salvation here and now.[106]

Thurman also affirmed the centrality of personality in forming a sense of community. He believed that community results from a sense of unity with life (inter- and intra-relatedness). This is only possible if the individual has a sense of "self" (inner-relatedness). The development of Thurman's theology begins with the individual. He believed that the individual personality is of infinite worth, and that its significance and nurture are essential concerns of religion. In understanding the principles that affirm, sustain and give meaning to the individual, one has the key to understanding that which affirms, sustains and gives meaning to community and ultimately to the universe.[107]

The essence of evangelical liberalism affirms a religious teleology in which Christianity wins the world to profess Jesus Christ as Lord. The saved community is the Christian community. The Kingdom of God is more precisely the Kingdom of God in Christ. Christianity's goal is to convert individuals and societies to "the way" of Jesus; any achievement less than this is inadequate.[108]

This emphasis on the centrality of personality to religion puts Howard Thurman in the company of George Cross, Henry Robins, and Rufus Jones. Personality-centered Christianity is the basic tenet of liberalism. For Thurman, two matters are essential for a true sense of self. First, since a person's inherent worth is of ultimate value, it is important that one's self-image conforms to one's own sense of reality. Thurman is convinced that an accurate sense of self is the only "basis that the dignity of man, the individual, can be restored."[109]

Secondly, though one's sense of reality is inherent, the nurture of this reality toward a healthy self-image is a social function. Thurman says, "We are all related either positively or negatively to some immediate social unit, which provides the other-than-self reference that in turn undergirds the sense of self. Such a primary group confers *persona* upon the individual; it fashions and fortifies the character structure."[110]

Love and freedom permit the individual to live the committed life that works for community. "Commitment" is a major theme of Thurman's theology.   In his book, *Disciplines of the Spirit,* it is the first discipline considered. Without commitment, the other disciplines, in Thurman's construct of community-building (growth, suffering, prayer, and love), are meaningless. Commitment orders, focuses, defines, and channels the use of one's resources. It also moves the individual from a false self-centerednesss. It illumines the reality that "our life is not our own" – that life is lived in inter-dependence with our fellow men and women, inter-dependence with nature, and most important of all, inter-dependence with God. This awareness not only devotes life to an other-than-self concern, but in devotion, the self is given a greater sense of its own meaning.[111]

Human freedom, then, is essential to love's commitment toward community-building. Howard Thurman felt that such freedom is not only essential, but is always operative. A person never loses the opportunity, and therefore the responsibility, for creating community. A person keeps the initiative over the living of his or her life.

Jesus of Nazareth, in Howard Thurman's mind, is the revelation of how personality creates community; Jesus personifies the transforming power of love. The conditions and circumstances of Jesus' life are significant in understanding Christianity and the meaning of Jesus in the world.[112] In *Jesus and the Disinherited,* Thurman emphasized the social circumstances of this poor and oppressed Jew, and then concluded that the religion of Jesus was a creative response which emerged from and dealt with transforming these conditions of oppression and sought to develop authentic community.

NOTES

[1] Alton Pollard, *Mysticism and Social Change: The Social Witness of Howard Thurman,* (New York: Peter Lang, 1992), 3.

[2] Michael I. N. Dash, et. al. *Hidden Wholeness: An African American Spirituality for Individuals and Communities* (Cleveland, OH: United Church Press), 1.

[3] Howard Thurman, *For the Inward Journey* (Richmond, IN: Friend United Press, 1984), x.

[4] Lerone Bennett, Jr. "Eulogy of Howard Thurman: Tributes to Genius," *The African American Pulpit*, p. 63, Lerone Bennett made reference to Thurman's perspective on life and personal identity at Thurman's funeral in 1981.

[5] Luther Smith, *Howard Thurman: The Mystic as Prophet* (Richmond, IN: Friends United Press, 1978), see pp. 15-20.

[6] Luther E. Smith and Alton B. Pollard are two of the scholars who have placed Thurman within the historic context of the mystical tradition.

[7] Pollard, 1.

[8] Cheslyn Jones, Jeffrey Wainwright and Edward Yarnold, SJ, eds. *The Study of Spirituality* (Oxford, UK: Oxford University Press, 1986), 19.

[9] Howard Thurman, "Mysticism and Social Change," *Eden Theological Seminary Bulletin* IV (Spring Quarter, 1939): 27.

[10] See Luther Smith, *The Mystic as Prophet*, see pp. 15-20.

[11] Walter Brueggemann, *The Prophetic Imagination* (Philadelphia: Fortress Press, 1978), 111.

[12] Jessie L. Jackson, "Eulogy of Howard Thurman: Tributes to Genius" in *The African American Pulpit,* p. 64. Jackson made reference to Thurman's notion of the "irreducible essence" at Thurman's funeral in 1981.

[13] Howard Thurman, This prayer appears in the *United Methodist Hymnal* (Nashville: United Methodist Publishing,

1989), 401.

[14] Howard Thurman, *Disciplines of the Spirit* (Richmond, IN: Friends United Press, 1987), 9.

[15] Howard Thurman, *Deep River and the Negro Spiritual Speaks of Life and Death* (Richmond, IN: Friends United Press, 1975), Thurman's thoughts on the river as metaphor for life and meaning is explicated throughout.

[16] Howard Thurman, *For the Inward Journey* (Richmond, IN: Friends United Meeting, 1984), 64.

[17] Howard Thurman, *Meditations of the Heart* (Richmond, IN: Friend United Press, 1953), 15.

[18] Luther Smith, 15.

[19] Thurman, "Mysticism and Social Change."

[20] Luther Smith, 17.

[21] Segundo Galilea, "Liberation as an Encounter with Politics and Contemplation," in *The Mystical and Political Dimension of the Christian Faith,* eds. Claude Gaffre and Gustavo Gutierrez (New York: Herder and Herder, 1974), 28.

[22] Ibid., 31-32.

[23] Pollard, 1.

[24] Ibid.

[25] Mozella Gordon Mitchell, *Spiritual Dynamics of Howard Thurman* (Bristol, IN: Wyndham Hall Press, 1985), 105. Alton Pollard also offers an exposition on this point in *Mysticism and Social Change,* 46.

[26] Luther Smith offers an explication on these four major influences in *Howard Thurman: The Mystic as Prophet.*

[27] Luther Smith, 23-24.

[28] George Cross, *What is Christianity: A Study of Rival Interpretations* (Chicago: University of Chicago Press, 1918), 187.

[29] Ibid., 193.

[30] George Cross, *Christian Salvation: A Modern Interpretation* (Chicago: University of Chicago Press, 1925), 133.

[31] Ibid., 33.

[32] Henry Robins believed that Christianity had the "Supreme Pattern" of the moral personality in the "Lord Jesus Christ." This view was explicated in his *Four Addresses Before the Burma Baptist Mission Conference* (Rangoon: American Baptist Mission Press, 1928).

[33] Both Henry Robins and George Cross defined "saved community" within the context of an environment of the growth of personality.

[34] Luther Smith, *The Mystic as Prophet,* 32. Smith recounts Thurman's views on Henry Robins from a 1978 personal interview.

[35] Pollard, 33. Pollard makes reference here to Howard Thurman, "Mysticism and Social Change," 15–part lecture series delivered at the Pacific School of Religion, Berkley, CA, July 5-28, 1978.

[36] Ibid., 33.

[37] Luther Smith, 33.

[38] Howard Thurman, *Mysticism and the Experience of Love* (Wallingford, PA: Pendle Hill, 1961), 4-5.

[39] Roberta Byrd Barr, interview with Howard Thurman, Seattle, Washington, January 1969.

[40] Wayne A. Meeks, *The Writings of St. Paul* (New York: Norton, 1978), xiv.

[41] Mary E. Goodwin, "Racial Roots and Religion: An Interview with Howard Thurman," *Christian Century,* 9 May 1973, 534.

[42] Ibid., 533.

[43] Elizabeth Yates, *Howard Thurman: Portrait of a Practical Dreamer* (New York: John Day, 1964), 23.

[44] Ibid., 47-48.

[45] Luther Smith, 138, see also Howard Thurman, *Deep is the Hunger: Meditations of Apostles of Sensitiveness* (New York: Harper and Brothers, 1951), pp. 10-11.

[46] Ibid., 173.

[47] Ibid.

[48] Pollard, 6, Pollard makes reference to the work to this effect by Vincent Harding, C. Eric Lincoln, and Gayraud Wilmore.

[49] Ibid.

[50] Ibid., 7-8.

[51] Ibid., 10.

[52] Yates. 95.

[53] Howard Thurman, *Footprints of a Dream: The Dawn of the Idea of the Church for the Fellowship of All Peoples: Letters Between Alfred Fisk and Howard Thurman, 1943-1944.* (San Francisco: Lawton and Alfred Kennedy, 1975), 24.

[54] Ibid., 24.

[55] Ibid., 23.

[56] Luther Smith, 9.

[57] Yates, 95.

[58] Thurman, *Footprints of a Dream*, 46.

[59] Howard Thurman, *With Head and Heart: The Autobiography of Howard Thurman* (New York: Harcourt, Brace, and Jovonovich, 1979), 144.

[60] Thurman, *Footprints of a Dream,* 13.

[61] Mark L. Chapman, *Christianity on Trial: African-American Religious Thought Before and After Black Power* (Maryknoll, NY: Orbis Books, 1996), 28.

[62] Thurman, *Footprints of a Dream,* 65.   Thurman's conception and practice of "church" is further developed in the works of Dennis Wiley, *The Concept of the Church in the Theology of Howard Thurman,* Ph.D. Dissertation (Union Theological Seminary, N.Y., 1988), and in Mark L Chapman, *Christianity on Trial.*

[63] Thurman, *Footprints of a Dream*, 109.

[64] Pollard, 79.

[65] Luther Smith, 11.

[66] Ibid.

[67] Thurman, *With Head and Heart,* 144.
[68] Thurman, *Disciplines of the Spirit,* 114-115.
[69] Ibid., 122.
[70] Thurman, *Deep is the Hunger,* 109.
[71] Luther Smith, 50.
[72] Lerone Bennett, Jr. "Eulogy of Howard Thurman: Tributes to Genius," p. 63.
[73] Luther Smith, 202.
[74] Olin Moyd, *Sacred Art,* 22.
[75] Luther Smith, 107.
[76] Howard Thurman, *Jesus and the Disinherited,* 74.
[77] See Howard Thurman's analysis of hate (hatred) in *Jesus and the Disinherited,* pp. 77-78.
[78] Luther Smith, 107.
[79] Ibid.
[80] Thurman, *The Mood of Christmas* (Richmond, IN: Friends United Press, 1969), 19.
[81] Thurman, *Jesus and the Disinherited,* 89.
[82] Ibid.
[83] Ibid., 89-90.
[84] Ibid., 92.
[85] Luther Smith, 133. Smith makes reference to Thurman's "Peace Tactics and a Racial Minority," *The Wold Tomorrow,* December, 1928, 505-507.
[86] See Thurman, *Jesus and the Disinherited,* pp. 89-109.
[87] See Thurman, *Disciplines of the Spirit,* pp. 104-127.
[88] Howard Thurman, *The Search for Common Ground: An Inquiry into the Basis of Man's Experience of Community* (Richmond, IN: Friends United Press, 1971), 104.
[89] Henry Nelson Wieman, *Methods of Private Religious Living* (New York: MacMillan Co., 1929), 140.
[90] Luther Smith, 73.
[91] Howard Thurman, "The Fascist Masquerade," pp. 82-100, in *The Church and Organized Movements,* Chapter 4, ed. Randolph Crump Miller (New York: Harper and Broth-

ers, 1946).

[92] Ibid.

[93] Howard Thurman, "The Will to Segregate," *Fellowship* (New York: Fellowship of Reconciliation, August, 1943).

[94] Ibid.

[95] Thurman, *The Creative Encounter,* 140-145.

[96] Thurman, *Jesus and the Disinherited,* 98.

[97] Thurman, *The Search for Common Ground,* 103.

[98] Ibid., 104.

[99] Luther Smith, 48.

[100] Thurman, *Disciplines of the Spirit,* pp, 104-105.

[101] Luther Smith, 49.

[102] Ibid., 50.

[103] Mark L. Chapman, 28.

[104] Howard Thurman, *The Luminous Darkness,* (New York: Harper and Row, 1965), 98-99.

[105] Luther Smith, 51.

[106] Thurman, *The Mood of Christmas,* 9.

[107] Luther Smith, 54

[108] Ibid., 93.

[109] Howard Thurman, *Deep is the Hunger,* 62.

[110] Ibid., 63.

[111] Ibid., 94-95.

[112] Luther Smith, 62.

CHAPTER THREE

THE SPIRITUAL AND INTELLECTUAL DEVELOPMENT OF MARTIN LUTHER KING, JR.

Throughout his public life, Martin Luther King, Jr. consistently reached down into the deep streams of the religious experience and social integration that had been so integral to his early formation. It was within these streams that he seemed to consistently discover and re-discover the essence of a faithfulness in God, which would ultimately sustain him in his constant beckoning for persons in the church and society to heed the words of the Prophet Micah, to "love kindness, and to do justice, and to walk humbly with God." (Micah 6:8)

Any examination of King's public intellectual life is to be understood within the context of the faith that he lived, the lessons of theology and fellowship that he taught, and the hope of the *Beloved Community* that he perpetually sought to convey to the whole of humanity. In order to comprehend Martin Luther King, Jr.'s intellectual development, his public achievements, and his conceptions of peaceful community, it is critical to first consider the early spiritual, social and psychological influences on his life.

In most of the biographical works written on King over the past thirty years, a great deal of attention has been given to his intellectual development at Morehouse College in Atlanta, at Crozer Seminary in Philadelphia, and at Boston University where he completed his doctoral studies in 1955. Certainly, King's spiritual, emotional and intellectual encounters at these institutions, along with additional academic work at Harvard University and the University of Pennsylvania, were critical to his intellectual development and public identity. King's studies at these institutions would provide the "fertile ground" necessary for progress in what he would refer to as "a serious intellectual quest for a method to eliminate social evil."

But in order to comprehend King's movement toward a theological praxis of non-violent social resistance and peaceful community, King's experiences and development at these academic institutions should be considered within the context of his earlier development.

I. Early Spiritual Development

There were essentially three major influences present in King's early life that would shape his later attitudes and behavior. These were: (1) his black middle class family (which included his extended family) and the family/community ethos in which he was raised; (2) the religious ethos and *mores* of the southern black Baptist church; and (3) the ongoing patterns of racial segregation and discrimination in the South.

Foundational to his early development were King's family experiences. Robert Franklin, in *Liberating Visions,* suggests that King's fundamental character was shaped and nurtured within the valuing context of the southern middle-class Black family structure.[1]   The Kings and Williamses were prominent leaders in the "new South." His family tree included a long line of Baptist preachers (his father, grandfather and great-grandfather were ministers), and outspoken advocates for freedom and justice.

King's father and grandfather were not only Baptist ministers but also pioneering exponents of a distinctively African-American version of social gospel Christianity. When King's grandfather, the Reverend A. D. Williams, arrived in Atlanta in 1893, social gospel activism was becoming increasingly common among both black and white urban clergymen. After taking over the pastorate of Atlanta's Ebeneezer Baptist Church in March 1894, Williams built a large congregation through forceful preaching that addressed the everyday concerns of poor and working-class residents. Baptist denominational practices encouraged ministers such as Williams to retain the support of occasionally rebellious congregations through charismatic leadership that extended beyond purely spiritual matters. Having arrived in Atlanta on the eve of a major period of institutional development among African-American Baptists, Williams joined two thousand other delegates and visitors who met at Atlanta's Friendship Baptist Church in September 1895, to organize the National Baptist Convention, the largest black organization in the United States.[2]

When Martin Luther King, Jr. was very young, his parents noticed that M.L. (as he was affectionately known) possessed an unusual ability to endure pain. Although obvious during spankings, M.L. refused to cry. Robert Franklin suggests that this ability to endure pain would become evident again, as he would later face the injury of American racism.[3]

King's later views on racism in America are clearly traced to his early development. In his biography on King, *Let the Trumpet Sound,* Stephen B. Oates reports on King's preschool years, when his closest playmate was a white boy whose father owned the store across the street from the King family home. When the two friends entered school in 1935, they attended separate schools. One day, the parents of his friend announced that M.L. could no longer play with their son. Their explanation was, "Because we are white and you are colored."[4]

Later, around the dinner table, his parents responded to his hurt by telling him the story of the black experience in America. It was typically through conversations such as this (around the dinner table) that black youth would be socialized into the protest traditions of the black community and church.[5]

Benefiting from extensive exposure to proponents of the African-American social gospel, King was able to perceive theological training as a means of reconciling his inclination to follow his father's calling with his desire for intellectual acceptability. King's descriptions of his decision to enter the ministry reveal that he had accepted the social mission of the church even though he had not yet resolved his theological doubts. He realized that the Baptist religion he had absorbed during his youth had derived mainly from daily contact with church life rather than from theological reflection. Growing up in the church provided a substitute for orthodox theological convictions; born a Baptist, he never felt the need to affirm all the tenets of the denomination. In his "Autobiography of Religious Development," King explained: "Conversion for me was never an abrupt something. I have never experienced the so-called 'crisis moment.' Religion has just been something I grew up in. Conversion for me has been a gradual intaking of the noble ideals set forth in my family and my environment, and I must admit that this intaking has been largely unconscious."[6]

Although King's published descriptions of his "pilgrimage to non-violence" generally emphasized the impact of his academic training, King also was careful to acknowledge his black Baptist roots. "I am many things to many people," King acknowledged in 1965, "but in the quiet recesses of my heart, I am fundamentally a clergyman, a Baptist preacher. This is my being and my heritage, for I am also the son of a Baptist preacher, the grandson of a Baptist preacher, and the great-grandson of a Baptist preacher."[7]

II. Intellectual Development

The intellectual formation of Martin Luther King, Jr. is to be seen within the context of his earlier development. King's later formal education was predicated upon and guided by the more informal learning and personal experiences of his early years within the nurturing context of a close-knit family, church, and community. King's early childhood experiences with racism predisposed him to study and address the psychological and social effects of oppression on human development.

Clayborne Carson asserts that King was deeply influenced by his childhood immersion in African-American religious life, but his years at Crozer and Boston increased his ability to incorporate aspects of academic theology into sermons and public speeches.[8] His student papers demonstrate that he adopted European-American ideological ideas that ultimately reinforced rather than undermined the African-American social gospel tradition embraced by his father and grandfather. Although King's advanced training in theology set him apart from most African-American clergymen, the documentary evidence regarding his formative years suggests that his graduate studies engendered an increased appreciation for his African-American religious roots. From childhood, King had been uncomfortable with the emotionalism and scriptural literalism that he associated with traditional Baptist liturgy, but he was also familiar with innovative, politically active, and intellectually sophisticated African-American clergymen who had themselves been influenced by European-American theological scholarship. These clergymen served as role models for King as he mined theological scholarship for nuggets of insight that could enrich his preaching. As he sought to resolve religious doubts that had initially prevented him from accepting his calling, King looked upon European-American theological ideas not as alternatives to traditional black Baptist beliefs but as necessary correctives to those beliefs.[9]

Although King had been reared in the fundamentalist, simplistic piety of the black Baptist Protestantism of the South, a fact that almost dissuaded him from entering Christian ministry, he was introduced in his undergraduate studies at Morehouse College and later in his graduate studies at Crozer Seminary to theological liberalism. In a speech before the American Baptist Convention, shortly after the Montgomery Bus Boycott had been completed in 1956, King publicly stated:

> I gained my major influences from…Morehouse and Crozer – and I feel greatly indebted to them. They gave me the basic truths I now believe…the worldview which …I have…the idea of the oneness of humanity and the dignity and worth of all human personality…At Crozer I found the actual living out of Christian beliefs.[10]

Clayborne Carson further suggests that King's graduate studies and ongoing intellectual development should be viewed within the context of his struggle to synthesize his father's Christian practices and his own theological skepticism. Seen from this perspective, King's experiences at Crozer and Boston constituted neither a pilgrimage toward the social gospel views of his Crozer professors, nor a movement toward the personalism of those at Boston. Instead, King eclectically drew upon the writings of academic theologians, and he moved away from Christian liberalism toward a theological synthesis closer to aspects of his father's religious faith, particularly toward a conception of God as a source of support in times of personal need. Rather than becoming more liberal in college and seminary, he became increasingly skeptical of intellectualized conceptions of divinity. As King became increasingly aware of the limitations of liberal Christian thought, he acquired a renewed appreciation for his southern Baptist roots.[11]

King's intellectual development is specifically evident in his attraction to: (1) a model of the rational, black minister as organic intellectual as epitomized by Benjamin E. Mays at Morehouse College; (2) the evangelical liberalism of George Washington Davis; (3) the philosophy of Personalism of L. Harold DeWolf and Edgar Brightman at Boston University; (4) the Liberalism and Social Gospel of Walter Rauschenbusch, (5) the Christian Realism of Reinhold Niebuhr; and (6) the nonviolent, social transformation model of Mohandas Gandhi. The first five of these influences will be discussed here, with a complete analysis of Mohandas Gandhi - his philosophy and influence upon Martin Luther King, Jr. and Howard Thurman - in Chapter Four.

A. Benjamin E. Mays

After entering Morehouse College in 1944 at the age of fifteen, Martin Luther King, Jr. was profoundly influenced by the example of the college's president, Benjamin Elijah Mays, a family friend who was the kind of dedicated, intellectually sophisticated religious leader that King wished to emulate. Selected in 1940 to succeed John Hope as head of Morehouse, Mays was the first Morehouse president with a Ph.D. (University of Chicago). Although not a graduate of Morehouse himself, Mays had internalized the Morehouse tradition calling for students to use their skills on behalf of the black community.[12]

In his article, "The Christian Way in Race Relations: Benjamin E. Mays and the Theology of Race Relations," Mark L. Chapman points out the significant impact that Mays had on the thinking of Martin Luther King, Jr. Mays focused a great deal of his work on seeking to bring comprehension to the race problem in America. This focus is reflected in his 1954 comment:

> We are what we do and not what we say. We are as democratic as we live and we are as Christian as we act. If we talk brotherhood and segregate human beings, we do not believe in brotherhood. If we talk democracy and deny it to certain groups, we do not believe in democracy. If we preach justice and exploit the weak, we do not believe in justice. If we preach truth and tell lies, we do not believe in truth. We are what we do.[13]

Mays viewed Christianity as the means of addressing the race problem. He is quoted again in 1957:

> It is not enough for us to call upon members of different races to be decent toward one another for the sake of humanity, science or democracy. The basis for good relations is found in Christian religion, in the proper understanding of the Christian doctrine of man, Christ, and God, and in the application of Christian insights and convictions in everyday living.[14]

King's attraction to Benjamin Mays and other African-American intellectuals and ministers was affected by the early influence of his father, grandfather, and great-grandfather who were, before him, Baptist ministers. This model of ministry and intellectual engagement is rooted in the notion of what Cornel West refers to as the "organic intellectual."[15]　In contrast to the traditional western model of intellectual life where one's intellectual identity and development remains connected to academic life as a primary source - the "organic intellectual" remains connected to priestly (and other public) institutions (like the church).

King's intellectual life is thus viewed in this organic, public dimension as exemplified by his ongoing connection with the Black Baptist church, and later to public institutions such as the Southern Christian Leadership Conference, which he helped to found.

Benjamin Mays also served as president of Howard University, in Washington, DC and was considered to be a major Black public intellectual of the early and middle twentieth century. His work exemplified that of an organic intellectual. Before Martin Luther King, Jr.'s rise to international prominence in the wake of the 1955 Montgomery Bus Boycott, Benjamin Mays was the most assertive public spokesman for the theology of race relations; his active participation in ecumenical conferences throughout the world made him one of the most visible Negro churchmen of his time.[16] As scholar Keith D. Miller notes in his study of King's language and its sources, "What Mays has been to liberal black (and to a lesser degree white) religious and academic circles, King – with the benefit of a huge political movement and television – would be to America."[17]

B. George Washington Davis

George Washington Davis, Martin Luther King, Jr.'s professor of Christian Theology at Crozer Seminary, was known as one of the major proponents of "evangelical liberalism." Davis was a dynamic embodiment of "evangelical liberalism" at its very best. Kenneth Smith and Ira Zepp, Jr., in *Search for the Beloved Community,* assert that Martin Luther King, Jr. very clearly found some of the answers he had been searching for in the courses that he took from Davis. [18]

The degree of Davis' attachment to evangelical liberalism is evident in the textbooks he used in his courses: William Newton Clarke's *An Outline of Christian Theology* and William Adam Brown's *Christian Theology in Outline.* Davis' methodology and content paralleled the texts very closely. The volumes of Clarke and Brown were classical texts in the liberal tradition; both authors had served as theological mentors to a whole generation of liberals like Davis. [19]

In an article published in *Theology Today* in 1948, Davis identified several cardinal tenets of liberalism. They are summarized as follows:

(1) *The existence of a moral order in the universe (cosmos)* - For Davis, God has a purpose for the human race, and history moves toward a moral goal. Progress toward that goal may appear to be slow, but the outcome is certain; for there is a moral order "which is relevant to the corporate life of men and the ordering of human society." If mankind is to escape chaos and recurrent war, social and political institutions must be brought into conformity with the moral order. [20]

(2) *The activity of God in history* – Religious humankind, Davis argues, has always affirmed that there is a divine purpose in history, and the evidence proves that this is a rational belief.

(3) *The value of the personal* – For Davis, a high priority is assigned to the value of personality in Christian faith. Davis linked his belief in the value of the personal, with Jesus of Nazareth and Jesus' emphasis upon the ethic of love. In Jesus of Nazareth we perceive the divine in the human and the intention of God for human life. God's love for humankind was revealed in the

life and death of Jesus, and Jesus' sacrifice on the cross attested to the fact that every person is a being of infinite worth. The greatness of Christianity lies in its faith that the proper category of understanding the nature of ultimate reality is personality.

(4)   *The social character of human existence* – According to Davis, human existence is fundamentally social in character and human solidarity is the goal toward which history evolves. People are essentially social animals, and it is only within the context of fellowship and cooperation that an individual's character can evolve the way God intended it to evolve. It is much more likely to grow in democratic, cooperative, and Christian societies where people are constantly exhorted to manifest regard for the personal rights and opportunities of others.[21]

(5)   *The ethical nature of Christian faith* – For Davis, Christianity is essentially a moral and ethical religion. The goal and test of the Christian faith are its ethical fruits. Davis was concerned throughout his thought to balance the traditional supernatural interpretation of salvation with the ethical interpretation because he felt that the latter had been overshadowed by the former. He approached this subject by observing that Jesus "makes the goal of human character likeness in moral quality to God himself."[22]

Many of the major themes of Martin Luther King, Jr. were the themes of evangelical liberalism. His stress upon the parenthood of God and the unity of humankind, the centrality of religious experience, the concern of God for all life, the rights of humankind and moral feeling, the humanity of Jesus and his emphasis upon love, the dynamic nature of history and God's action therein, his essential optimism about human nature and history, the tolerance and openness of the liberal spirit, his tolerance toward a pluralism of world religions – all of these were key themes of evangelical liberalism embraced quite early in his intellectual pilgrimage. Davis, representing the distillation of liberal thought and the irenic spirit of the liberal mind, introduced King to the major motifs that would become integral to King's mature thought. King would continue to develop, to synthesize, and to criticize these themes, but he found them first in clearly articulated form in the evangelical liberalism of George Washington Davis.[23]

King's conception of personalism can be understood in light of George Davis's notion of the value of the personal. King defined personalism as "...the theory that the clue to the meaning of ultimate reality is found in personality. This personal idealism remains today my basic philosophical position."[24]   It seems apparent that when Davis claims, "We know now that we must live together or perish. If we will not have one world, we may have no world" – he presages one of the main themes of King, the oft-quoted statement that "the choice of humankind is not between violence and nonviolence, but between nonviolence and nonexistence."[25]   When a person becomes like God in his or her ethical orientation (i.e. exhibits the qualities of love and forgiveness), he or she becomes a child of God. Jesus' words, Davis argues, are explicit: "Love your enemies...that you may be sons." The Christian's ineradicable interest in the good life for all human beings stems from the ethical nature of the Christian faith and the moral foundation of Christian salvation. This theme is explicit in King's emphasis upon the Sermon the Mount as the ethical and spiritual model for Christian behavior.

C. Edgar Sheffield Brightman and L. Harold DeWolf

Martin Luther King, Jr.'s attraction to the personalism of L. Harold DeWolf and Edgar Sheffield Brightman can be viewed within the context of King's consistent striving to develop approaches for framing human relations with each other, to the world of nature, and to God. King was introduced to the thinking of Brightman and DeWolf while studying with George W. Davis at Crozer Seminary. In her autobiography, *My Life with Martin Luther King, Jr.,* Coretta Scott King explained that King chose Boston University as the institution where he would pursue his doctoral degree because he wanted to study the philosophy of personalism with L. Harold DeWolf and Edgar S. Brightman.[26]   This school of thought provided the broad horizon for King's theological, political and pastoral orientation.

Personalism is founded on the doctrine of the sanctity and inviolability of the person. According to one of the founders of the school, Ralph Flewelling, in religious terms, personalism is theistic, holding that "the more a person can reach the highest selfhood, the greater his harmony with the Divine nature.[27]   Because it is known as the "philosophy of freedom," from a political perspective it holds that society should be so organized as to "provide the best possible opportunity for the self-development of every human being, as the basis of all true democracy."[28]   Edgar Brightman defined *Personalism* as a "system of philosophy that regards the universe as an interacting system of persons (or selves)." Everything that exists is either a person or some experience, process, or aspect of a person or persons in relation to each other. All of reality is social or interpersonal. Consequently, "a person is taken to be a complex unity of thought and ideal values."[29]

The impact of Brightman and DeWolf, personally and intellectually, upon King's thought was recorded by King in these words:

> Both men greatly stimulated my thinking. It was mainly under these teachers that I studied personalistic philosophy – the theory that the clue to the meaning of ultimate reality is found in personality. This personal idealism remains today my basic philosophical position. Personalism's insistence that only personality – finite and infinite – is ultimately real strengthened me in two convictions; it gave me metaphysical and philosophical grounding for the idea of a personal God, and it gave me a metaphysical basis for the dignity and worth of all human personality.[30]

King's reading of Brightman led him to discover his own spirituality:

> How I now long for that religious experience which Dr. Brightman so cogently speaks of through his book. It seems to be an experience, the lack of which life becomes dull and meaningless. As I reflect on the matter, however, I do remember moments that I have been awakened; there have been times that I have been carried out of myself by something greater than myself and to that something I gave myself. Has this great something been God? Maybe after all, I have been religious for a number of years, and am now only becoming aware of it.[31]

For King, personalism validated the notion that experience rather than intellectual reflection should be the basis of religious belief. "It is through experience that we come to realize that some things are out of harmony with God's will," King wrote in reference to personalism. "No theology is needed to tell us that love is the law of life and to disobey it means to suffer the consequences."[32] King's adoption of personalism as a theological orientation enabled him to reject abstract conceptions of God while continuing his search for cogency and intellectual sophistication.

D. Walter Rauschenbusch

At Crozer, Martin Luther King, Jr. continued a search begun at Morehouse for a philosophical method to eliminate social evil. He studied the history of philosophy and the thought of Walter Rauschenbusch. In King's first book, *Stride Toward Freedom,* he acknowledged that Rauschenbusch's *Christianity and the Social Crisis* left "an indelible imprint" on his thinking by providing him with a theological base for the social concern he had developed as a result of his early experiences.[33]

One of the manifestations of evangelical liberalism was the social gospel movement. King acknowledged a great debt to the social gospel movement and to Walter Rauschenbusch. King's consistent synthesis and appropriation of the liberal social gospel perspective of Rauschenbusch can be viewed within the context of the complex nature of the southern Black (often fundamentalist, yet liberation/transformation-oriented) Christianity of King's upbringing in the Baptist Church. King noted that he had found the theological basis for his social concern in the thought of Rauschenbusch:

...Rauschenbusch gave to American Protestantism a sense of social responsibility it should never lose. The gospel at its best deals with the whole man, not only his soul but also his body, not only his spiritual well-being but also his material well-being. A religion that professes a concern for the souls of men and is not equally concerned about the slums that damn them, the economic conditions that strangle them, and the social conditions that cripple them, is a spiritually moribund religion.[34]

In arriving at a theological/philosophic construct for the social gospel movement - Rauschenbusch viewed religion as essentially ethical and social within the context of a prophetic model. He outlined his perspectives on ethical and social religion in *Christianity and the Social Crisis.*[35] Rauschenbusch traced the historical roots of Christianity and argued that Jesus stood squarely in the tradition of the Old Testament prophets, and that Christianity was the direct heir of the priority assigned to the social dimension of life by the prophets of Israel. Moreover, whenever Christianity has attempted to change social and political conditions for the betterment of humankind, it has manifested its indebtedness to the social ideals of the Old Testament because they have made, when properly understood and interpreted, positive contributions to the development of democracy and social justice culture.[36]

The essence of the prophetic principle, according to Rauschenbusch, is the affirmation of historical relativity – everything in history stands under the judgment of God. For this reason the prophet cannot put a stamp of approval upon anything "as it is." The prophet must always point out the gap between the will of God and "the present things." No person who calls himself or herself a Christian can accept "things as they are"; instead, one must condemn them on the basis of the values enunciated by the prophets and Jesus.[37]

Rauschenbusch offers several corollaries of the prophetic model. One is the *inseparability of religion and ethics.* If one believes in the social gospel, any method of cultivating the spiritual life may be chosen provided it has an ethical outcome. Righteousness is what God commands; an ethical life is the appropriate act of worship; and the amelioration of social injustice is the goal of the religious person. Another corollary of the prophetic model of religion for Rauschenbusch is the *affirmation of the fundamental social character of religion.* He claimed that the social nature and dimensions of religions should be the major norm for evaluating religious systems.[38]

The views of Martin Luther King, Jr. on the relationship between the church and society were significantly influenced by Walter Rauschenbusch. Like Rauschenbusch, King firmly believed that the church should take the lead in programs of social action and societal change. The church should engage in combating injustices that people confront in the areas of housing, education, employment, and health-care. For King, it was essential for the church to capture its prophetic vision and to actively participate in the struggle for economic and racial justice, and peace in communities and among the nations of the world.

E. Reinhold Niebuhr

It was through a study of Walter Rauschenbusch and the Social Gospel that Martin Luther King, Jr. would recall that he learned that "the gospel deals with the whole man, not only his soul but his body." His professors, however, told him that Social Gospel progressivism was out of touch with many of society's hard realities and injected him with a dose of Reinhold Niebuhr's "Christian realism."[39] King's respect for the writings of Niebuhr derived from the pleasure he felt in finding a theological stance that synthesized faith and intellect. In Niebuhr's Christian realism, King probably heard echoes of his father's fundamentalism, which affirmed the limits of human perfectibility. Niebuhr provided an intellectual rationale for King's recognition of the limits of liberal theology. As King wrote, he had become "so enamored of the insights of liberalism that I almost fell into the trap of accepting uncritically everything it encompasses."[40] After reading Niebuhr, King recalled becoming aware of the "depth and strength of sin" and:

> the complexity of man's social involvement and the glaring reality of collective evil. I realized that liberalism had been all too sentimental concerning human nature and that it leaned toward a false idealism. I also came to see that the superficial optimism of liberalism concerning human nature overlooked the fact that reason is darkened by sin. The more I thought about human nature, the more I saw how our tragic inclination for sin encourages us to rationalize our actions. Liberalism failed to show that reason by itself is little more than an instrument to justify man's defensive ways of thinking. Reason, devoid of the purifying power of faith, can never free itself from distortions and rationalizations.[41]

Niebuhr's Christian realism or "realistic theology" was explicated in his seminal work, *Moral Man and Immoral Society (1932)*. Christian realism was a more moderate reaction to liberalism than the more severe reactions of the neoorthoxy of Karl Barth, Emil Brunner and others. Also, Christian realism retained a far greater concern for social ethics. King noted his affinity for the thinking of Niebuhr in seeking to distinguish between neoorthodoxy and Christian realism:

> Niebuhr's great contribution to contemporary theology is that he has refuted the false optimism characteristic of a great segment of Protestant liberalism, without falling into the anti-rationalism of the continental theologian Karl Barth, or the semi-fundamentalism of other dialectical theologians.[42]

For King, a religion that focuses exclusively upon the individual is a truncated form of religion. King applauded Niebuhr's rigorous analysis of "the fundamental weaknesses and inevitable sterility of the humanistic emphasis" of liberalism in the twentieth century.[43] He was drawn to Niebuhr's economic and moral analysis of capitalism, such as the notion that modern industrial civilization was responsible for the "appalling injustices," particularly the "concentration of power and resources in the hands of a relatively small wealth class."[44] Injustices are inherent in human society, Niebuhr argued, because humans engaged in collective activity are essentially immoral, whereas individuals acting on their own possess a moral conscience. Niebuhr sought to resolve the tension between "moral man and immoral society" by reinterpreting the traditional Christian notion of *agape,* or divine love.[45] Agreeing with Niebuhr's analysis, King stated that *agape* may not be achievable in an immoral society but "remains a leaven in society, permeating the whole and giving texture and consistency to life."[46]

The exponents of Christian realism argued that the biblical understanding of human nature, symbolized by the myth of the Fall, is a far more accurate, more realistic, understanding of the human situation than either the pessimism of Christian orthodoxy or the optimism of Christian liberalism. The one objective and empirically verifiable base, from which most realistic theologians operated because they thought it could be clearly documented as a fact of human experience, was the doctrine of original sin (i.e., the egotistic predicament of every human being). In short, Christian realism was the theological expression of a general revolt against the romanticism, the idealism, and the liberalism of the nineteenth century. Rienhold Niebuhr was the moving spirit of theological realism. Martin Luther King, Jr. was an heir of this new school of thought through the influence of Rienhold Niebuhr.[47] By the time King wrote *Where Do We Go From Here: Chaos or Community?* in 1967, he had arrived at a position on the relationship between power, justice, and love which was similar to that of Rienhold Niebuhr. Although there were differences in emphasis and mode of expression at some points, the substance was quite similar. King understood and agreed with the necessity of power, as Niebuhr had stated it, as necessary to facilitate constructive change.[48] King concluded that is was utopian to believe "that ethical appeals and persuasion alone will bring about justice. This does not mean that ethical appeals must not be made. It simply means that those appeals must be undergirded by some form of constructive coercive power." [49]

With regard to Niebuhr's critique of the optimistic doctrine of humankind in Protestant liberalism, King argued:

> Niebuhr has extraordinary insight into human nature, especially the behavior of nations and social groups. His theology is a persistent reminder of the reality of sin on every level of man's existence...While I still believed in man's potential for good, Niebuhr made me realize his potential for evil as well.[50]

And yet, King remained concerned with Niebuhr's apparent overemphasis on the corruption of human nature. King said, "His pessimism concerning human nature was not balanced by an optimism concerning divine nature. He was so involved in diagnosing man's sickness of sin that he overlooked the cure of grace."[51]

King remained particularly receptive to Niebuhr's criticism of love and justice as conceived in both liberal and orthodox theology. In orthodoxy, "individual perfection is too often made an end in itself," whereas liberalism "vainly seeks to overcome justice [through] purely moral and rational suasions." Liberalism, King would write, "confuses the ideal itself with the realistic means which must be employed to coerce society into an approximation of that ideal." King agreed with Niebuhr's emphasis on making realistic moral choices and with his social analysis, but he believed that Niebuhr lacked an adequate explanation of how *agape* operates in human history: "He fails to see that the availability of the divine *agape* is an essential [affirmation] of the Christian religion."[52]

III. Development of Peaceful Community in the Thinking of Martin Luther King, Jr.

A. Notion of the Integrative Person

Robert L. Franklin offers the notion of the *Integrative Person* as that which best captures the essence Martin Luther King, Jr.'s ongoing development and thinking.[53] In the summer of 1958, King was invited to deliver two devotional addresses at the first National Conference on Christian Education of the United Church of Christ, at Purdue University. In one of his addresses, "The Dimensions of a Complete Life," he offered a vision of human fulfillment by using geometry as an organizing paradigm. King conceived the complete life to be a process, a quest, rather than an achievement. This is clearly evident in Franklin's construct of the *Integrative Person*. Inspired by the geometric perfection of the New City of God described in the Book of Revelation (chapter 21), King suggested that the complete life was analogous to a cube. Each of its three dimensions represents a significant individual commitment. (1) The length of life corresponds to a person's inner concern for his or her own welfare and development, (2) breadth corresponds to concern for the welfare of others, and (3) height refers to concern for reconciliation and communion with God.

With regard to the notion of the length of life, King stressed that it "... is not its duration or its longevity, but it is the push forward to achieve life's personal ends and ambitions." It is the inward concern for a person's own welfare and the realization of his own purposes. The individual is concerned with developing his inner powers. It is that dimension of life in which the individual pursues personal ends and ambitions. King said, "Love yourself, if that means rational and healthy self-interest. You are commanded to do that."[54]

King pointed out that length without breadth, the second dimension of the complete life, is like a self-contained tributary having no outward flow to the ocean. Stagnant, still, and stale, it lacks both life and freshness.[55]   The "I" cannot attain fulfillment without the "thou." For its full development, the self needs other selves. Paul Tillich had observed that only a "thou" can make man realize he has an ego.[56]   The breadth of life is that dimension of life in which we are concerned about others.   An individual has not started living until one can rise above the narrow confines of individualistic concerns to the broader concerns of all humanity.

Finally, there is a third dimension, the height of life. King pointed out that some people never get beyond the first two dimensions, and thus life remains incomplete.   They develop their inner powers, they love humanity, but they stop right there. Without God, even the most brilliant achievements on the other two dimensions soon prove to be empty and disillusioning. King pointed out that if persons are to live the complete life they must reach up and discover God.[57]

In challenging everyone to live an integrative life of *agape,* King developed the Christian implications of the second and third dimensions of the complete life and in effect maintained that at times the practice of *agape* may require suspension of the first dimension, immediate self-interest. As part of the challenge, he called for a "creative altruism" that makes concern for others the first law of life.   He indicated that Jesus had revealed the meaning of this altruism in his parable about the Good Samaritan who was moved by compassion to care for "a certain man" who had been robbed and beaten on the road to Jerico.[58]

King asserted that the altruism of the Samaritan was *universal, dangerous and excessive.*[59]   His altruism was *universal* since he did not seek to inquire into the nationality of the wounded man to determine whether he was a Samaritan or a Jew.   He saw that he was "a certain man" in need, and that was sufficient for him to intervene. The Samaritan was a good neighbor who demonstrated dangerous and excessive altruism because, unlike the priest and the Levite who passed by the wounded man, he was willing to help any person in distress under any conditions, and he was able to look beyond external accidents to regard the stranger in need as his brother. Jesus gave the command to love one's neighbor, and King explained that through this parable Jesus disclosed his definition of neighbor: He is neither Jew nor Gentile; he is neither Russian nor American; he is neither Negro nor white. He is "a certain man" – any needy man – on one of the numerous Jerico roads of life.[60]

B. Philosophy of Nonviolence

Owing to the eloquence of Martin Luther King, Jr.'s words, it is easy to lose sight of his singular vision of nonviolent social resistance as a means of realizing peaceful community. It is critical, at the genesis of a new millennium, not to lose sight of the prophetic vision of King and his understanding of Christian faith, which led him to stand up against the most dominant and insipid social reality of his day - racism. This profound understanding of faith highlighted the God-giftedness of all persons, the equality that is inherent in all humanity, and the unending hope that we as a society – amidst the inexhaustible power of this God-giftedness, and despite the existential and communal fallenness that is evidenced in the perpetuation of the race line in America – possess the grace, if not yet the will, to overcome race division.

King's theological project to link his conception of God-giftedness – as rooted in his early intellectual and spiritual development - to dialectical Christian praxis led him to call the Christian community to a form of sacrificial witness that would move persons of all races and nationalities beyond existing paradigms of ritual and theology, and toward authentic community. If the church were to be the church, it would engage in an evangelical liberal witness that would prophetically and progressively bring its spiritual, social, economic and political resources to bear in ways that would be truly transforming, liberating, reconciling and redeeming.

James Cone speaks of the impact of Martin Luther King's

prophetic witness in writing:

> As a prophet, with a charisma never before witnessed in
> this century, King preached black liberation in the light of
> Jesus Christ and thus aroused the spirit of freedom in the
> black community. To be sure, one may argue that his method
> of nonviolence did not meet the needs of the black commu-
> nity in an age of black power; but it is beyond question that
> it was King's influence and leadership in the black commu-
> nity which brought us to the period in which we now live,
> and for that we are in debt. His life and message demon-
> strate that the "soul" of the black community is inseparable
> from liberation, but always liberation grounded in Jesus
> Christ...[61]

King's prophetic vision of nonviolence would spawn a religious and social movement unparalleled in American history. The
roots of the struggle for women's rights (feminism and womanism),
the rights of gays and lesbians, the rights of workers and the dis-
abled, and the rights of immigrants of various hews of brown, red,
yellow, white and black can be traced to the prophetic vision of
King. It was he who espoused a form of nonviolent social resistance – a construct that would ultimately lead to the passage of the
Civil Rights Act (1964) and the Voting Rights Act (1965) by the
Congress of the United States. The epistemological foundations of
affirmative action – however it might be conceived in contemporary socio-political context – is rooted in King's prophetic vision of
equality and justice throughout society.

As much as nonviolence was the foundation that brought
about social change, King viewed nonviolence as a process toward
spiritual growth and the realization of authentic community. For
King, nonviolence was not an end in itself – but a means for the
church and society to appropriate community; for him it was a philosophy that clearly had its roots in the black church. In a speech
to the National Conference on Religion and Race in 1963, King
said:

> I am happy to say that the nonviolent movement in America
> has come not from secular forces but from the heart of the
> Negro church... The great principles of love and justice

which stand at the center of the nonviolent movement are deeply rooted in our Judeo-Christian heritage. [62]

While rooted in the church, Martin Luther King, Jr.'s philosophy of nonviolence was derived from numerous other sources, as well. King received early exposure to civil disobedience by observing and hearing about the defiance of black people in Southern communities who refused to conform to Jim Crow laws. Later, he found in Henry David Thoreau a model and language to legitimate the practice before the dominant culture. He possessed firsthand knowledge of the social and political power of the Christian church and found in Walter Rauschenbusch a more complete elaboration of the prophetic and redemptive social mission of the church. As a sensitive and observant youth, he had learned that social change always entails conflict, and in the philosophy of Georg Wilhelm Hegel he discovered the dialectical analysis of history that reinforced his faith and hope in the future. Although he had observed examples of social evil all of his life, King found in Reinhold Niebuhr a biblically informed theological analysis of collective sin and evil. Indeed, this understanding of the logic and rhythm of King's informal and formal learning can be applied to all of the major sources he embraced in shaping his own eclectic moral philosophy.[63] Although Martin Luther King, Jr. learned much about the power of self-discipline and nonviolence from his father and extended family, Mohandas Gandhi embodied the ideal of nonviolence in a socially transformative manner.

The Montgomery Bus Boycott, which began in 1955, captured the fancy and support of the nation and much of the world. It would serve as the impetus for King's theo-praxis of nonviolent social resistance. What had begun as a demonstration for a better form of segregation (first-come-first-serve basis) developed under King's skillful and charismatic leadership into a holy cause. What was aimed at a week's duration stretched into 385 days of "tired feet and rested souls." Jim Crow was very much alive in the Deep South, but major surgery was performed at Montgomery. At the end of the bus boycott, almost half of Black America had been involved in one way or another. The period ushered in by the Montgomery bus protest is of enormous significance. There is very little question that Montgomery opened the door to a period of the most frenetic activity in the history of race relations in America. Martin Luther King, Jr., a Black Brahmin of well-to-do parentage, credentialed at Boston University, young, gifted, and a Black preacher, introduced the modern techniques of Gandhi, wrapped up in the religion and morality of the folk churches. King's nonviolent program of attack against an old enemy (segregation) on a scale of mass involvement, constructively channeled the bitter and frustrated energies of a people too often betrayed.[64]

Nonviolence played a critical role in the thinking and practice of Martin Luther King, Jr., and was integral to the Montgomery Movement. This philosophy had several elements that King would continue to develop throughout his life, and which were codified into a set of principles in his book *Stride Toward Freedom* in 1958.[65] An analysis of King's thinking indicate six general characteristics of nonviolent resistance as a means of protest and community-building.

First, according to King, *it must be emphasized that nonviolent resistance is not a method for passive cowards*; it was conceived by King and those who were a part of the Civil Rights movement as a method of active resistance. Persons were not to engage in nonoviolent resistance because they were afraid or merely because of a lack of the instruments of violence. Mohandas Gandhi often said that if cowardice is the only alternative to violence, it is better to fight. He made this statement conscious of the fact that there is always another alternative to violence. Nonviolence is ultimately the way of the strong person. It is not a method of stagnant passivity. The phrase "passive resistance" is often used in conjunction with nonviolent resistance. But a distinction should be made in that the notion of "passive resistance" gives the impression of a lack of active involvement in which the resister quietly and passively accepts evil. While the nonviolent resister is passive in the sense that he or she is not physically aggressive toward the opponent, the resister's mind and emotions are always active, constantly seeking to persuade his opponent of the evil that is present. The method is passive physically, but strongly active spiritually. It is not passive nonresistance to evil, it is active nonviolent resistance to evil.

A second basic characteristic of nonviolent resistance, according to King, is that *it does not seek to defeat or humiliate the opponent, but to win his friendship and understanding.* In this regard, King stated:

> The nonviolent resister most often expresses his protest through non-cooperation or boycotts, but he realizes that these are not ends themselves; they are merely means to awaken a sense of moral shame in the opponent. The end is redemption and reconciliation. The aftermath of nonviolence is the creation of the *Beloved Community*, while the aftermath of violence is tragic bitterness.

A third characteristic of this method is that *the attack is directed against forces of evil rather than against persons who happen to be doing evil.* Regarding this distinction, King pointed out: It is evil that the nonviolent resister seeks to defeat, not the persons who are the perpetrators of evil. If one is opposing racial injustice, the nonviolent resister has the vision to see that the basic tension is not between the persons of different races. King continued by pointing out:

> As I like to say to the people of Montgomery: "The tension in this city is not between white people and Negro people. The tension is, at bottom, between justice and injustice, between the forces of light and the forces of darkness. And if there is victory, it will not be merely for fifty thousand Negroes, but a victory for justice and the forces of light. We are out to defeat injustice and not white persons who may be unjust."

A fourth characteristic of nonviolent resistance is *a willingness to accept suffering without retaliation, to accept blows from the opponent without striking back.* Here, King refers to the thinking of Mohandas Gandhi to make his point about the suffering of the resister:

> Gandhi said to his countrymen, "Rivers of blood may have to flow before we gain freedom, but it must be our blood." The nonviolent resister is willing to accept violence if necessary, but never to inflict it. He does not seek to dodge jail

if going to jail is necessary to meet the objectives of social change through nonviolence.

The nonviolent resister's justification for this is found in the notion that unearned suffering is redemptive. The nonviolent resister realizes that suffering has tremendous educational and transformational possibilities. Gandhi said:

> Things of fundamental importance to people are not secured by reason alone, but have to be purchased with their suffering…. Suffering is infinitely more powerful than the law of the jungle for converting the opponent and opening his ears which are otherwise shut to the voice of reason.

In an article in the *Christian Century* in 1960, entitled "Suffering and Faith," Martin Luther King, Jr. personally reflected further upon the matter of the redemptive and transformational qualities of suffering:[66]

> Some of my personal sufferings over the last few years have also served to shape my thinking. I always hesitate to mention these experiences for fear of conveying the wrong impression. A person who constantly calls attention to his trials and sufferings is in danger of developing a martyr complex and of making others feel that he is consciously seeking sympathy. It is possible for one to be self-centered in his self-denial, and self-righteous in his self-sacrifice. So I am always reluctant to refer to my personal sacrifices. But I feel somewhat justified in mentioning them in this article because of the influence they have had in shaping my thinking.

> Due to my involvement in the struggle for the freedom of my people, I have known very few quiet days in the last few years. I have been arrested five times and put in Alabama jails. My home has been bombed twice. A day seldom passes that my family and I are not the recipients of threats of death. I have been the victim of a near-fatal stabbing. So in a real sense I have been battered by the storms of persecution. I must admit that at times I have felt that I

could no longer bear such a heavy burden, and have been tempted to retreat to a more quiet and serene life. But every time such a temptation appeared, something came to strengthen and sustain my determination. I have learned now that the Master's burden is light precisely when we take his yoke upon us.

My personal trials have also taught me the value of unmerited suffering. As my sufferings mounted I soon realized that there were two ways that I could respond to my situation: either to react with bitterness or seek to transform the suffering into a creative force. I decided to follow the latter course. Recognizing the necessity of suffering, I have tried to make of it a virtue. If only to save myself from bitterness, I have attempted to see my personal ordeals as an opportunity to transform myself and heal the people involved in the tragic situation, which now obtains. I have lived these last few years with the conviction that unearned suffering is redemptive.

King persistently sought to articulate a theodicy (rationale for the justice of God) which coherently spoke to the suffering and injustices inflicted upon oppressed and marginalized persons. He sought to make a clear connection between spirituality and suffering. Gustavo Gutierrez speaks of the challenge of making this connection in *On Job: God-talk and the Suffering of the Innocent:*

This then is the question: Are suffering human beings able to enter into an authentic relationship with God and find a correct way of speaking about God? If the answer is yes, then it will be a priori possible to do the same in other human situations. But if the answer is no, then it will be irrelevant that persons living in less profound and challenging situations "appear" to accept the gratuitousness of God's love and claim to practice a disinterested religion. Human suffering is the harsh, demanding ground on which the wager about talk of God is made; it is also that which ensures that the wager has universal applicability.[67]

In historical context and philosophical perspective, suffering may be viewed in dialectical terms. Perhaps the most perpetual dilemma has been seeking to address for people of faith the question, "Why do bad things happen to good people?" There are several theological views that have been posited to address this dilemma. Suffering might be seen as a means of spiritual growth. Through suffering, persons may gain spiritual refinement. Suffering might also be understood eschatologically as it could be understood as preparation for a "reward" to be received in the next world. Suffering might also be viewed within the context of vicarious suffering (atonement) where one suffers sacrificially for the benefit of another person or some greater cause.

There have been a number of philosophical perspectives that speak to the matter of suffering among persons of faith. The philosophic dilemma seems to derive from the question, "If God is all-powerful and all-loving, then why is there suffering and injustice in the world?" Given the existence of suffering and evil, one might be led to question the presence of God, or at the very least, to question the all-powerful, all-loving nature of God. The conclusion here is that evil and injustice may be the very absence of God. Viktor Frankl sought to speak to the matter of suffering within the context of his experiences during the Jewish Holocaust. In *Man's Search for Meaning,* Frankl posits that we can discover meaning in life by the attitude we take toward unavoidable suffering. With regard to this, Frankl offers:

> We must never forget that we may also find meaning in life even when confronted with a hopeless situation, when facing a fate that cannot be changed. For what then matters is to bear witness to the uniquely human potential at its best, which is to transform a personal tragedy into triumph, to turn one's predicament into a human achievement. When we are no longer able to change a situation – just think of an incurable disease such as inoperable cancer – we are challenged to change ourselves... In some ways, suffering ceases to be suffering at the moment that it finds meaning, such as the meaning of sacrifice.[68]

Martin Luther King, Jr. suggests that a fifth characteristic of nonviolent resistance is that *it avoids not only external physical violence but also internal violence of the spirit.* The nonviolent resister not only refuses to shoot his opponent, but he also refuses to hate him. At the center of nonviolence stands the principle of love. King elaborates on love as the center of nonviolence:

> The nonviolent resister would contend that in the struggle for human dignity, the oppressed people of the world must not succumb to the temptation of becoming bitter or indulging in hate campaigns. To retaliate in kind would do nothing but intensify the existence of hatred in the universe. Along the way of life, someone must have sense enough and morality enough to cut off the chain of hate. This can only be done by projecting the ethic of love to the center of our lives.

In speaking of love at this point, we are not referring to some sentimental and affectionate emotion. It would be nonsense to urge persons to love oppressors in an affectionate sense. Love in this context means understanding, redemptive goodwill. Here the Greek language comes to our aid. There are three words for love in the Greek New Testament. First, there is *eros.* In platonic philosophy *eros* meant the yearning of the souls for the realm of the divine. It has come now to mean a sort of aesthetic or romantic love. Second is *philia*, which means intimate affection between personal friends. *Philia* denotes a sort of reciprocal love; the person loves because he is loved. When we speak of loving those who oppose us, we refer to neither *eros* nor *philia;* we speak of a love that is expressed in the Greek word *agape. Agape* means understanding, redeeming goodwill for all men. It is an overflowing love, which is purely spontaneous, unmotivated, groundless, and creative. It is not set in motion by any quality or function of its object. It is the love of God operating in the human heart.

Agape is disinterested love. It is a love in which the individual seeks not his own good, but the good of his neighbor. (1 Cor. 10:24) *Agape* does not begin by discriminating between worthy and unworthy people, or any quality people possess. It begins by loving others for their sakes. It is an entirely "neighbor-regarding concern for others," which discovers the neighbor in every man it meets. Therefore *agape* makes no distinction between friend and enemy; it is directed toward both. If one loves an individual merely on account of his friendliness, he loves him for the sake of the benefits to be gained from the friendship, rather than for the friend's own sake. Consequently, the best way to assure oneself that love is disinterested is to have love for the enemy-neighbor from whom you can expect no good in return, but only hostility and persecution.

Another basic point about *agape* is that it springs from the need of the other person – his need for belonging to the best in the human family. The Samaritan who helped the Jew on the Jerico Road was "good" because he responded to the human need that he was presented with. God's love is eternal and fails not because man needs his love. St. Paul assures us that the loving act of redemption was done "while we were yet sinners" - that is, at the point of our greatest need for love. Since the white man's personality is generally distorted by segregation, and his soul is greatly scarred, he needs the love of the Negro. The Negro must love the white man, because the white man needs his love to remove his tensions, insecurities and fears.

King points out that a sixth characteristic of nonviolent resistance is that *it is based on the conviction that the universe is on the side of justice.* With regard to this, King says:

Consequently, the believer in nonviolence has deep faith in the future. This faith is another reason why the nonviolent resister can accept suffering without retaliation. For he knows that in his struggle for justice, he has cosmic companionship. It is true that there are devout believers in nonviolence who find it difficult to believe in a personal God. But even those persons believe in the existence of some creative force that works for universal wholeness. Whether we call it an unconscious process, an impersonal Brahman, or a Personal Being of matchless power and infinite love, there is a creative force in this universe that works to bring the disconnected aspects of reality into a harmonious whole.

In 1963, while imprisoned in a Birmingham, Alabama jail, King wrote a letter that was first published in *The Christian Century*. It became a classic appeal for rights denied blacks for 340 years. In what is commonly referred to as "The Letter from the Birmingham Jail," King stated, "There are *just* laws and there are *unjust* laws." With St. Augustine, King reasoned that a truly unjust law was no law at all. As he argued his case, King called attention to the burgeoning and potentially violent Black Muslim movement, which loomed as a threat should white Americans continue to deny rights. "It is made up of people who have lost faith in America, who have absolutely repudiated Christianity, and who have concluded that the white man is an incurable 'devil,'" asserted King. The Negro church offered the best hope for nonviolent change.[69]

C. National and International Perspectives

Martin Luther King, Jr. exhibited a form of national and international socio-political concern similar to that of Mohandas Gandhi, which constantly called people of the nation to rise above the ills of racial discord and class division. Although King's message is often depicted as being directed exclusively toward African Americans – and the call for their freedom from racial injustice – a careful analysis of his message points to his nationalist passion, a vision of unity, peace and quality of life for all Americans – Jews, Protestants, Catholics, Muslims, and for the many nationalities, ethnic and religious groups present in America. There is clear evidence that King's broader concerns included all persons who were in some way marginalized and disenfranchised in America. While his concern was certainly for the eradication of poverty for urban African Americans in cities like Chicago and Memphis, Tennessee, he expressed concern for all persons affected by poverty. For instance, King's leadership in 1968 of the campaign on behalf of sanitation workers in Memphis would serve to impact the quality of life for all sanitation workers in that city.

Like Jesus Christ in the temple that had become a den of thieves, King realized that the church and society are fertile ground for corruption. He viewed God as the source for overcoming such corruption. King shared this perspective in the connection of God with society:

> There is much frustration in the world because we have relied on gods rather than God. We have genuflected before the god of science only to find that it has given us the atomic bomb…We have worshipped the god of pleasure only to discover that thrills play out and sensations are short-lived. We have bowed before the god of money only to learn that there are such things as love and friendship that money cannot buy and that, in a world of possible depressions, stock market crashes and bad business investments, money is a rather uncertain deity. These transitory gods are not able to save or to bring happiness to the human heart. Only God is able. It is a faith we must rediscover."[70]

When King gave the commencement address at Lincoln University in Pennsylvania on June 6, 1961, he said that in order for the American public to realize "The American Dream," the first thing that needed to be affirmed is that the dream is universal, and comes out of the struggles of all persons. King further declared that each person has certain basic rights that are rooted in the interrelatedness of all persons. King stated:

> All this is simply to say that all life is interrelated. We are caught in an inescapable network of mutuality; tied in a single garment of destiny. Whatever affects one directly, affects all indirectly… This is the way the world is made. I didn't make it that way, but this is the interrelated structure of reality. [71]

He pointed out that the United States professes a balance between the whole and the individual, yet practices the exact opposite. King asserted that American society has a "schizophrenic personality." While our scientific genius and research may have made us a world community or neighborhood, we must open ourselves to a spiritual reality that surrounds us in order to regain a truly inter-connected society.[72]

King viewed peace as the highest calling of the nation. In his last Christmas Eve sermon on December 24, 1967, he said:

It is one of the strangest things that all the great military geniuses of the world have talked about peace. The con-querors of old who came killing in pursuit of peace – Alexander, Julius Caesar, Charlemagne, and Napoleon – were akin in seeking a peaceful world order. If you will read *Mein Kampf* closely enough, you will discover that Hitler contended that everything he did in Germany was for peace. And the leaders of the world today talk elo-quently about peace. Every time we drop bombs in North Vietnam, President Johnson talks eloquently about peace. What is the problem? They are talking about peace as a distant goal, as an end we seek, but one day we must come to see that peace is not merely a distant goal we seek, but that it is a means by which we arrive at that goal. We must pursue peaceful ends through peaceful means. One of the most persistent ambiguities we face is that everybody talks about peace as a goal, but among the wielders of power, peace is practically nobody's business. Many men cry "Peace! Peace!" but they refuse to do the things that make for peace.[73]

King's nationalist passion was perhaps most demonstratively articulated in his famous "I Have a Dream" speech, delivered on the steps of the Lincoln Memorial in Washington, DC on August 28, 1963.[74] At this – the largest protest march in the history of the United States - King began the address by drawing on the collective conscience of all of America:

Fivescore years ago, a great American, in whose symbolic shadow we stand today, signed the Emancipation Procla-mation. This momentous decree came as a great beacon light of hope to millions of Negro slaves who have shared in the flames of withering injustice. It came as a joyous daybreak to end the long night of their captivity.

King continued by pointing America's sights toward the condition of African Americans at the time of the March on Washington in 1963:

But one hundred years later, the Negro still is not free, one hundred years later, the life of the Negro is still sadly crippled by the manacles of segregation and the chains of discrimination; one hundred years later, the Negro lives on a lonely island of poverty; one hundred years later, the Negro is still languishing in the corners of American society and finds himself in exile in his own land.

King's plea to the nation continued:

So we've come here today to dramatize a shameful condition. In a sense, we've come to our nation's capital to cash a check. When the architects of our republic wrote the magnificent words of the Constitution and the Declaration of Independence, they were signing a promissory note to which every American was to fall heir. This note was the promise that all men, yes black men as well as white men, would be guaranteed the unalienable rights of life, liberty and the pursuit of happiness.

It's obvious today that America has defaulted on this promissory note in so far as her citizens of color are concerned. Instead of honoring the sacred obligation, America has given the Negro a bad check; a check, which has come back marked "insufficient funds." We refuse to believe that there are insufficient funds in the great vaults of opportunity of this nation. And so we've come to cash this check, a check that will give us, upon demand the riches of freedom and the security of justice.

King continued by speaking of his dream of a nation united in a freedom that rings on behalf of all persons. He closed his address by recalling his dream of unity in poetic form with a repeated exhortation of "Let freedom ring":

So let freedom ring from the prodigious hills of New Hampshire.
Let freedom ring from the mighty mountains of New York.
Let freedom ring from the heightening Alleghenies of Pennsylvania.

Let freedom ring from the snow-capped Rockies of Colorado.
Let freedom ring from the curvaceous slopes of California.
But not only that.
Let freedom ring from the Stone Mountain of Georgia.
Let freedom ring from the Lookout Mountain of Tennessee.
Let freedom ring from every hill and molehill of Mississippi,
from every mountainside, let freedom ring.

And when we allow freedom to ring, when we let it ring from every village and every hamlet, from every state and city, we will be able to speed up that day when all of God's children – black men and white men, Jews and Gentiles, Catholics and Protestants – will be able to join hands and to sing in the words of the old Negro spiritual, "Free at last, free at last, thank God Almighty, we are free at last."

Evidence of King's nationalistic perspective, and developing conception of the love-ethic and the call for peace in the church and society, is also found in his views on the Vietnam War. He came to see a direct correlation between the Civil Rights movement in America and the War in Asia.[75] King stated:

For those who ask the question, "Aren't you a Civil Rights leader?" and thereby mean to exclude me from the movement of peace, I have this further answer. In 1957 when a group of us formed the Southern Christian Leadership Conference, we chose as our motto: "To save the soul of America." We were convinced that we could not limit our vision to certain rights for black people, but instead affirmed the conviction that America would never be free or saved from itself unless the descendants of its slaves were loosed completely from the shackles they still were in. In a way we were agreeing with Langston Hughes, that black bard of Harlem, who had written earlier:

O yes,
I say it plain,
America never was America to me,
And yet I swear the oath –
America will be!

Regarding the War in Vietnam, King continued:

> Now, it should be incandescently clear that no one who has any concern for the integrity and life of America today can ignore the present war. If America's soul becomes totally poisoned, part of the autopsy must read "Vietnam." It can never be saved so long as it destroys the deepest hopes of men the world over. So it is that those of us who are yet determined that America *will* be are led down the path of protest and dissent, working for the health of our land.

As if the weight of such a commitment to the life and health of America were not enough, another burden of responsibility was placed upon me in 1964; and I cannot forget that the Nobel Prize for Peace was also a commission – a commission to work harder than I had ever worked before for the "brotherhood of man." This is a calling that takes me beyond national allegiances, but even if it were not present I would yet have to live with the meaning of my commitment to the ministry of Jesus Christ. To me the relationship of this ministry to the making of peace is so obvious that I sometimes marvel at those who ask me why I am speaking against the war. Could it be that they do not know that the good news was meant for all men – for communist and capitalist, for their children and ours, for black and for white, for revolutionary and conservative? Have they forgotten that my ministry is in obedience to the one who loved his enemies so fully that he died for them? What then can I say to the "Viet Cong" or to Castro or to Mao as a faithful minister of this one? Can I threaten them with death or must I not share with them my life?[76]

D. The Christian Love-Ethic and the Search for Beloved Community

Martin Luther King, Jr.'s perspective on the Christian love-ethic was perhaps most clearly explicated in his sermon entitled, "Loving Your Enemies."[77] The sermon was based on Jesus's admonition to his disciples in Matthew 5:43-45:

> "You have heard that it was said, 'You shall love your neigh-

bor, and hate your enemy.' But I say to you, love your
enemies, and pray for those who persecute you, so that you
may be children of your Father which is in heaven; for he
makes his sun rise on the evil and the good, and sends rain
on the righteous and on the unrighteous."

King pointed out that probably no admonition of Jesus has
been more difficult to follow than the command to "love your enemies." Loving one's enemies is not an option, but is essential to
building authentic Christian community. King offered a model for
how one is to love an enemy.[78] First, *we must develop the capacity
to forgive.* He who is devoid of the power to forgive is devoid of
the power to love. It is impossible even to begin the act of loving
one's enemies without the prior acceptance of the necessity, over
and over again, of forgiving those who inflict evil and injury upon
us. It is also necessary to realize that the forgiving act must always
be initiated by the person who has been wronged, the victim of
some great hurt, the recipient of some tortuous injustice, the ab-
sorber of some terrible act of oppression.

Second, *we must recognize that the evil deed of the enemy-
neighbor, that thing that hurts, never quite expresses all that he is.*
An element of goodness may be found in even the worst enemy.
Each of us is something of a schizophrenic personality, tragically
divided against ourselves. A persistent civil war rages within all
our lives, King said. Something within us causes us to lament with
Ovid, the Latin poet, "I see and approve of better things, but follow
worse," or to agree with Plato that human personality is like a chari-
oteer having two headstrong horses, each wanting to go in a different direction, or to repeat the Apostle Paul, "The good that I would
I do not; but the evil which I would not, that I do."

Third, *we must not seek to defeat or humiliate the enemy
but to win his friendship and understanding.* At times we are able
to humiliate our worst enemy. Inevitably, his weak moments come
and we are able to thrust inside the spear of defeat. But this we
must not do. Every word and deed must contribute to an understanding with the enemy and release those vast reservoirs of goodwill which have been blocked by impenetrable walls of hate.

King concluded by defining love (*agape*) as the means by
which we overcome the propensity toward hatred and humiliation:

Agape is the love of God operating in the human heart. When we rise to love on the *agape* level, we rise to the position of loving the person who does the evil deed, while hating the deed which the person does.[79]

William Shannon in *Seeds of Peace* offers a perspective on the nature of this unconditional love:

Unconditional love is love that makes demands on oneself more than on the other. It is a love that brooks no "if" clauses. It does not say: "I love you, if you do this or that." Instead it says: "I love you regardless of what you do or say. I love you because, no matter what you say or do, you are the icon, the image of God. Precisely because I love you, I will confront you with the truth and challenge you with its demands. But I will also be a listener. I will try to hear what you are saying. For I realize that I do not possess all the truth; and there may well be things you have to say to me that I need to hear. But regardless of how much we may differ, I shall try always to remember the contemplative vision: that you and I are one in God. That oneness exists at a level of perception that perhaps we do not often enough achieve. But I know in faith that that oneness is a reality. And since we are one, I must love you as my other self. There can be no strings attached to my love for you."[80]

Agape is not a weak, passive love. It is love in action. *Agape* seeks to preserve and create community. It is insistent on community even when one seeks to break it. *Agape* entails a willingness to go to any length to restore community. It doesn't stop at the first mile, but it goes the second mile to restore community. It is a willingness to forgive, not seven times, but seventy times seven to restore community.

The Cross is the eternal and divine expression of the length to which God will go in order to restore broken community. The Resurrection is symbolic of God's triumph over all forces that seek to block community. The Holy Spirit is the continuing community-creating reality that moves through history. Those who work against community are working against the whole of creation. Therefore, if the response to hate is reciprocal hate, then there is nothing but intensification of the cleavage in broken community. If hate is met with hate, persons become depersonalized because creation is so designed that human personality can only be fulfilled in the context of community. Booker T. Washington once said: "Let no man pull you so low he brings you to the point of working against community; he drags you to the point of defying creation, and therefore becoming depersonalized."[81]

Kenneth Smith and Ira Zepp, Jr. in *Search for the Beloved Community,* suggest that Martin Luther King, Jr.'s perspective on the Christian love-ethic provides critical insight into understanding his persistent search for the *"Beloved Community."*[82] A recurring theme in King's sermons, throughout his career, was what he called *Beloved Community.* It was the ultimate goal for which he worked. For King, the *Beloved Community* was an integrated community in which persons of all races and creeds lived together harmoniously as sisters and brothers in peace. It was the Kingdom of God on earth. King stated, "I do not think of political power as an end. Neither do I think of economic power as an end. They are ingredients in the objective we seek in life. And I think that end, that objective, is a truly brotherly society, the creation of *Beloved Community.*"[83]

In the final analysis, Martin Luther King, Jr. asserted, *agape* is recognition of the fact that all life is interrelated. One of his fundamental beliefs was the kinship of all persons. He believed all life is part of a single process; all living things are interrelated; and all persons are sisters and brothers. All have a place in the *Beloved Community.* Because all are interrelated, one cannot harm another without harming oneself. King said:

> To the degree that I harm my brother, no matter what he is doing to me, to that extent I am harming myself. For example, white men often refuse federal aid to education in order to avoid giving the Negro his rights; but because all men are brothers they cannot deny Negro children without harming themselves. Why is this? Because all men are brothers. If you harm me, you harm yourself. Love, *agape*, is the only cement that can hold this broken community together. When I am commanded to love, I am commanded to restore community, to resist injustice, and to meet the needs of my brothers.[84]

The quest for the *Beloved Community* – through *agape* - would lead King to take a consistently prophetic stance, armed with his faith in God, against the powerful, progressive and ideological apparatus of the Jim Crow racism of the Southern church and society, and the more apathetic, sophisticated brand of racism experienced in the North.

When the Montgomery Bus Boycott ended, Martin Luther King, Jr. spoke at a victory rally on December 3, 1956. He pointed out that the goal had not been to defeat other persons, but to awaken the conscience of others to challenge the false sense of superiority that persons might harbor. Now that victory had been achieved, King said, it was time for reconciliation. "The end is reconciliation; the end is the creation of *Beloved Community*."

And it is in the God-giftedness of humanity, as manifest in the perpetual striving toward *Beloved Community*, through the appropriation of the Christian love-ethic, that the church and society can begin to constructively address disintegration and disunity such as racism and its concomitant twin evil - economic deprivation - that continue to serve as hindrances to true peace and authentic community.

NOTES

[1] Robert L. Franklin, *Liberating Visions: Human Fulfillment and Social Justice in African-American Thought* (Minneapolis: Fortress Press, 1990), 105.

[2] Clayborne Carson, "Martin Luther King, Jr. and the African-American Social Gospel" in *African-American Religion: Interpretive Essays in History and Culture,* eds. Timothy Fulop and Albert Raboteau (New York: Routledge, 1997), 345-6.

[3] Franklin, 106.

[4] Stephen B. Oates, *Let the Trumpet Sound* (New York: HarperPerennial, 1982), 10.

[5] Ibid.

[6] Carson, 349. Carson makes reference to King's paper, "Autobiography of Religious Development," *Papers of Martin Luther King, Jr.,* vol. 1, ed. Clayborne Carson

(Berkley, CA: University of California Press, 1992), 361.
[7] Martin Luther King, Jr. "The Un-Christian Christian," *Ebony* 20 (Chicago: Johnson Publishing, August 1965), 76.
[8] Carson, 344.
[9] Ibid.
[10] Kenneth Smith and Ira Zepp, Jr., *Search for the Beloved Community: The Thinking of Martin Luther King, Jr.,* (Valley Forge, PA: Judson Press, 1974, 1998), 3. Here, Smith and Zepp make reference to a speech made by King to the American Baptist Convention shortly before the start of the Montgomery Bus Boycott.
[11] Carson, 351.
[12] Ibid., 349.
[13] Mark L. Chapman, *Christianity on Trial,* 15.
[14] Ibid.
[15] Cornel West, *Prophetic Fragments: Illuminations of the Crisis in American Religion and Culture* (Grand Rapids, MI: Eerdmans, 1988), pp. 271-272, West alludes to Italian philosopher Antonio Gramsci's distinction between "organic" and "traditional" intellectuals, as fully enumerated in Gramsci's *Prison Notebooks.*
[16] Chapman, 27.
[17] Ibid., 16. Here, Chapman makes reference to Keith D. Miller's landmark study of King's language and its sources. See Keith D. Miller, *Voice of Deliverance: The Language of Martin Luther King, Jr., and Its Sources* (New York: The Free Press, 1992), 44.
[18] Smith and Zepp, 18.
[19] Ibid.
[20] Ibid.
[21] Ibid., 21.
[22] Ibid., 22.
[23] Ibid., 23.
[24] Ibid., 20.
[25] Ibid., 21.
[26] Franklin, 109.

[27] Ibid.

[28] Ibid.

[29] Ibid.

[30] Martin Luther King, Jr., *Stride Toward Freedom: The Montgomery Story* (New York: Harper and Row, 1958), 100.

[31] Martin Luther King, Jr., "Conceptions and Impressions of Religion," *Papers of Martin Luther King, Jr.,* ed. Carson, vol. 1, 415-416.

[32] Carson, 352, Here, Carson makes reference to King's perspectives on Personalism in the "Place of Reason and Experience," *Papers of Martin Luther King, Jr.,* vol. 1, p. 234.

[33] Franklin, 107.

[34] Smith and Zepp, 26

[35] Smith and Zepp, 31. Smith and Zepp offer an analysis of Rauschenbusch's perspectives on ethical and moral religion as outlined in *Christianity and the Social Crisis.*

[36] Ibid., 32.

[37] Ibid.

[38] Ibid., 33.

[39] Martin E. Marty, *Pilgrims in Their Own Land: 500 Years of Religion in America* (New York: Penguin Books, 1984), 441.

[40] Carson, 354.

[41] Martin Luther King, Jr., "How Modern Christians Should Think of Man," in ed. Carson, *Papers of Martin Luther Kings, Jr.,* vol.1, 273.

[42] Smith and Zepp, 73.

[43] Martin Luther King, Jr., "Reinhold Niebuhr," April 2, 1952, in ed. Carson, *Papers of Martin Luther King, Jr.,* Vol. 2.

[44] Martin Luther King, Jr., "Reinhold Niebuhr's Ethical Dualism," May 9, 1952, in ed. Carson, *Papers of Martin Luther King, Jr.,* Vol. 2.

[45] See Smith and Zepp, 73f., and Reinhold Niebuhr, *Moral*

Man and Immoral Society (New York: Scribner, 1933).

[46] Carson, 353.

[47] Smith and Zepp, 73.

[48] Ibid., 88.

[49] Ibid., 89.

[50] Ibid., 74.

[51] Martin Luther King, Jr., "My Journey to Nonviolence," *Fellowship* (New York: Fellowship of Reconciliation, September 1958).

[52] Carson, 353. Here Carson makes reference to Martin Luther King, Jr., "Reinhold Niebuhr's Ethical Dualism."

[53] Martin Luther King, Jr., "Three Dimensions of the Complete Life," in *Strength to Love* (New York: Harper and Row, 1963), 69-73.

[54] Smith and Zepp, 76.

[55] Ibid., 71.

[56] See, Robert Franklin, *Liberating Visions,* 109f. Franklin points out that King, in his conception of the "Three Dimensions of the Complete Life," makes reference to Paul Tillich, *Love, Power and Justice,* (London: Oxford University Press, 1954), 78.

[57] King, "Three Dimensions of the Complete Life," *Strength to Love,* 69-73.

[58] John J. Ansbro, *Martin Luther King, Jr.: Nonviolent Strategies and Tactics for Social Change* (Maryknoll, NY: Orbis Books, 2000), 30.

[59] King. *Strength to Love,* 17-24.

[60] Ibid., 17.

[61] James Cone, *A Black Theology of Liberation,* 37.

[62] Smith and Zepp, 2.

[63] Franklin, 108-109.

[64] Carson, 356f.

[65] King, *Stride Toward Freedom.* It is in this work that King outlines his doctrine of nonviolence.

[66] Martin Luther King, Jr. "Suffering and Faith" *The Christian Century* (Chicago: Christian Century, April 27, 1960).

See also *A Testament of Hope: The Essential Writings of Martin Luther King, Jr.*, ed. James Melvin Washington (New York: Harper and Row, 1986), 41.

[67] Gustavo Gutierrez, *On Job: God-talk and the Suffering of the Innocent* (Maryknoll, NY: Orbis Books, 1985), 15.

[68] Viktor Frankl, *Man's Search for Meaning* (New York: Washington Square Press, 1984), 135.

[69] Marty, 442, Martin Marty here refers to Martin Luther King Jr.'s famous "Letter from the Birmingham Jail." See also *A Testament of Hope,* ed. James Melvin Washington, 289.

[70] King, "Our God is Able," *Strength to Love,"* see pp.124-130 for King's complete manuscript of this sermon.

[71] King, "The American Dream," in *A Testament of Hope,* ed. James Melvin Washington, 210.

[72] Ibid.

[73] Martin Luther King, Jr., *Where Do We Go from Here: Chaos or Community?* (Boston: Beacon Press, 1967), 182.

[74] Martin Luther King, Jr., "I Have a Dream," in *A Testament of Hope,* ed. James Melvin Washington, 217f.

[75] Martin Luther King, Jr., "Beyond Vietnam," *Brotherman: The Odyssey of Black Men in America – An Anthology* (New York: Ballentine, 1995), eds. Herb Boyd and Robert L, Allen, 393-394.

[76] Ibid.

[77] King, "Loving Your Enemies," *Strength to Love,* 41-50.

[78] Ibid.

[79] Ibid.

[80] William Shannon, *Seeds of Peace,* 116.

[81] Ibid.

[82] Smith and Zepp, in *Search for the Beloved Community,* the matter of King's development of the concept of *Beloved Community* within the context of the Christian love- ethic is explicated at various points throughout the book.

[83] Martin Luther King, Jr., in *The Christian Century,* (Chicago, IL: Christian Century, July 13, 1966).

CHAPTER FOUR

THE INFLUENCE OF MOHANDAS GANDHI ON
HOWARD THURMAN AND MARTIN LUTHER KING, JR.

I. Toward a Spirituality and Philosophy of Nonviolence

A. Gandhi's Early Development

Mohandas Gandhi provided a deep reservoir of ideas from which both Howard Thurman and Martin Luther King, Jr. drank. Thurman and King may or may not have been equipped with the most rigorous understanding of nonviolent principles before their exposure to Gandhi, but both had been committed – at least to some degree - to the transforming ideals of nonviolence prior to encountering the thought of Gandhi. Their respective contacts with him would serve to codify their thinking with regard to nonviolence, while also serving as an impetus for their ongoing search of peaceful community.

Gandhi was born in India in 1869 into the Vaisa caste (merchants, farmers, and craftspeople). [1] His father, however, was involved in law and politics. His mother was a very religious person. A devout Hindu, she engaged in self-discipline, purification and other religious observances. Gandhi's India was dominated by British colonialism. In Rajkot, he experienced early segregation. The British reserved for themselves the best part of town; Indians were restricted to the slums. At school, he was taught in English, under the assumption that everything Indian was inferior. Gandhi disliked this arrangement. He felt that Indians needed the pride of language, custom and history. With his pride of self and people, Gandhi studied both Sanskrit and Persian.[2]

When he decided to go to England to study law, Gandhi came up against the stark reality of the caste system. His family told him that if he crossed the ocean to a foreign land, he would become an outcast. Gandhi, however, did not yield to this threat and vowed to be a Hindu wherever he was. A family priest intervened on his behalf and assured everyone that, if Gandhi kept his vow, he could remain a Hindu. This led Gandhi to declare war against the strictures and harshness of the caste system, and this conviction remained with him for the rest of his life.

In England, Gandhi's philosophy of nonviolence began to take shape. He studied the ideas of Hindus, Buddhists and Christians. He was moved as well by the writings of American authors such as Ralph Waldo Emerson and Henry David Thoreau. Thoreau's ideas, especially on civil disobedience, impressed him. His encounter with the New Testament, especially with Jesus and the Sermon on the Mount, had a profound impact on his thinking.

B. Development of Satyagraha

Faith was the center of life for Gandhi. Gandhi believed in God, and in truth. "What I want to achieve, what I have been striving and pining to achieve these thirty years," he wrote in his autobiography, "is self-realization, to see God face to face. I live and move and have my being in pursuit of this goal. All that I do by way of speaking and writing, and all my ventures in the political field, are directed to the same end." Gandhi saw the face of God in the poorest peasant and in the struggle of nonviolent resistance and love in the public realm. He sought to uncover truth at every turn and found that justice and nonviolence spring from the journey in truth. "You may be sent to the gallows, or put to torture, but if you have truth in you, you will experience an inner joy." Truth, for Gandhi, was the essence of life.[3]

The formative ideas of Gandhi's philosophy began to take shape in the years he worked to better the social and economic conditions of Indians in South Africa. Gandhi spent 20 years of his life in South Africa as an acknowledged leader of the Indian people.[4] Rajmohan Gandhi, research professor at the Center of Policy Research, New Delhi, India suggests that much of Gandhi's view on nonviolence can be traced to his personal experiences and early encounters with bigotry on his journey to South Africa in 1893. [5] Rajmohan Gandhi offers an account, depicted in the Attenborough film, of the well-know incident when Mohandas Gandhi was ejected from the railway train at the station of Pietermaitzburg in the year 1893:

> The barrister trained in London, he was holding a first-class ticket and had just arrived in South Africa – he had been there hardly a week. Because he did not have the right skin color and did not move to the van compartment when asked, he was thrown out. Then he made a journey by train, coach, and train again, eventually arriving, via Johannesburg, Pretoria. Along the way he was roughly beaten on the coach because he refused to sit as ordered on the floor. He tried to spend the stopover night in Johannesburg in a hotel, but was told that there was no room. He had experiences that were not very pleasant. On a Sunday evening he arrived in Pretoria, his destination. Not sure of what lay ahead of him, and remembering that he could not get accommodations in Johannesburg, he wondered where he would spend his first night in Pretoria. He decided to consult the man who was checking tickets at the exit for ideas. While he was having this conversation, a Black American noticed the predicament of the young man from India (Gandhi was only 23 at this time), went up to Gandhi, and asked the young man if he could help.[6]

Mohandas Gandhi explained his anxiety. The African American said, "I have an American friend, Mr. Johnston, who has a hotel in Pretoria. He might put you up." So they walked from the station to the hotel, this man whose name is not known and Gandhi. Gandhi describes the incident in his autobiography, written 33 years later, but does not give the name of the good Samaritan. At the hotel the man introduced Gandhi to Mr. Johnston, who said: "You can stay in the hotel if you are willing to eat in your room. If I took you to the dining room, the other guests might not like it." Gandhi hated conditions of this sort but he made the compromise. "All right," he said. A little later there was a knock on the door, and Gandhi thought it was a man with a tray. But it was Mr. Johnston himself, who said: "I have spoken to the other guests in the hotel and they are willing for you to eat in the dining room." As far as I know it was Gandhi's first encounter with Americans, one Black and the other White.[7]

Rajmohan Gandhi points out that it remains an interesting fact of history that the man who enabled Gandhi to have a roof and a bed in Pretoria was an African American.[8]   As is evident from a sketch of Gandhi's early life, he was "born to rebel." His philosophy would inevitably be a philosophy for action. It was to be more than a philosophy for social engagement; it was to become a philosophy for social transformation. He came to believe that every person was of equal value, and that oppressed people should struggle for their equality. According to Gandhi, they must fight peacefully and they must not hurt others while doing so. He strongly believed that unjust laws should not be obeyed, but that people should not be violent in their attempt to change the law.

In 1907, Mohandas Gandhi, who was still in South Africa, read Henry David Thoreau. In seeking to conceptualize his philosophy, Gandhi borrowed the anglicized term "civil disobedience" from Thoreau, which was more often referred to as "passive resistance." But Gandhi was not satisfied with either. Both were too narrowly conceived; they appeared to be negative, passive, and weak. They could easily denigrate into hatred and would likely opt, finally, for violence. Thus, civil disobedience and passive resistance became obsolete for Gandhi.

In a magazine called *Indian Opinion,* which he edited for a time in South Africa, Gandhi offered a small prize to be "awarded to the reader who invented the best designation for our struggle." One of his cousins, Maganlal Gandhi, produced a word that seemed almost right, *sadagraha,* which means "firmness in a good cause." Gandhi corrected it to *satyagraha... Satya* means "Truth"; *graha* means "firmness, tenacity, holding on." [9]

"I thus began," Gandhi says, "to call the Indian movement *Satyagraha,* that is to say the Force that is born in truth and love, or non-violence," and gave up the use of the phrase "passive resistance." On other occasions, Gandhi called it "Soul Force," or "Love Force," or "Truth force." *Sat* in *satyagraha* means "being," "that which is," "truth." For Gandhi, *Sat* was "the only correct and fully significant name for God.[10]

The conception of s*atyagraha* became fundamental to Gandhi's life and activity.[11]   It is "truth-taking" or "the taking of vows of truthfulness." Its root and meaning is "holding on to truth" and, by extension, resistance to evil by nonviolent means. This "truth force" is possible because it excludes the use of violence, because humans are capable of grasping the truth (but not in an absolute sense) and are not competent to punish. Theologically, truth in an absolute sense is God or Ultimate Being.

In Gandhi's writings, teachings and actions in South Africa *satyagraha* became manifest as a technique for action. It is not dogma; it is neither static nor substantial. It is, rather, a dynamic and spiritual concept and a technique and process for action leading to personal and social transformation. As Gandhi saw it, s*atyagraha* is not intended to overwhelm one's opponent. It should not be used in an arbitrary way to rectify a situation. *Satyagraha* must appear to be a last resort in an unbearable situation that merits the commitment of unlimited suffering. All would-be participants must be thoroughly prepared to know the factuality of the grievances being set forth. Participants must be willing to join in the conclusion that the cause is just and attainable, and they must be on the side of truth, which transcends facts. In other words, the truth being sought must be of such dimension that the practice of "soul-force" might give opponents concern. Opponents should be moved to seek the opportunity to change sides, and to approximate the higher goal or good that beckons all to become involved for human betterment and fulfillment.

A related concept used by Gandhi in the discussion of the meaning of nonviolent action was the principle of *ahimsa* (non-injury). This term is borrowed from the Jains. Jainism, founded by Mahavira, is one of the oldest personally founded religions in India. The Jains were known for their doctrine of the non-injury of all forms of life. It was this religious concept of *ahimsa* that attracted Gandhi. Historically, Jains became merchants rather than farmers because they did not wish to destroy any form of (sentient) life. Even today, Jaina women wear veils over their noses and mouths to avoid breathing in any form of insect life.[12]

For Gandhi, *ahimsa* was the basic law of being. It can be used as the most effective principle for social action, since it is ingrained deeply in human nature and corresponds to humanity's innate desire for peace, justice, freedom and personal dignity. *Himas* (violence or injury) is just the opposite – it degrades, corrupts and destroys. It feeds on the tendency to meet force with force, hatred with hatred. This plan of action leads to progressive denigration. Nonviolence, on the other hand, heals and restores humanity's best nature, while providing the best means of restoring a social order of justice and freedom. *Ahimsa* is not preoccupied with the seizure of power as an end in itself; it is a way of transforming relationships in order to bring about a peaceful transfer of power.[13]

Gandhi was convinced of the power of nonviolence, through the principles of *satyagraha* and *ahimsa,* as the key to achieving the aims of peace. In 1926, he wrote:

> Nonviolence is the greatest force humanity has been endowed with. Truth is the only goal we have. For God is none other than Truth. But Truth cannot be, never will be reached except through nonviolence. That which distinguishes us from other animals is our capacity to be nonviolent. And we fulfill our mission only to the extent that we are nonviolent and no more. We have no doubt many gifts. But if we do not serve the main purpose – the development of the spirit of nonviolence in us – they but drag us down lower than the brute, a status from which we have only just emerged. The cry for peace will be a cry in the wilderness, so long as the spirit of nonviolence does not dominate millions of men and women. An armed conflict between nations horrifies us. But the economic war is no better than an armed conflict. This is like a surgical operation. An economic war is prolonged torture. And its ravages are no less terrible than those depicted in the literature on war properly so called. We think nothing of the other because we are used to its deadly effects.[14]

Gandhi's conception of nonviolence began with the spiritual disciplines of prayer, solitude, and fasting. By avoiding power in all its forms of violence and control, and by renouncing the desire for immediate results, Gandhi discovered that one could be reduced to zero. From this ground zero of emptiness, the compassionate love of God - nonviolence – could grow. At this point, Gandhi wrote, the individual becomes "irresistible" and one's nonviolence becomes "all-pervasive." [15] Nonviolence, the power of the powerless, Gandhi believed, is the power of God, the power of truth and love that goes beyond the physical world into the realm of the spiritual. This power can overcome death, as God revealed through the nonviolence of Jesus, his crucifixion, and subsequent resurrection in the resisting community.[16]

Gandhi's experiments in Truth revealed that the mandate of the Sermon on the Mount – to love one's enemies – is of critical importance. In all of Gandhi's public uses of nonviolence, he always manifested a desire for reconciliation, friendship with his opponent. He also always tried to stand with the outcasts of society and to speak up for the rights of the marginalized. In India, such solidarity primarily meant taking the radical and scandalizing public stand on behalf of the so-called untouchables. Gandhi called them *harijans,* or "children of God," and begged his fellow Indians to banish untouchability from their hearts and lives.[17]

Gandhi warned against what he called the seven social sins, which served ultimately to divide society into the powerful and the powerless. He identified these sins as: (1) politics without principle, (2) wealth without work, (3) commerce without morality, (4) pleasure without conscience, (5) education without character, (6) science without humanity, and (7) worship without sacrifice. Jim Wallis, in *The Soul of Politics,* suggests that these social sins today... are the accepted practices of the life of the nation.[18]

William Shannon asserts that no one has found an English equivalent for *Satyagraha.* Hence, we are still obliged to content ourselves with the word "nonviolence." But we need continually to make clear the positive meaning it intends to convey as a translation of *ahimsa.*[19]

Nonviolence is the essence of truth; one cannot seek truth, Gandhi discovered, and still continue to participate in violence and injustice within one's heart and in the world. Nonviolence is the power of the powerless, the power of God, the only power that overcomes evil. "Nonviolence is the greatest and most active force in the world... One person who can express nonviolence in life exercises a force superior to all the forces of brutality... Nonviolence cannot be preached. It has to be practiced," Gandhi insisted. "If we remain nonviolent, hatred will die as everything does, from disuse."[20]

The first commitment of a nonviolent person is to the truth, according to Gandhi. Quoted by Thomas Merton, Gandhi sums up the heart of his teaching about nonviolence: "The way of peace is the way of truth." He even says: "Truthfulness is more important than peacefulness... A truthful person cannot long remain violent." Gandhi offers his reason for saying this: "A person will perceive in the course of his research that he has no need to be violent, and he will further discover that so long as there is the slightest trace of violence in him, he will fail to find the truth he is searching for." At the deepest level of our being we are in touch with God and there- fore with truth itself. That is why at the core of our being we are nonviolent..." [21]

Gandhi viewed the problem of violence as being rooted in the hearts of men and women. Thus, the means of realizing nonvio- lence and peace were through transforming the hearts of persons. In 1926, he stated:

> I observe, in the limited field in which I find myself, that unless I can reach the hearts of men and women, I am able to do nothing. I observe further that so long as the spirit of hate persists in some shape or other, it is impossible to es- tablish peace or to gain our freedom by peaceful effort. We cannot love one another if we hate Englishmen. We cannot love the Japanese and hate the Englishmen. We must either let the law of love rule us through and through or not at all. Love among ourselves based on hatred of others breaks down under the slightest pressure. The fact is, such love is never real love. It is an armed peace. And so it will be in this great movement in the West against war. War will only be stopped when the conscience of humankind has become sufficiently elevated to recognize the undisputed supremacy of the Law of Love in all the walks of life. Some say this will never come to pass. I shall retain the faith till the end of my earthly existence that it shall come to pass.[22]

In 1929, Dr. John Mott met Gandhi in India. Mott asked: "What causes you solicitude, concern, for the future of India?" That was on the eve of Gandhi's Salt March to the Sea, so that Gandhi was close to a high point on his freedom movement. He responded:

"Our apathy and hardness of heart, if I may use the biblical phrase, toward the masses and their poverty."[23]

Dr. Mott also asked him about what India was meant to contribute to the world. Gandhi answered: "Nonviolence, which the country is exhibiting at the present day on a scale unprecedented in history." He added that nonviolence has "so permeated our people that an armed revolution has almost become an impossibility in India, not because, as some would have it, we as a race are physically weak, for it does not require much physical strength so much as a devilish will to press a trigger to shoot a person, but because the traditions of *ahimsa* (nonviolence/non-injury) have struck deep roots among the people."

In 1945, two African Americans met Gandhi. One was Deton Brooks of the *Chicago Defender,* who asked if Gandhi had a message for America. In his well-known answer, Gandhi said, "My life is its message." Also in the summer of 1945, a man named Bolden of the National Negro Press Association went to interview Gandhi, who however, interviewed Bolden on the condition of Blacks in the United States. Writes Bolden on Gandhi's reaction to the story: "All during our discussion I noticed the great Mahatma's face registering first sorrow, then disgust, then agreement, followed by humor, and ending in pleasure."[24]

Once two of Gandhi's close friends, Charles F. Andrews and Rabindranath Tagore, who had won a Nobel Prize for literature in 1913, expressed their unhappiness at one of Gandhi's methods in the nonviolent battle for freedom: the burning of foreign cloth. Tagore and Andrews said to Gandhi: "How can you do this? You are burning something valuable and beautiful." Gandhi gave his answer: "I want to care for the starving Indian peasant. He has nothing. I want him to spin and weave and to make cloth. Nobody will buy his cloth if mass-produced cloth from Manchester is sold in India." Also, said Gandhi: "Indians hate the British. I want to deflect their hate from people to things."

Decades later, Martin Luther King, Jr. expressed similar thoughts. He saw a distinction between violence against people and violence on things.[25] He likened things to the earth we walk on: "Humans are different from what they walk on," King said. Gandhi saw national self-respect as a religious and spiritual virtue.

India was the embodiment of such truth and virtue to him. However, he knew well that national self-respect could cloak cruelty and hatred.

Gandhi was a strong Indian nationalist. He said in 1940: "my mission is to convert every Indian, whether he is a Hindu, Muslim or any other, even Englishmen and finally the world to non-violence for regulating mutual relations whether political, economic, social or religious." The phrase "even ...and finally" revealed his priority toward serving and leading Indians to liberation. "I can't find Him apart from the rest of humanity," he said. "My countrymen," he added, "are my nearest neighbors." He had to serve people if he was to serve God; and his nearest neighbors were Indians. He would say in 1931, "My nationalism, fierce though it is, is not exclusive, is not devised to harm any nation or individual." A core of nationalism always resided in him, rallying Indians, inspiring colonized people everywhere to rise above the social ill and violence that was so much a part of Indian reality under British domination.[26]

Mohandas Gandhi realized that the spirituality of nonviolence begins within persons and moves out from there. The life of active nonviolence is the fruit of an inner peace and spiritual unity already realized in us, and not the other way around... through our personal, inner conversion, our own inner peace, we are sensitized to care for God, ourselves, each other, for the poor, and for our world. Gandhi taught that nonviolence does not mean passivity. It is the most daring, creative, and courageous way of living, and it is the only hope for the world. Nonviolence demands creativity. It pursues dialogue, seeks reconciliation, listens to the truth in opponents, rejects militarism, and allows God's Spirit to transform us socially and politically.[27]

II. Gandhi's Influence on Howard Thurman

By 1936, Mohandas Gandhi was not certain that India was going to demonstrate nonviolence to the world.[28] He had noticed deep layers of violence in India. During the 1935-36 academic year, Howard Thurman headed an African-American delegation to South Asia, lecturing at some 45 institutions.[29] While on this trip,

Thurman met for several hours with Gandhi in Bardoli, India; re-
markably, Gandhi broke his fast for the duration of the delegation's
visit. By all accounts, Thurman's conversation with Gandhi represented the first formal exchange between an African-American religious leader and the great Indian prophet of nonviolent revolution.
It was Gandhi's first opportunity to engage African Americans in
discussion concerning their respective struggles for freedom. An
outspoken critic of traditional Christianity, Gandhi believed that
western interpretations of Christianity contributed to racial, economic, and sexual discrimination, and led to segregation of the
world's people.

Howard Thurman, then dean of Rankin Chapel at Howard
University, was accompanied by his wife Sue Bailey Thurman, who
was an historian and singer; and another Black couple from the
United States, Edward and Phenola Carroll (Edward would eventually become one of the first African-American bishops in the United
Methodist Church). They had asked for a chance to meet Gandhi.
He had written welcoming them. When the four Americans arrived, Gandhi went out of his way to greet them. He didn't always
do that to visitors. His secretary, Mahadev Desai, told Thurman
that he had never seen Gandhi greet a visitor so warmly in his many
years with the Mahatma. Thurman later recalled that Gandhi asked
persistent, pragmatic questions about American Negroes, about the
course of slavery, and how they had survived it.[30]

Gandhi asked about the plight of blacks in the United States
with respect to issues such as economics, interracial marriage and
politics. Howard Thurman asked Gandhi whether South African
Blacks had joined his movement. Gandhi replied: "No, they hadn't."
Gandhi said he deliberately did not want to amalgamate those two
struggles at that time. He added that this was due to their lack of
understanding of the meaning and methods of nonviolence. But
Gandhi's work there had an impact on influential leaders in South
Africa such as Albert Luthuli who, like Martin Luther King, Jr. was
awarded the Nobel Peace Prize.

Asked by Thurman to define nonviolence, Gandhi said he
hoped it would be love in the Pauline sense, love as spelled out in
the letter to the Corinthians, plus the struggle for justice. Gandhi
asked his American visitors if they would sing a Negro spiritual for

him. The Thurmans and the Carrolls gave two. Gandhi was greatly moved as Mrs. Thurman sang two typical Negro spirituals: "Were You There When They Crucified My Lord" and "We Are Climbing Jacob's Ladder." To all who heard them, these spirituals expressed the hopes and aspirations of the oppressed to climb higher and higher until freedom's goal has been reached.[31]

After he had heard the spirituals, Gandhi said to the four: "Well if it comes true it may be through the Negroes (in America) that the unadulterated message of nonviolence will be delivered to the world."[32] In other words, by this time in 1936, Gandhi was not sure that it would be India that would deliver a model of nonviolence, and he gave expression to a prophetic intuition that African Americans would demonstrate nonviolence to the world.

The conversation between Thurman and Gandhi continued. Thurman inquired about the nature of nonviolence. Gandhi replied: … without direct, active expression of it, nonviolence to my mind is meaningless. One cannot be passively nonviolent. In fact, nonviolence is a term I had to coin in order to bring out the root meaning of *ahimsa*. In spite of the negative particle "non," it is no negative force. Superficially, we are surrounded in life by strife and bloodshed, life living upon life. But some great seer, who ages ago penetrated the center of truth, said, "It is not through strife and violence but through nonviolence that man fulfills his destiny and his duty to his fellow creatures." It is a force that is more positive than electricity, and more powerful than either. At the center of nonviolence is the force, which is self-acting. *Ahisma* means "love" in the Pauline sense, and yet something more than love defined by St. Paul, although I know St. Paul's beautiful definition is good enough for all practical purposes. *Ahisma* includes the whole creation, and not only humans.[33]

Thurman asked: "How are we to train individuals and communities in this difficult act?" Gandhi replied:

> There is no royal road, except through living the creed in your life, which must be a living sermon. Of course, the expression in one's life presupposes great study, tremendous perseverance, and thorough cleansing of one's self of all impurities. If for mastering the physical sciences you have to devote a whole lifetime, how many lifetimes may

be needed for mastering the greatest spiritual force that mankind has ever known? But why worry even if it means several lifetimes? For, if this is the only permanent thing in life, if it is the only thing that counts, then whatever effort you bestow on mastering it is well spent. "Seek ye first the Kingdom of Heaven and everything else will be added unto you." The Kingdom of Heaven is *ahimsa.*[34]

Mrs. Sue Bailey Thurman asked, "How am I to act, supposing my own brother was being lynched before my very eyes?" Gandhi responded:

There is such a thing as self-immolation. Supposing I was a Negro, and my sister was ravished by a white and lynched by a whole community, what would be my duty? I ask myself. And the answer comes to me: I must not wish ill to these, but neither must I cooperate with them. It may be that ordinarily I depend on the lynching community for my livelihood. I refuse to cooperate with them, refuse to touch food that comes from them, and I refuse to cooperate with even my brother Negroes who tolerate the wrong. This is the self-immolation that I mean. I have often in my life resorted to this plan. Of course, a mechanical act of starvation will mean nothing. One's faith must remain undimmed while one's life ebbs out minute by minute.[35]

Howard Thurman was extremely impressed with Gandhi's ideas on the power of nonviolence as a method which positively responds to the spiritual needs of humanity, while at the same time accomplishing the necessary political transformation of the social order.[36] Certainly, Gandhi's success in India was solid evidence for nonviolence. Gandhi reinforced, confirmed and provided deeper insights about nonviolence for Thurman.

The end result of the conversation was that Thurman felt assured that nonviolence could transform whatever difficulties it confronted. The techniques might have to be refined, individuals would need to go through radical preparation to be faithful disciples of the method, large numbers of people might suffer and die, but the moral and spiritual imperatives for nonviolence would prevail over experiences of violence.[37]

In formulating his response to Gandhi's critique of Christianity, Thurman began to integrate Gandhian principles of unity and nonviolent social change into his own Christian pacifism and mysticism.[38]   Thurman returned to the United States with "an enhanced interpretation of the meaning of nonviolence."[39]   He learned from Gandhi, "a man who (was) rooted in the basic mysticism of the [Hindu] Brahma," the life-affirming concepts of *ahimsa* and s*atyagraha*.   Thurman found in Gandhi a kindred mind and spirit who refused to think in terms of a disconnected Truth, God, or Ultimate reality but focused his attention on that which was pre-eminently practical and spiritual.   For Thurman as for Gandhi, unwavering sincerity in the face of strident opposition was grasped as an intensely active and revolutionary endeavor.[40]

The other important contribution that Gandhi made to Thurman's work was in offering a global perspective on the human condition.   The anti-imperialist movement then surging through South Asia, exemplified by the implementation of ethical nonviolence and non-cooperation on the part of the masses, provided the first critical international referent for Thurman's understanding of the relationship that exists between religion and the social world. Thurman's wartime essay, "The Fascist Masquerade," affords a glimpse into this aspect of his development.[41]   Later, other arenas of protest – colonial Africa, Nazi Germany, the Native American communities of Canada and the United States – would further sensitize Thurman's thinking in this regard.

III. Gandhi's Influence on Martin Luther King, Jr.

Martin Luther King, Jr. was introduced to the thinking of Mohandas Gandhi in a sermon that he heard by Mordecai Johnson, while King was a student at Crozer Seminary in Philadelphia. President of Howard University, Johnson was one of the greatest orators and preachers in black history, and always held his audiences spellbound. Johnson had just returned from India when King heard him lecture on Gandhi.   King offers an account of his first encounter with the thought of Gandhi[42] :

...to my great interest, he spoke of the life and teachings of Mahatma Gandhi. His message was so profound and electrifying that I left the meeting and brought a half dozen books on Gandhi's life and works. Like most people, I had heard of Gandhi, but I had never studied him seriously. As I read, I became deeply fascinated by his campaigns of non-violent resistance. I was particularly moved by the Salt March to the Sea and his numerous fasts. The whole concept of *satyagraha* was profoundly significant to me. As I delved deeper into the philosophy of Gandhi, my skepticism concerning the power of love gradually diminished, and I came to see for the first time its potency in the area of social reform. Prior to reading Gandhi, I had about concluded that the ethics of Jesus were only effective in individual relationship. The "turn the other cheek" philosophy and the "love your enemies" philosophy were only valid, I felt, when individuals were in conflict with other individuals; when racial groups and nations were in conflict, a more realistic approach seemed necessary. But after reading Gandhi I saw how utterly mistaken I was.

King encountered Gandhi's thinking at a time when American civil rights leaders were in the midst of a profound intellectual and spiritual quest. King sought an ethical framework that could serve as the foundation for tackling massive social evils such as racism. Mordecai Johnson's presentation on Gandhi convinced King that Gandhi's thought and action crowned his search, and would help him formulate his Christian understanding of nonviolence.

J. Deotis Roberts asserts that William Stuart Nelson is a key person in understanding the link between Gandhi and King.[43] Nelson was a graduate of Yale Divinity School, and studied in Paris and Berlin. He was an administrator at Shaw and Dillard Universities before going to Howard University to work with Mordecai Johnson. At Howard, Nelson served as professor of theology and philosophy, dean of the divinity school and vice president of the university.

Nelson researched and reflected on nonviolence throughout his life. He studied in India on several occasions and was a personal friend of Mohandas Gandhi. For Nelson, nonviolence was an active protest against injustice. Nelson can be seen as the bridge between Gandhi and African Americans, and as a scholar, devoted more attention to Gandhian nonviolence than any other African American. At Howard University, Nelson was also associated with Howard Thurman and Benjamin Mays, who was president of Morehouse College during King's student days.[44]

Nelson studied Hindu literature and traced in it the roots of nonviolence. He also studied the life of Mohandas Gandhi whom he met and marched with in India. He found the major influences shaping the Gandhian concept of nonviolence in a number of documents: *The Vedas, The Upanishads, The Ramayana, The Mahabharta, The Bhagavid-Gita, The Laws of Manu,* as well as in Jaina and Buddhist documents. His search led him to the writings of Leo Tolstoy, Henry David Thoreau, and many other sources. As a Jaina and Buddhist theologian, Nelson also searched the Bible, especially the Sermon on the Mount, for clues to understanding Gandhi's philosophy.[45]

In 1947, William Stuart Nelson visited Gandhi.[46] That was the year when India became independent, but in October and November 1946, Hindu-Muslim killings had started in India and what was to be Pakistan. Two or three days after Indian independence, in Calcutta, Nelson asked Gandhi: "Why is it that Indians who had more or less successfully gained independence through peaceful means are now unable to check the tide of civil war through the same means?" Gandhi replied that it was indeed a searching question, which he must answer. He confessed that it had become clear to him that what he had mistaken for *satyagraha,* or holding on to truth, was not *satyagraha,* but a weapon of the weak. Indians, he said, "harbored ill-will and anger" against their erstwhile rulers while claiming to resist them nonviolently. Their resistance was therefore "inspired by violence" and not by regard for the humanity in the British whom they should convert through *satyagraha.* Gandhi argued:

> The attitude of violence which we had secretly harbored, in spite of the restraint imposed by the Indian National Congress, now recoiled upon us and made us fly at each other's throats when the question of the distribution of power came

up. It was the passivity of the weak and not the nonviolence of the stout in heart who would never surrender their
sense of human unity and brotherhood even in the midst of
conflict of interests, and would never try to convert and not
coerce their adversary.[47]

The attraction of Martin Luther King, Jr. to the thought and
theo-praxis of Mohandas Gandhi can be traced to models of social
activism inculcated throughout the southern Black church and culture, to which King was exposed during his earlier intellectual and
spiritual development. King's sense of justice and his passionate,
prophetic stance for peace were values transmitted to him within
the common ethos of his upbringing.

Behind King's interpretations and use of nonviolent resistance were the traditional black family and church. It was the black
family and church that provided the context and support for King's
effective use of nonviolent action.[48] He did his best work in the
South where family and church traditions for blacks were strongest.
The role of black educational institutions, especially black colleges,
should also be considered. From this spiritual and intellectual base,
King's influence was both national and international. Thus, he drew
upon the long prophetic or protest principles in the black church,
and transformed them into an operational paradigm of liberation
mainly from racist oppression. For King, this resource of black
religious experience – and by extension black community - stood
alongside the legacy of Gandhi and Jesus.

Martin Luther King, Jr. had become very skeptical of dis-
covering an ethical framework that would help him face massive
social evils. He was encouraged and fascinated by Gandhi's campaigns of nonviolent social resistance against colonialism and the
caste system in India.

King's attraction to the thought of Gandhi was somewhat
surprising when considered within the context of the intense study
King had already undertaken of Western history and its religious,
philosophical and ethical thought. He had studied utilitarianism,
Marxism, Hobbes, Rousseau and Nietzsche, and had also taken seriously the thought of theologians like Rauschenbusch and Reinhold
Niebuhr. But it was in Gandhi's philosophy that King found a mor-

ally and practically sound method open to oppressed people in their struggle for freedom.   In a very clear way, King stated his discovery: "Gandhi gave me the Method and Jesus gave me the Message."

King points out his particular attraction to Gandhi's notion of the love-ethic:

> Gandhi was probably the first person in history to lift the love-ethic of Jesus above a mere interaction between individuals to a powerful and effective social force on a larger scale. Love, for Gandhi, was a potent instrument for social and collective transformation. It was in this Gandhian emphasis on love and nonviolence that I discovered the method for social reform that I had been seeking for so many months. The intellectual and moral satisfaction that I failed to gain from the utilitarianism of Bentham and Mill, the revolutionary methods of Marx and Lenin, the social contracts theory of Hobbes, the "back to nature" optimism of Rousseau, and the superman philosophy of Nietzsche, I found in the nonviolent resistance philosophy of Gandhi. I came to feel that this was the only morally and practically sound method open to oppressed people in their struggle for freedom. [49]

It was characteristic of King that he thought through any system of thought and any form of action before embracing or employing it. Thus, Gandhi's concept of *satyagraha,* or truth-force, was understood almost immediately as "love-force" by King. J. Deotis Roberts asserts that one important sign of the transformative power of Christianity upon Gandhi's Hindu faith is manifest in his interchangeable use of "Truth" and "Love."[50] In fact, according to Roberts, one might correctly refer to "truth-force" as "love-force." Gandhi viewed nonviolence as an expression of love that grows out of the central truth of one's inner being and the unity of all existence. Love is kindness, compassion, and helpfulness. There is no room for hatred and violence in a world where truth is recognized and love is practiced. Whereas violence calls forth violence, love calls forth love.

King saw a direct connection between Truth and Love, and like Gandhi, essentially equated the two. He saw in Gandhi the means by which the love-ethic in the teaching of Jesus could become effective for social change, even transformation. King also saw that it was not necessary to limit the Christian love-ethic to individual relationships; the love-ethic could be applied to conflicts between races, cultures and nations.

It is known that some Christians in England strongly urged Gandhi to convert to Christianity. He did read the Bible carefully. He found the Old Testament to be more difficult than the New Testament. Jesus, and the Sermon on the Mount, impressed Gandhi more than any other part of the Christian Scriptures. He never was convinced that it was necessary to abandon Hinduism for Christianity, however. He could not accept Christianity as a perfect religion. Gandhi also saw defects in Hinduism but, for him, Hinduism was all that was necessary to satisfy his soul. He had some leanings toward Christianity, but was never moved to make an all-out commitment to it.

Nevertheless, throughout his life, Gandhi was able to defend the best that he had gleaned from the study of Christianity. He urged people to live more like Jesus Christ, practice the Christian faith without adulterating it or toning it down, and to emphasize love and make it the driving force of life and action. It is not surprising that Gandhi asserted that his encounter with Christianity made him a better Hindu. His attention to some of the noblest principles of Christianity enriched his life as a religious person. Although he remained a Hindu, his understanding and expression of religious experience was more profound.

In his reflections on the significance of Gandhi within the context of religious life throughout the world, King wrote:
It is ironic, yet inescapably true that the greatest Christian of the modern world was a man who never embraced Christainity... I believe that in some marvelous way, God worked through Gandhi, and the spirit of Jesus Christ saturated his life. [51]

King felt that Gandhi was probably the first person in history to lift the love-ethic of Jesus Christ into a context where it could become an effective instrument for collective transformation. Thus, the method of social reform, which had eluded King, was now found in the way in which Gandhi understood truth (as love). The mission and ministry of Martin Luther King, Jr. in Montgom-

ery, Alabama gave him the opportunity to test the Gandhian principles of nonviolent social resistance (*satyagraha and ahimsa*). It
has been appropriately observed that "if Rosa Parks had not sat
down, King would not have stood up."   King was immediately
drafted as the leader of the Montgomery Bus Boycott. He points
out the significance of Gandhi's teachings on the events in Montgomery:

> When I went to Montgomery as a pastor, I had not the slight-
> est idea that I would later become involved in a crisis in
> which nonviolent resistance would be applicable. I neither
> started the protest nor suggested it. I simply responded to
> the call of the people for a spokesman.   When the protest
> began, my mind, consciously or unconsciously, was driven
> back to the Sermon on the Mount, with its sublime teach-
> ings on love, and the Gandhian method of nonviolent resis-
> tance. As the days unfolded, I came to see the power of
> nonviolence more and more. Living through the actual ex-
> perience of the protest, nonviolence became more than a
> method to which I gave intellectual assent; it became a com-
> mitment to a way of life. Many of the things that I had not
> cleared up intellectually concerning nonviolence were now
> solved in the sphere of practical action.[52]

King also discussed how his exposure to Gandhi helped
him to reconcile in his thinking the power of pacifism and nonviolent social resistance as a force for change:

> My study of Gandhi convinced me that true pacifism is not
> nonresistance to evil, but nonviolent resistance to evil.
> Between the two positions, there is a world of difference.
> Gandhi resisted evil with as much vigor and power as the
> violent resister, but he resisted with love instead of hate.
> True pacifism is not unrealistic submission to evil power
> (as Reinhold Niebuhr contends). It is rather a courageous
> confrontation of evil by the power of love, in the faith that
> it is better to be the recipient of violence than the inflicter
> of it, since the latter only multiplies the existence of vio-
> lence and bitterness in the universe, while the former may
> develop a sense of shame in the opponent and thereby bring

about a transformation and change of heart. [53]

For Mohandas Gandhi, Howard Thurman, and Martin Luther King, Jr., ideas had practical consequences. The issue then is one of identifying what in their thought was behind their action, in light of what J. Deotis Roberts conceives as the "moral suasion" espoused by leaders like King and Thurman.[54]   Both were Christian ministers and theologians for whom the love-ethic of Jesus was foundational, but the Gandhian influence was direct and powerful, as well.

In light of the widespread contemporary conflicts between races, ethnic groups and nations, it is important to revisit the universal insights of Gandhi, and their impact upon the thinking and praxis of Thurman and King. Howard Thurman wrote and spoke out vehemently against racial hatred in the church and society. And under great duress, Martin Luther King, Jr. opposed racism, poverty and other matters of social and political concern like the war in Vietnam. It cost King support among black and white national leaders. But, as a Christian ethicist and theologian, King felt compelled to apply the Gandhian philosophy of nonviolence to the conflict among nations, as he had done to the conflicts among races and classes in America. Just four days before his death, before an audience of more than 4,000, King spoke out against the Vietnam War in the Washington National Cathedral. Thus, one of King's final messages to our world in the nation's capital was against war, as he urged persons and nations to diligently seek an alternative to war in the settlement of international disputes.

NOTES

[1] See Thomas Merton, *Gandhi on Nonviolence* (New York: New Directions, 1964). Merton offers details on the life of Mohandas Gandhi.

[2] Ibid.

[3] John Dear, "The Experiments of Gandhi: Nonviolence in the Nuclear Age," *Fellowship* (New York: Fellowship of Reconciliation, January/February, 1988).

[4] J. Deotis Roberts, "Gandhi and King: On Conflict Resolution," in *Shalom Papers: A Journal of Theology and Public Policy,* ed. Victoria J. Barnett (Washington, DC: Church's Center for Theology and Public Policy, Vol. 11, No. 2, Spring 2000), 36.

[5] Rajmohan Gandhi, "Gandhi's Unfulfilled Legacy: Prospects for Reconciliation in Racial/Ethnic Conflict," (1995 Cynthia Wedel Lecture, Church's Center for Theology and Public Policy, Wesley Theological Seminary, Washington, DC, April 27, 1995). In this lecture, Rajmohan Gandhi offers a view of Mohandas Gandhi's life and unfinished legacy from the perspective of a contemporary Indian scholar.

[6] Ibid.

[7] Ibid.

[8] Ibid.

[9] William Shannon, *Seeds of Peace*, 154.

[10] Ibid., 153.

[11] See Thomas Merton, *Gandhi on Nonviolence,* for details on Gandhi's development of the conceptualization of *Satyagraha.*

[12] Roberts, 37.

[13] Ibid.

[14] Mohandas K. Gandhi, "Nonviolence – the Greatest Force," *The World Tomorrow,* (October 1926).

[15] John Dear, "The Experiments of Gandhi."

[16] Ibid.

[17] Ibid.

[18] Jim Wallis, *The Soul of Politics* (New York: The New Press, 1994), xiii.

[19] Shannon, 154.

[20] Dear, "The Experiments of Gandhi."

[21] Shannon, 154.

[22] Gandhi, "Nonviolence – The Greatest Force."

[23] Ibid.

[24] Ibid.

[25] Ibid.

[26] Ibid.

[27] Mairead Corrigan Maguire, "Gandhi and the Ancient Wisdom of Nonviolence," *Fellowship* (New York: Fellowship of Reconciliation, June 1988).

[28] Rajmohan Gandhi, "Gandhi's Unfulfilled Legacy."

[29] Luther Smith, *The Mystic as Prophet,* pp. 7-8. Smith offers an account of Thurman's visit with Gandhi, and the impact that this visit had on Thurman's concept and practice of prophetic mysticism.

[30] Ibid.

[31] Roberts, 32.

[32] Mohandas K. Gandhi, *Non-violence in Peace and War,* Vol. 1 (Ahmedabad: Navajivan Publishing House, 1942), 124.

[33] Gandhi, "Nonviolence – The Greatest Force," 121.

[34] Ibid., 123.

[35] Ibid., Mrs. Sue Bailey Thurman's response fits with the conceptualization of the "moral suasion" as discussed by J. Deotis Roberts. See, Roberts, "Moral Suasion as Non-violent Direct Action," *Journal for Religious Thought* (Vol. 35, No. 2, Fall /Winter 1978-79), 29-43.

[36] Elizabeth Yates, *Howard Thurman: Portrait of a Practical Dreamer*, 104-109.

[37] Ibid., 105-106.

[38] Walter E. Fluker and Catherine Tumber, eds., *A Strange Freedom: The Best of Howard Thurman* (Boston Beacon Books, 1998), 7.

[39] Alton B. Pollard, III., *Mysticism and Social Change,* 37.

[40] Ibid.

[41] Ibid., 38. Pollard here makes reference to Thurman's essay "The Fascist Masquerade" which appears as Chapter 4 in *The Church and Organized Movements,* ed. Randolph C. Miller (New York: Harper Brothers, 1946), pp. 82-100.

[42] Martin Luther King, Jr., "My Pilgrimage to Nonviolence," *Fellowship* (New York: Fellowship of Reconciliation, September 1958).

[43] Roberts, 31.

[44] Ibid., 32.

[45] Ibid.

[46] See Roberts, 31-32.

[47] Ibid.

[48] Lewis V. Baldwin, *There is a Balm: The Cultural Roots of Martin Luther King, Jr.* (Minneapolis: Fortress Press, 1991), Baldwin offers a complete analysis of the impact of the black family and church on thinkers like King and Thurman in this work.

[49] King, "My Pilgrimage to Nonviolence."

[50] Roberts, 38.

[51] See Martin Luther King, *Stride Toward Freedom,* pp. 85-97.

[52] King, "My Pilgrimage to Nonviolence."

[53] Ibid.

[54] Roberts, 30-31, J. Deotis Roberts offers an extensive analysis of "moral suasion" in his article "Gandhi and King: On Conflict Resolution." Roberts asserts that moral suasion assumes that there are people of good will of all races.

CHAPTER FIVE

A COMPARISON OF THE CONCEPTIONS OF PEACEFUL COMMUNITY IN THE THINKING OF HOWARD THURMAN AND MARTIN LUTHER KING, JR.

I. Early Influences

Howard Thurman and Martin Luther King, Jr. were both African Americans whose earliest experiences of community and non-community in the segregated South had a profound impact on their respective quests and interpretations of human community. Those early experiences and later ones are given in autobiographical statements throughout their writings, sermons and speeches. Walter E. Fluker, in *They Looked For a City,* suggests that the experiential and intellectual sources of the ideal of community in Thurman and King demonstrate that their respective understandings of community arose initially from the common experience of oppression and segregation in the Deep South.[1]

For King and Thurman, the conception of the inherent dignity and worth of all human beings developed very early out of their respective experiences in the black family and church. Their parents' and grandparents' teachings on the sacredness of humanity were reinforced by what they heard in church concerning the Judeo-Christian view of humanity being created in the image of God. This concept of *imago dei* in the black church developed out of a heritage of the slaves, who despite their untutored state, caught the significance of the fact that every human soul is a part of God and is therefore dear to the heart of God.[2]

Out of the particularity of the experiences of Thurman and King emerged a universal vision of human community which transcended race, class, religion, and other forms of sectarianism. Their early childhood experiences in the contexts of family, the black church, and the black communities of Daytona, Florida (Thurman), and Atlanta, Georgia (King), provided them with a sense of personal worth and an awareness of the interrelatedness of life which became central elements in their respective views of community.[3]

Howard Thurman was a family friend of the Kings, and had attended Morehouse College with Martin Luther King, Sr. He remained close to the elder King throughout his lifetime. When Thurman became Boston University's dean of the chapel, he developed a personal acquaintance with Martin Luther King, Jr. who was attending the university.[4] He noted that King visited his home at least once during the final year of King's residency work in Boston. Thurman also said that he visited King during his stay in Harlem Hospital. He was moved to visit King in the hospital because of his concern about King's mental, spiritual, and physical health.[5]

Thurman's tribute to King offers a sense of the separate paths the two men took. Thurman wrote:

> Perhaps the ultimate demand laid upon the human spirit is the responsibility to select where one bears witness to the truth of his spirit. The final expression of the committed spirit is to affirm: I choose! And to abide.[6]

While the focus of Thurman's lifetime quest was to bring coherency to the nature of the inner spiritual life within the context of racism and disunity in the church and society, King was true to his spirit, which led him to pursue a prophetic ministry in the struggle for human rights. Thurman had great respect for King's vocational choice and for his method of addressing the race problem and seeking to develop authentic and peaceful community.   As Thurman said, "I felt myself a fellow pilgrim with King and with all the host of those who shared his dream and shared his vision."[7]

II. Philosophy of Nonviolence

Luther Smith asserts that contrary to most public perceptions, it was Howard Thurman's conception of community that served as the primary philosophic foundation for the Civil Rights movement of the 1950s and 1960s.[8] According to Smith, Thurman's concept of community tied the black struggle for freedom to divine will and destiny. The black struggle then became a holy struggle. In defining the ethic of nonviolence, he gave the freedom movement a holy mechanism. This identification of Thurman as the creative mind behind the development of a philosophy of nonviolence for the black struggle underscores the significant contribution of his social witness. The beginning of a philosophy of nonviolence in the civil rights struggle of black America is often traced to Martin Luther King, Jr. and the Montgomery Bus Boycott, which began in 1954. Although the boycott may represent the most successful, notable and visible application of this nonviolent philosophy, nonviolence as a means of addressing the race problem in America received considerable discussion and shaping beginning in the 1930s through the work of persons like Howard Thurman and Benjamin Mays.

Despite his identification with King's vision, Thurman's approach to the subject of human oppression was different. Nothing makes this point more aptly than Thurman's assessment of the spiritual dimensions of the Civil Rights struggle.[9] According to Thurman, the key to King's contribution was that he always ... Spoke from within the context of his religious experience, giving voice to an ethical insight that sprang out of his profound brooding over the meaning of his Judeo-Christian heritage. And this indeed is his great contribution to our times. He was able to put at the center of his personal religious experience a searching ethical awareness.[10]

Thurman's approach to civil rights was less direct, and much less confrontational than was King's.[11] Walter E. Fluker suggests that Thurman and King – and their respective approaches to community-building - complement each other. He asserts that Thurman's more spiritualized, personal, and individualistic approach to transformation and community-building should be viewed as a corrective balance to King's more aggressive and organized practice of nonviolent direct social action. It is evident that both Thurman and King consistently made the connection between religious experience and the demand for social transformation. Their goals were similar, but their methods were different.[12]

Synthesis was a key element in the nonviolent philosophy of both Howard Thurman and Martin Luther King, Jr. Both used synthesis to resolve difficult philosophical, ideological and sociopolitical issues. Synthesis was derived from the dialectical method made famous by the German philosopher Georg Wilhelm Hagel, known for his formulation "thesis-antithesis-synthesis."

Thurman and King tried to avoid extremes, which they saw as the thesis and the antithesis. They sought to arrive at the synthesis that combined aspects of the thesis and antithesis. Both avoided extreme "either-or" viewpoints about black and white, rich and poor, materialism and humanism, pessimism and optimism, communism and capitalism, liberalism and conservatism. Instead of "either-or," they sought "both-and" solutions of synthesis by combining conflicting prospects to create a greater, more harmonious whole - a synthesis.

Racial integration was one form of synthesis championed by both King and Thurman as a solution to racial conflict. The development of the *Beloved Community* in the case of King, and *Multicultural Fellowship* in Thurman's case embodied and exemplified their respective synthetic approaches. King viewed nonviolent resistance as another aspect of synthesis. He said, "Like the synthesis of Hagelian philosophy, the philosophy of nonviolent resistance seeks to reconcile the truths of two opposites – acquiescence and violence – while avoiding the extremes and immoralities of both."[13]

III. Evangelical Liberalism

It has been suggested that the theological perspectives of both Howard Thurman and Martin Luther King, Jr. fall within the tradition of evangelical liberalism. Kenneth Cauthen in his book, *The Impact of American Religious Liberalism* defines the tradition in the following way:

> The [evangelical liberals] stood squarely within the Christian traditions and accepted as normative for their thinking what they understood to be the *essence* of historical Christianity. The men had a deep consciousness of their continuity with the mail line of Christian orthodoxy and felt that they were preserving its *essential* features in terms that were suitable to the modern world. One of the evidences of the loyalty of the evangelical liberals to the historic faith is the place that they give to Jesus. Through his person and work there is mediated to men both knowledge of God and saving power. He is the source and norm of the Christian's

experience of God. In short, evangelical liberalism is Christocentric.[14]

Both Thurman and King placed a high value on the human personality, regarding personality as a reflection of the soul and therefore an image of the divine. The personality is not only an expression of the soul's individuality; it is a unique image of God. Because every personality is divine in essence, every personality is endowed with dignity and worth. In an article entitled, "The Ethical Demands of Integration," King wrote, "Deeply rooted in our political and religious heritage is the conviction that every (person) is an heir to a legacy of dignity and worth...This innate worth referred to in the phrase *image of God* is universally shared in equal portion by all (persons)."[15]

Both Thurman and King focused on the nature of the person as the central focus of religion in the context of community-building. Thurman, perhaps to a greater degree than King, proposed that spiritual impoverishment, deriving from an improper sense of self, was the fundamental cause of moral decay in society. Where individuals have a proper sense of self, the stage is set for strong moral forces to shape a moral and secure society.

This reasoning faced sharp criticism from Reinhold Niebuhr who continually spoke to the defects in Christian liberalism. Niebuhr, in *Moral Man and Immoral Society,* argued that the ethical considerations which govern relations between individuals are not the same as those which govern inter-group relations. One may be willing to make all kinds of personal sacrifices to live the ethical life (moral man), but the same sacrifice may be too much to expect of a body politic (immoral society). As an individual, one may have the right to face emaciating and abusive conditions as a symbol of protest against politics, but the same individual may decide that a more violent response is required if those conditions threaten his/her fellows. A group is not just the sum total of its individual members. A group can have a consciousness and value system which differs from those of individual members.[16]

When this problem was posed to Thurman, he admitted the difficulties that arose in his moral position. He stated that while he might be certain about a nonviolent response to an act of violence perpetrated against him, he might react differently if his wife were in the same danger.[17]   Niebuhr's thesis raised serious dilemmas for Thurman's focus on the ethical individual as the key to the ethical society. The ethical individual may be very responsible in interpersonal relations, and be ill-prepared to be the ethical social or political leader of other decision-makers for society.

In contrast to Thurman's conception of the Christian love-ethic, Niebuhr believed life must not only be governed by a concept of love but also by a distinct and profound concept of justice.[18] It is necessary for love to be accompanied by justice. Niebuhr's perspective is more in concert with the assertion of Martin Luther King, Jr. that "true peace is not merely the absence of tension, it is the presence of justice." King agreed with Niebuhr that justice could be a fulfillment of love. Niebuhr said, "Yet the law of love is involved in all approximations of justice, not only as the source of the norms of justice, but as an ultimate perspective by which their limitations are discovered."[19]

Like Howard Thurman, Martin Luther King, Jr. was aware that spiritual transformation was necessary for lasting social change. Speaking about what he conceived as the means of addressing oppression, King said:

> The ultimate solution to the race problem lies in the willingness of men to obey unenforceable laws…Desegregation will break down the legal barriers and bring men together physically, but something must touch the hearts and souls of men so that they will come together spiritually because it is natural and right.[20]

In a more pronounced manner than Thurman, King came to understand some of the possible flaws in extreme liberalism as well as extreme neoorthodoxy. In seeking to arrive at a synthesis in his thinking, King said, "An adequate understanding of man is found neither in the thesis of liberalism nor in the antithesis of neoorthodoxy, but in a synthesis which reconciles the truths of both."[21]

While Howard Thurman and Martin Luther King, Jr. agreed that spirituality is the basis for social transformation, this theme is more pronounced in Thurman's treatment of individual and social responsibility.[22]   Thurman maintained that the movement from the inner experience of community within the self is the basis for social transformation. His understanding of the movement from the "inner" to the "outer" dimensions of religious experience has profound implications for spirituality and social change, and serves as a corrective to the tendency of one-dimensional theological discourse that exalts the social dynamics of community at the expense of the individual relationship between God and the self. Mozella Gordon Mitchell suggests that Thurman's contribution to black theology rests on his provision of an intellectual framework for a proper *sense of self* and *urge toward community.*[23]   Thurman's shamanistic endeavor to lead the individual to the inner resources of being, which he described as "the hunger of the heart," is a cogent reminder that the work for harmony and wholeness in the world cannot be accomplished without the cultivation of the inner life.[24]

IV. Christian Love-Ethic

Howard Thurman and Martin Luther King, Jr. understood nonviolence to be the only Christian means of struggle validated in Scripture. Indeed for King, Thurman and other black religious thinkers prior to Black Power movement and the advent of Black liberation theology of the late 1960s, the praxis of Jesus was the authoritative source for Christian living in the area of race relations and building inclusive, peaceful community. Therefore, these thinkers rejected hatred, bitterness, and violence as acceptable Christian behavior. For them, nonviolence was the only way Christians could be true to the love- ethic of Jesus. These views are expressed throughout the writings of both Thurman and King, and can also be found in the writings of persons like Benjamin Mays and George Kelsey. While both Thurman and King were clearly influenced by the thinking of Mohandas Gandhi, and gleaned a great deal from social critics such as Henry David Thoreau and A.J. Muste, from long-time social activists like Bayard Rustin and Glenn Smiley, and from Jesus' Sermon on the Mount in the New Testament, it is critical to understand their respective concepts of nonviolence in relation to the southern black Christian tradition.[25]   Both were influenced by southern black Christians like Mordecai Johnson and Benjamin Mays whose traditional form of nonviolence had long represented moderation in the midst of the violence of white America. The respective decisions of King and Thurman to embrace nonviolence in its personal and social ethical dimensions resulted more from their experiences with the practical applications of the method of nonviolence among black southerners than from any other intellectual or spiritual source. King clearly points this out when reflecting upon the Montgomery Bus Boycott:

> The experience in Montgomery did more to clarify my thinking than all the books that I had read. As the days unfolded, I became more and more convinced of the power of nonviolence. Nonviolence became more than a method to which I gave intellectual assent; it became a commitment to a way of life. Many issues I had not cleared up intellectually concerning nonviolence were now resolved within the sphere of practical action.[26]

King and Thurman viewed the challenge to act nonviolently as one of the most formidable challenges facing society on the brink of the new age. Nonviolence, through the appropriation of the Christian love-ethic, was critical to the realization of peaceful community. King's views summarize this perspective:

> This simply means that the Christian virtues of love, mercy, and forgiveness should stand at the center of our lives. There is the danger that those of us who have lived so long under the yoke of oppression, those of us who have been exploited and trampled over, those of us who have had to stand amid the tragic midnight of injustice and indignities will enter the new age with hate and bitterness. But if we retaliate with hate and bitterness, the new age will be nothing but a duplication of the old age. We must blot out the hate and injustice of the old age with the love and justice of the new. This is why I believe so firmly in nonviolence. Violence never solves problems. It only creates new, more complicated ones. If we succumb to the temptation of using violence in our struggle for justice, unborn generations will be the recipients of a long and desolate night of bitterness, and our chief legacy to the future will be an endless reign of

meaningless chaos.[27]

Underlying the thinking of Thurman and King on love, reconciliation, and nonviolence was the firm belief in the power of Christianity to transform lives. Both men interpreted Jesus' teachings on forgiveness, reconciliation and love for one's enemies quite literally, pointing out that Christian nonviolence is an act of profound love that seeks to redeem oppressors, not to humiliate or destroy them.

In addition to the teachings of the Christian scriptures, Thurman and King noted that nonviolence was rooted in the history of the black experience of protest and resistance. Thurman - to a greater extent than King – contended that the Negro spirituals were to be understood as a critical means of nonviolent protest and a source of strength in the praxis of the Christian love-ethic over the ages.[28]   The spirituals are not songs of hate, revenge or conquest, but rather songs of the soul that helped slaves survive and protest oppression without bitterness and violence.[29]   James Cones elaborates on Thurman's perspective on the Negro spirituals as a source of protest and means of moving toward freedom:

> Howard Thurman was one of the first scholars to use religion as the starting point in his interpretation of the black spirituals. According to Thurman, "The clue to the meaning of the spirituals is to be found in religious experience and spiritual discernment." In the spirituals, he perceives "the elemental and formless struggle to a vast consciousness in the mind and spirit of the individual." According to Thurman, the black spiritual is an expression of the slave's determination to *be* in a society that seeks to destroy their personhood. It is an affirmation of the dignity of the black slaves, the essence of humanity of their spirits. Where human life is regarded as property and death has no dignity, "the human spirit is stripped to the literal substance of itself." Deprived of power, the slaves found ways to hold together their personhood. To be sure, the insights reflected in the slaves' struggle for being may not have been original, but, in the presence of the naked demand upon the primary sources of meanings, even without highly specialized

tools or skills, the universe responded... with overwhelming power.[30]

Thus, for Thurman, spirituals like "We are Climbing Jacob's Ladder," and "Swing Low, Sweet Chariot," and "Go Down Moses, and later songs like "We Shall Overcome" which became the "anthem" of the Civil Rights movement, were to be understood within the context of nonviolent protest and the historic quest for freedom and authentic peaceful community.[31]   Both Thurman and King often pointed to the strength and leadership of historic black figures like Frederick Douglass, Harriet Tubman, Booker T. Washington, W.E.B. Dubois, to show that a tradition of nonviolence and the Christian love-ethic – rooted in the black church - has shaped the ongoing praxis of nonviolence as a means of survival, actualization, peace and community-building for marginalized persons in America.

The respective encounters of Howard Thurman and Martin Luther King, Jr. with the thinking of Mohandas Gandhi also helped to shape their understanding and philosophy of nonviolence as an "active force" of resistance. As Sudarshan Kapur has demonstrated in his book *Raising Up a Prophet: The African-American Encounter with Gandhi* (1992), black intellectuals' encounter with Gandhi beginning in the 1930s (including Benjamin Mays, William Stuart Nelson, and Edward Carroll) laid the theological foundation that Thurman, and later King, were able to develop with regard to the Christian love-ethic and peaceful community.[32]

One of the books that King read during the Montgomery Bus Boycott was Howard Thurman's *Jesus and the Disinherited*.[33] Thurman devoted a major portion of this book to addressing the nature of Christian love and presented several ideas that are found in King's philosophy of nonviolence. Thurman indicated how Jesus used the Parable of the Good Samaritan to reveal how love of neighbor should respond directly to human need, permitting no barriers of class, race, and condition.[34]

Thurman asserted that, "Every man is potentially every other man's neighbor."[35]   He stressed that Jesus practiced a love not only for those who acted as personal enemies, but also for persons who made it difficult for the Israelites to live without shame and humiliation. In Jesus' day, the tax collectors helped perpetuate the Roman oppression of Israel. They were despised for helping the enemy, and to be seen in their company meant the loss of status and respect in the community.[36] Yet Jesus invited Matthew, a tax collector to become his disciple:

> When Jesus became a friend to the tax collectors and se-
> cured one as his companion, it was a spiritual triumph of
> such staggering proportions that after nineteen hundred years
> it defies rational explanation.[37]

Thurman maintained that in every ghetto and dwelling place of the disinherited throughout the ages, there have been those who have tried to prosper by the betrayal of their own people:

> To love such people requires the uprooting of the bitterness
> of betrayal, the heartiest poison that grows in the human
> spirit... To love them means to recognize some deep re-
> spect and reverence for their persons. But to love them
> does not mean to condone their way of life.[38]

Thurman emphasized that the love that Jesus practiced ex-
tended also to the Roman, the political enemy. When Jesus spoke with the Roman captain who sought healing for his servant, he claimed that he had not found such faith in all of Israel. Thurman explained that in this encounter the Roman, in seeking help from a Jewish teacher, put aside his status as a Roman, and Jesus did not regard him as an enemy but as a human being:

> The concept of reverence for personality, then is applicable
> between persons from whom, in their initial instance, the
> heavy weight of status has been sloughed off. Then what?
> Each person meets the other where he is and there treats
> him as if he were where he ought to be. Here we emerge
> into an area where love operates, revealing a universal char-
> acteristic unbounded by special or limited circumstances.[39]

King could easily identify with and apply the insights of Thurman to his relationship with the segregationist. When King was confronted with the deliberate misinterpretations of his position by some in the civil rights movement during the Montgomery Bus Boycott and in later crusades, he had to rely on Christian Personalism to avoid experiencing the bitterness of betrayal.[40]   While denouncing the segregationist's acts, King could still revere the personality of the segregationist as an image of God, and regard him as a brother, and potential member of the *Beloved Community.*

Howard Thurman synthesized his treatment of Christian love by referring to the need to forgive the enemy for injury. He contended that in the insistence of Jesus that persons develop the capacity to forgive seventy times seven, there seemed to be the assumption that forgiveness is mandatory for three reasons: (1) God forgives us again and again for what we do intentionally and unintentionally; (2) no evil deed represents the full intention of the person; (3) and the evil doer will be punished.[41] In the wide sweep of the ebb and flow of moral law our deeds track us down, and doer and deed meet.[42] Martin Luther King, Jr. similarly appealed to three reasons for forgiveness of oppressors, although he tended to stress the eventual defeat of injustice rather than the punishment of the persons who perpetrated and perpetuated injustice as the third reason for forgiveness.[43]

V. Conceptions of Peaceful Community

Although focused on eradicating racism and economic oppression, Martin Luther King, Jr.'s vision for humanity was not confined to black prosperity and position, nor was it confined to removing barriers that denied individuals an opportunity to "succeed." Rather, his movement consisted of incremental steps that would ultimately lead to the actualization of the *"Beloved Community"* in which all human beings had value in and of themselves, and were subjects worthy of love. King challenged African Americans – and all persons – to lay full claim to their identity as relational beings. He believed that people live in an inescapable network of mutuality, noting that even when one sits down at the breakfast table a host of persons in the global community have participated in bringing together the necessary elements for early morning preparations for the day.[44] King understood that the network of mutuality was there, but that people failed to recognize it. It was this failure, he believed, that was the primary impediment to the realization of peaceful community.

Like King, Howard Thurman shaped his ministry out of the firm conviction that "all life is interrelated." But unlike King, he was not primarily interested in exposing America's racial sins before the world community; nor did Thurman spend a great deal of time making impassioned appeals to the moral conscience of the nation, seeking to remind the church and the government of their Christian and democratic principles.

Thurman sought to demonstrate human interrelatedness, and test the capacity to build authentic peaceful community through the practice of religious experience. In this regard, Thurman sought to be more intentionally multicultural than King in his practice of the inclusive Christian church. In his pastoral work in Ohio and San Francisco, and in his teaching and campus ministries at Howard and Boston Universities, Thurman experimented with creative worship styles that would appeal to congregants from diverse cultural, religious, social, and ethnic backgrounds. Essentially, he believed that authentic religious experience transcends "all superficial categories that separate and divide people and allows them to sense their relatedness to all humanity."

Thurman felt that one potential vehicle for effecting constructive change was nonviolence, not as employed by movement leaders – Martin Luther King, Jr. being a conspicuous exception – but a more involved commitment to nonviolence as personal, spiritual discipline and technique. He casts nonviolence as a creative, ethical approach to change, capable of producing specific ramifications in society. [45] In the first place, it is immanently practical: "the purpose of shock treatment is … to hold before the offender a mirror that registers an image of himself, that reflects an image of those who suffer at his hands." While at the same time, it serves an explicitly transcendent function, which "is to tear men from any alignments that prevent them from putting themselves in the other person's place (and) to remove anything that prevents the individual from free and easy access to his own altar-stair that is in his own heart." The importance of both factors must not, however, be misconstrued, for as Thurman makes manifestly clear, not even nonviolence as a collective device can guarantee social change. Rather, the major contribution of nonviolence is that it creates and maintains a "climate" wherein protagonists may be brought into a single commitment. To paraphrase Thurman, nonviolence affirms the existence of the "other," however defined, whereas violence embodies a will to non-existence which, translated at the level of society, means non-community.

Although Martin Luther King, Jr. sought to address issues of cultural diversity, inclusiveness and the interrelatedness of persons in the context of the broader society, there is little evidence in his pastoral ministries at Dexter Avenue Baptist Church in Montgomery, Alabama or Ebeneezer Baptist Church in Atlanta, Georgia that he ever sought to intentionally create a multicultural religious community.

The ministries of Thurman and King were similar in seeking to move persons – across cultures – toward community defined by relationships rather than accomplishment. This is most clearly evident in Thurman's multicultural pastoral ministry at the Church for the Fellowship of All Peoples in San Francisco, and King's leadership of the Southern Christian Leadership Conference. Both Thurman and King called for new attitudes as well as new achievements. They called for new partnerships as well as new prosperity. They saw the need for interracial, intercultural, and interclass cooperation that reflected a healthy respect for persons and a commitment to work on their behalf. King stated that the struggle for civil rights was not a racial one. "In the end, it is not a struggle between people at all, but a tension between justice and injustice. Nonviolent resistance is not aimed against oppressors but against oppression. Under its banner, consciences - not racial groups - are enlisted."[46]

Like Martin Luther King, Jr., Howard Thurman brought the black religious experience to the forefront of his theological project. Both of their perspectives were rooted in the black nationalist's accent on the idea of black genius and uniqueness. They also consistently attributed the problems of the African-American community to centuries of American slavery, segregation, and oppression. Thurman's progressive and insightful interpretation of the slave Spirituals as a source for doing theology, coupled with his appropriation of themes of the black religious tradition served as a spiritual and intellectual model for King and other leaders of the Civil

Rights movement. King did not focus a great deal in his writing and speaking on "spirituality" - as it is generally understood - as a means of constructively developing peaceful communitiy. He spoke more to the problem of racism in its moral, ethical and socio-cultural dimensions than did Thurman. Both, Thurman and King, however, took every opportunity to show how the historical experiences of African Americans, particularly their religious experiences, spoke to the prevailing situation in American life, and how this religious experience could thus serve as an impetus to building authentic peaceful community.

Thurman was not adverse to nonviolent social action and protest as a means of moving persons toward a more profound sense of community and away from what he referred to as the "will to segregate."[47] With regard to this, Thurman said:

> What do I do then? I may resort to the exercise of some form of shock by organizing a boycott, or widespread non-cooperation, or the like. The function of these techniques is to tear people free from their alignments to the evil way, to free them so that they may be given an immediate sense of acute insecurity and out of the depths of their insecurity be forces to see their kinship with the weak and the insecure. People do not voluntarily relinquish their hold on their place. It is not until something becomes movable in the situation that they are spiritually prepared to apply Christian idealism to un-ideal and unchristian situations. Examples of these techniques are being developed by (groups) in different parts of the world even now. Action of this kind requires great discipline of mind, emotions, and body to the end that forces may not be released that will do complete violence both to one's ideals and one's purpose. All must be done with the full consciousness of the Divine Scrutiny.[48]

Howard Thurman and Martin Luther King, Jr. both held a vision of humanity as united community. For them, the key to overcoming social disintegration and developing peaceful community is the actualization of *agape*. *Agape* involves the recognition of the fact that all human life is interrelated. Thurman and King asserted that humanity must be seen as a single process. All persons belong to the family of God and therefore whatever directly affects one person affects all indirectly.[49]   For example, both recognized that not only did the American slavery of blacks adversely affect the freedom of white labor, which had to bargain from the depressed economic base imposed by slavery, but also *de facto* discrimination affects poor whites who have to exist within the same economic confines as poor blacks. In referring to the effects of racial and economic oppression on white persons in America, King once noted that the weight of discrimination "corrupts their lives, frustrates their opportunities, and withers their education."[50]

King's interpretation of *agape* is decidedly Christocentric. *Agape* requires that we be "our brother's keeper." King stated, "His agony diminishes me, and his well-being enlarges and enriches me. When a police dog is used to attack a child in a Birmingham demonstration, it attacks every citizen." [51]

Thurman concentrated on the power of *agape* as a means of overcoming the internal barriers of deception, fear and hate. King emphasized *agape* with respect to social justice and the organization of power in the creation of a responsible society. King identified the major crisis of our times as the collision between immoral power and powerless morality. His resolution of the dialectic created by this crisis was rooted in his understanding of *agape*.

King and Thurman differed with regard to the notion of "*moral suasion*", whose proponents espoused belief in the power of rational and moral reasoning as a means toward constructive change and overcoming injustice.[52]   While Thurman, out of his liberal theological perspective, believed that *moral suasion* was a legitimate (and perhaps) sufficient means to facilitate large-scale social change and build community among persons, King came to the conclusion that though appeals to morality are an appropriate beginning step toward transformation, coercive power is often necessary to overcome oppression.

Walter G. Muedler succinctly states that the central question for King in his quest for a method to eliminate social evil is "How was love as redemption related to just power? Is there a loving way to change unjust expressions of power and powerful embodiments of injustice?"[53]   Although Thurman recognized the necessity of the just and equitable distribution of power in social relationships, his primary concern was with the individual's response to unjust political and economic arrangements, which is equally important in the quest for social justice.[54]

Thurman and King were both aware that the existence of injustice anywhere is a threat to justice everywhere. The pervasiveness of non-community and social disintegration threatened the actualization of true community among all persons. It is then not only appropriate, but also necessary for each person in society to be actively concerned about the injustice that affects other persons, and to then work diligently and constructively to promote peaceful community.

Although their methods were different, the ends sought by Martin Luther King, Jr. and Howard Thurman were very similar. King and Thurman pushed persons and institutions to comprehend the connections between all human beings, with the tradition of the black church as the common backdrop. King and Thurman consistently affirmed that the essential mark of the black church is that it offered unconditional love as its central tenet. Love is the expression of the theological concept of related "being," and is the context for all relationships of Christian nurture. It was love for one another, Jesus said, that identified his disciples to the world. (John 13:35)

NOTES

[1] Walter E. Fluker, *They Looked For a City,* 156.
[2] Howard Thurman, *Deep River and the Negro Spiritual Speaks of Life and Death,* 17-18.
[3] Ibid.
[4] Clayborne Carson, "Martin Luther King, Jr. and the African-American Social Gospel," in *African-American Religion: Interpretive Essays in History and Culture,* 348.
[5] Thurman, *With Head and Heart,* 255.
[6] Ibid.

[7] Ibid.

[8] See Luther E. Smith, *The Mystic as Prophet*, chapter 4.

[9] Alonzo Johnson, *Good News for the Disinherited: Howard Thurman on Jesus of Nazareth and Human Liberation* (New York: University Press of America, 1997), 126.

[10] Thurman, *With Head and Heart,* 233. Thurman offered these remarks during a tribute to King at the occasion of his death in 1968.

[11] Johnson, 126.

[12] Fluker, *They Looked for a City,* 174f.

[13] King, *Stride Toward Freedom,* 213.

[14] Kenneth Cauthen, *The Impact of American Religious Liberalism* (New York: Harper and Row, 1962), pp. 27-28.

[15] Martin Luther King, Jr., "The Ethical Demands of Integration," *Religion and Labor,* May 1963, 4.

[16] Reinhold Niebuhr, *Moral Man and Immoral Society,* pp. xxii-xxiii.

[17] Luther E. Smith, *The Mystic as Prophet,* 146. Based on Luther Smith's personal interview with Thurman.

[18] Niebuhr, *Moral Man,* pp. 249 and 273.

[19] Reinhold Niebuhr, *An Interpretation of Christian Ethics* (New York: Harper and Brothers, 1935), 140.

[20] King, *Where Do We Go From Here?*, pp. 100-101.

[21] King, Strength *to Love,* 136.

[22] Fluker, *They Looked for a City,* 174.

[23] Mozella Gordon Mitchell, *Spiritual Dynamics,* 52.

[24] Fluker, *They Looked for a City,* 174.

[25] Lewis V. Baldwin, *There is a Balm in Gilead,* 65.

[26] King, *Strength to Love,* 151-152.

[27] Martin Luther King, Jr. "Facing the Challenge of A New Age," *Fellowship* (New York: The Fellowship of Reconciliation, February, 1957).

[28] See Howard Thurman, *Deep River and the Negro Spiritual Speaks of Life and Death* for an explication of Thurman's perspective on the Negro Spirituals as a primary

source in nonviolent protest and survival for Blacks.
[29] Howard Thurman, *Deep River and the Negro Spiritual Speaks of Life and Death.* Thurman speaks of the place of the Negro Spiritual in community-building and in the inculcation of nonviolence and the Christian love ethic throughout this work.
[30] James Cone, *The Spirituals and the Blues* (Maryknoll, NY: Orbis Books, 1972), 16. Here Cone makes reference to Howard Thurman's thinking in *The Negro Spiritual Speaks of Life and Death* (New York: Harper and Row, 1947), see pp. 12-15.
[31] See Luther Smith, *The Mystic as Prophet,* 116-117. Smith points out that Thurman's two books that give full treatment of Negro Spirituals are *Deep River (*1945) and *The Negro Spiritual Speaks of Life and Death* (1947). These works speak to the plight of black people and their quest for freedom as articulated through the Negro Spirituals.
[32] Sudarshan Kapur, *Raising Up a Prophet: The African-American Encounter with Gandhi* (Boston: Beacon Press, 1992), see pp. 81-100. Also, Thurman discusses his encounter with Gandhi in *With Head and Heart*, pp. 130-35.
[33] King, *Strength to Love,* 20.
[34] John J. Ansbro, *Martin Luther King, Jr.: Nonviolent Tactics and Strategies for Social Change,* 27.
[35] Thurman, *Jesus and the Disinherited,* 89.
[36] Absbro, 28.
[37] Thurman, *Disinherited,* 93-94.
[38] Ibid., 94-95.
[39] Ibid., 104-105.
[40] Ansbro, 28.
[41] Ibid., 29.
[42] Thurman, *Disinherited,* 108.
[43] See Martin Luther King, Jr., "Loving Your Enemies" in *Strength to Love*, for King's thorough analysis of the Christian love-ethic and the rationale for forgiveness, based on

Matthew 5:43-45.

[44] King, "A Christmas Sermon on Peace," in *A Testament of Hope: The Essential Writings of Martin Luther King, Jr.,* ed. James Melvin Washington, 254.

[45] See Howard Thurman, *Disciplines of the Spirit,* 111-22, and Alton Pollard, *Mysticism and Social Change,* 109.

[46] King, "Stride Toward Freedom," in *A Testament of Hope,* 483.

[47] Howard Thurman, "The Will To Segregate," *Fellowship* (New York: The Fellowship of Reconciliation, August, 1943).

[48] Ibid.

[49] The views of Thurman and King with regard to *Agape* as a key to community-building are explicated at various places throughout their respective writings, but is clearly evident in Thurman, *Jesus and the Disinherited, and* King, *Strength to Love.*

[50] Martin Luther King, Jr., These comments about the effects of discrimination on white persons were made by King during an address at the Convocation on "Equal Justice Under Law" of the NAACP Defense Fund, May 28, 1964, New York City, King Collection, XIII, no. 27, p.8.

[51] King, *Strength to Love,* 23.

[52] See J. Deotis Roberts, "Moral Suasion as Non-violent Direct Action," *Journal for Religious Thought* (Vol. 35, No. 2, Fall/Winter 1978-79), 29-43.

[53] See Fluker, 177, cf. Walter G. Muedler, "Philosophical and Theological Influences in the Thought and Action of Martin Luther King, Jr., " ed. Ronald Lee Carter, *Debate and Understanding* (Fall 1977): 184.

[54] See Thurman, *Deep is the Hunger,* pp. 51-52, and *Disciplines of the Spirit,* pp.111-121.

CHAPTER SIX

TOWARD PEACEFUL COMMUNITY: IMPLICATIONS AND PRINCIPLES FOR THE TWENTY-FIRST CENTURY CHURCH AND SOCIETY

Both Howard Thurman and Martin Luther King, Jr. spoke to the need for overcoming racial hatred and social disintegration, and advanced the appropriation of the Christian love-ethic as foundational for constructively moving toward the development of peaceful community. For Thurman and King, the willingness and ability to overcome hatred and fear derived out of their respective conceptions of the love of God. God's love is redemptive in that God loves humanity so much that God demonstrated love for the world by offering His son Christ to the world.

Thurman and King sought to be instruments of peace. The words of St. Francis of Assisi speak to their commitment and vision for peaceful community:

Lord, make me an instrument of your peace,
Where there is hatred, let me sow love,
Where there is injury, pardon,
Where there is doubt, faith,
Where there is despair, hope,
Where there is darkness, light,
Where there is sadness, joy.[1]

The search for peace and community – the yearning for *shalom* – has been one of the most consistent strivings among humans over the course of history. The psalmist encouraged us to "seek peace and pursue it." (Psalm 34:14) And in another passage, the psalmist exclaimed, "how good and how pleasant it is for persons to dwell together in unity." (Psalm 133:1) Peaceful community is to be understood as God's ideal way of life for a heretofore broken and disintegrated humanity.

The apostle Paul's words to the church at Ephesus speak to the contemporary challenge of the church and society, and the common and persistent hope for peace that is found in Christ:

> "Christ Jesus is our peace; in his flesh he has made all groups
> into one and has broken down the dividing wall, that is, the
> hostility between us… and reconciles groups to God in one
> body through the cross. So then you are no longer strang-
> ers and aliens, but you are citizens with the saints and also
> members of the household of God, built upon the founda-
> tion of the apostles and prophets, with Christ Jesus himself
> as the cornerstone. In him the whole structure is joined
> together and grows into a holy temple in the Lord; in whom
> you also are built together spiritually into a dwelling place
> for God." (Ephesians 2:14-22)

Martin Luther King, Jr. offered that "Love is the most du-
rable power in the world. This creative force, so beautifully exemplified in the life of Christ, is the most potent instrument available
in (humanity's) quest for peace and security."[2]   King reiterated:

> We have before us the glorious opportunity to inject a new
> dimension of love into the veins of civilization. There is
> still a voice crying out the words that echo across the gen-
> erations, saying: "Love your enemies, bless them that curse
> you, pray for them that despitefully use you that you may
> be the children of your Father which is in Heaven." This
> love may very well be the salvation of our civilization.[3]

In the last sermon before his assassination, King commented
on the parable of the Rich Man and Lazarus. (Luke 16:19-31) He
spoke of the "long-distance" call between heaven and hell, as the
rich man pleads with Abraham. King pointed out that we must not
see this conversation as a rich man talking to a poor man. On the
contrary, Abraham was the richest man of his day. The conversation, King said, was between a millionaire in hell and a multi-mil-
lionaire in heaven. The point he wanted to make is that the rich
man did not go to hell because he was rich. He went to hell because
he did not realize that his wealth was his opportunity. It was his
opportunity to bridge the gulf that separated him from his brother
Lazarus. His problem was that he did not see Lazarus as a brother.
In fact, he did not see him at all. He allowed his brother to become

invisible. One of the worst expressions of violence against other persons is to forget they are there, to ignore that they are brothers and sisters whom we must love with a love that displays itself in deeds on their behalf.[4]

The prophet Zechariah lived at the end of the sixth century B.C.E. His prophetic book, written in a critical time in the life of his people, is a call for rebuilding the community of Israel and the ushering in of an era of peace. "It is," Zechariah writes, "the seedtime of peace" (Zech. 8:12) We live in times that are critical not just for our own country, but for the whole universe. Unprecedented ways of destruction are available that could bring an end to human life on this planet. But there are also unprecedented resources for creating and preserving peace. Our time can be a "seedtime of peace."

As this study has focused upon the nature of peace and community – with particular analysis of the thought and praxis of Howard Thurman and Martin Luther King, Jr. - there are several implications and principles for the search for peaceful community that emerge as we have moved into the 21st century. The ten principles that follow can be seen as a framework for bringing synthesis to the thinking of Thurman and King, while also serving as the foundation of a contemporary model for the church and society for developing peaceful community in the 21st century.

I. Imperative

Although as African Americans, both Howard Thurman and Martin Luther King, Jr. possessed a Christian faith that had been forged on the anvil of slavery, segregation, and violent forms of racial oppression, they both affirmed that all humankind was bound together through their common creator. Hence, the fundamental tenets of love, forgiveness, and prayer would become the spiritual means of addressing extant forms of oppression. In a world that is still plagued with brokenness, separation, suspicion, and deadly conflicts along racial, tribal, and ethnic lines, it remains the urgent calling of Christians to share that one God created all persons.

God intends for the human family to live in community as interrelated members. Jesus came into the world to call persons back into community. Christ's love for all humanity was redemptive in that despite human faults and frailties, Christ willingly gave his life for us. "God demonstrated love toward us, in that while we were yet sinners, Christ died for us." (Romans 5:8) Thus, hatred and fear are overcome in the various forms that they manifest themselves in human relationships – particularly racism and ethnocentricism – through God's redemptive love.

An imitation of the unconditional love revealed in the teachings and life of Jesus can be helpful in the search for peaceful community. Moving toward a deeper sense of who we are as individuals and community will enable us to live more shalom-filled lives, modeled on the life of Christ.

Henri J. M. Nouwen, in *The Road to Peace* (edited by John Dear) offers that peacemaking cannot be regarded as peripheral to being a Christian.[5] Nouwen elaborates:

> It is not something like joining the parish choir. Nobody can be a Christian without being a peacemaker. The issue is not that we have the occasional obligation to give some of our attention to war prevention, or even that we should be willing to give some of our free time to activities in the service of peace. What we are called to is a *life* of peacemaking in which all that we do, say, think, dream is part of our concern to bring peace to this world. Just as Jesus' command to love one another cannot be seen as a part-time obligation, but requires total dedication, so too Jesus' call to peacemaking is unconditional, unlimited, and uncompromising. None of us is excused! It isn't something limited to specialists who are competent in military matters, or to radicals who have dedicated themselves to leafletting, demonstrating, and civil disobedience. No specialist or radical can diminish the undeniable vocation of each Christian to be a peacemaker. Peacemaking is a full-time vocation that includes each member of God's people.[6]

Imperative involves the movement from ethnocentrism to ethnorelativism. Eric Law speaks to the theological predicament of ethnocentrism when he states:

> In our towers of ethnocentrism, we put God within our cultural frame. We may be unable to distinguish the differ-

ence between our culture and God's culture. We believe that God is on our side and therefore, we can judge those who are not like us as the enemies.[7]

Ethnocentrism ultimately limits our perception of God. Jesus' challenge for us to love our enemies is an invitation to enter into a new paradigm of ethnorelativism. For God does not favor one culture over another. Ethnorelativism leads to a perception and valuation of cultural differences as neither good nor bad, but only different. Milton J. Bennett, identified three theoretical stages of ethnorelativity: *Acceptance, Adaptation*, and *Integration*.[8] These stages are arranged progressively according to the intercultural sensitivity developmental process, and are helpful in the movement beyond narrow conceptions of cultural identity, and toward broader perspectives of what and whom God may be inviting persons to become as community.

Consequently, there is the obligation to treat every person as Christ Himself, respecting his/her life as if it were the life of Christ. Even if the other person proves to be unjust, wicked and odious to us, we cannot take upon ourselves a final and definitive judgment in his case. We still have an obligation to be patient, and to seek his highest spiritual interests. In other words, we are formally commanded to love our enemies, and this obligation cannot be met by a formula of words.[9]

Raleigh Washington and Glen Kehrein in *Breaking Down Walls: A Model for Reconciliation in the Age of Racial Strife,* refer to the concept of imperative as *"call."*[10] Addressing the divine imperative for persons to move toward peaceful community involves the process of answering the question, "What does God call the church to become as peaceful community?" A sense of divine calling has the purpose of leading us into critical and constructive reflection and action that is beyond our human initiative, desires, abilities, and comfort zone.

It is clear throughout Scripture that Christians are called to lives and lifestyles that are characterized by peacemaking. Christianity and peacemaking are to be synonymous. Christ came into the world as the Prince of Peace. Thomas Merton asserts that we know that Christ himself is our peace. We believe that God has chosen himself in the Mystical Body of Christ, an elect people, regenerated by the Blood of the Savior, and committed by their baptismal promise to wage war upon the evil and hatred that are in man, and help to establish the Kingdom of God and of peace.[11] This means a recognition that human nature, identical in all (persons), was assumed by the Logos in the Incarnation, and that Christ died out of love for all (persons), in order to live in all (human beings).[12]

The church is called to model the meaning of peaceful community for the broader world. In the commonality among persons, there is unity in Christ. The biblical record makes it clear that Christ intended for the church to be a unified and peaceful body. Some of the Lord's final words in his prayer for all were "That they may be one." (John 17:21)

In light of God's ideal of individual and communal wholeness (*shalom*) the church is called to be the Body of Christ. (1 Corinthians 12:27) Each member of the Body is connected to the others, as branches are connected to their root, or vine. As Christ's body, we are connected to each other in, for, and because of Christ, the "true vine." (John 15:1) The Body of Christ is then understood as an organic and living entity, dependent upon its vine as the source of its being – its energy and life. And as the body is dependent upon the vine for its existence, it also depends upon each of its members, or branches, which comprise community.

The nature of the members of the church as the community of faith – and the model of peaceful community – is that each member is intricately related and dependent upon the other parts of the Body. In this way, members of the Body of Christ are to be viewed as more than appendages, like the arms and legs of the human body. Instead it has been suggested is more appropriate to view members of the church – as the ideal of community – as "membranes," where life and relationships are intertwined and interdependent with the other "membranes" that comprise the Body of Christ. The unity that is the ideal of the church allows persons of faith to envisage common opportunities to experience the grace of God. The Body of Christ, then is called to be a reconciling, healing and transformational entity – a change agent – that seeks to perpetually bridge the gap between a broken humanity and a gracious God, for the peace and justice of the church and world.

While the Christian church seeks to promote unity around the common cause of peace with justice, it also affirms the diverse nature of the world and its people. The church was commissioned by Christ to offer the gospel, and love of God, to all humanity. It was Christ's intent that the church would be a universal body. In the Great Commission, Jesus instructed his disciples to "Go there-fore and make disciples of all nations, baptizing them in the name of the Father, and of the Son, and of the Holy Spirit." (Matthew 28:19) The church's universality is embodied in the Greek concept 'oikoumene,' from which the word ecumenics is derived. In the Great Commandment, Christ instructed persons that "You shall love the Lord your God with all your heart, and with all your soul, and with all your mind. This is the greatest and the first commandment. And a second is like it: You shall love your neighbor as yourself." (Matthew 22:37-39) Thus, the church's universal mission is one of love, and this love is directed to the whole world.

The decision of the (early) church to reach out to gentiles was predicated on its basic decision to be a universal church, and to set no limitations on this universality. Here, the church professed *in actu* the universal (parenthood) of God and sovereignty of Christ. But also introduced enormous geographical and historical diversity into the church: diversity of peoples, diversity of cultures, diversity of social classes. In order to open itself up to this way, the church had to accept the possibility that it would adopt a variety of histori-cal forms. It would be a church of women and men, single and married, poor and rich, a church of the periphery, and a church of the centers of power.[13]

Within the context of universality, we come to realize the synergistic effects of the Holy Spirit within the church where the whole of community becomes greater than the sum of the individual parts. Diverse individuals and churches come to understand that they are participants within the much broader scheme of God's di-vine will. God desires that human giftedness is utilized in ways that create and perpetuate peaceful community.

II. Inspiration

Jesus was aware of the cultural context of his ministry. He knew that his teachings regarding God's justice, love, mercy, forgiveness and peace would get him into trouble. Yet, he remained faithful to his mission, and sought to perpetually live the God-inspired message that he had been given. Jesus stated his mission by sharing the prophetic words of the prophet Isaiah (Isaiah 61:1-2):

> The Spirit of the Lord is upon me,
> because God has anointed me
> to bring good news to the poor.
> God has sent me to proclaim
> release to the captives
> and recovery of sight to the blind,
> to let the oppressed go free,
> to proclaim the year of the Lord's favor.
> (Luke 4:18-19)

Like Christ, Martin Luther King, Jr. and Howard Thurman offered paradigms of God-centered and God-inspired ministries of peacemaking. The effectiveness of their respective witness is to be viewed in light of their God-connectedness. With Christ as the center of their word and witness, both Thurman and King remained inspired to prophetically challenge principalities and powers of the church and society to work for peaceful community.

The story of Pentecost is the experience of God, through Jesus Christ, inspiring and challenging persons of different languages, cultures and backgrounds to move beyond familiar comfort zones and into a new communal reality. At Pentecost, persons from diverse backgrounds found themselves in the same place, with a common purpose of hearing the mysterious story of Christ. They were together, communicating around the common reality of Christ. As the contemporary church and society struggles to realize Pentecost, overcoming intercultural barriers, we are invited to recognize that each cultural group, with its unique context, may experience God in ways that might be somewhat different from other groups.

Developing peaceful community is intricately related to a conception of a spirituality of peace. The Spirit is life, *ruah,* breath, wind. To be spiritual is to be alive, filled with *ruah,* breathing deeply, in touch with the wind. Spirituality is a life-filled path, a spirit-filled way of living. What is common to all paths that are spiritual is, of course, the Spirit – breath, life, energy. That is why all true paths are essentially one path – because there is only one Spirit, one breath, one life, one energy in the universe. It belongs to none of us and all of us. Spirituality does not make us otherworldly; it renders us more fully alive. The path that spirituality takes is a path away from the superficial into the depths; away from the "outer person" into the "inner person"; away from the privatized and indi-vidualistic into the deeply communitarian.[14]   As Meister Eckhart put it, "The outward person is the old person, the earthly person, the person of this world, who grows 'from day to day.' That person's end is death... The inward person, on the other hand, is the new person, the heavenly person in whom God shines." To find this "God who shines" in ourselves is to find the Cosmic Christ and to find a life that binds all things together.[15]

As God disarms our hearts of inner violence, we are in-spired to become God's instruments for the peace of the world. Without this inner conversion, we run the risk of becoming embit-tered, disillusioned, despairing, or simply burnt out, especially when our work for peace and justice appears to produce little or no result, or seems trifling in comparison with the injustice we see all around us. With this conversion we learn to let go of "all desires" – includ-ing the destructive desire to see ourselves.[16]

Martin Luther King, Jr. and Howard Thurman viewed peace-ful community as a transformational process that needed to be un-derstood within the context of salvation. King said, "Neither God nor man will individually bring the world's salvation. Rather, both Man and God, made one in a marvelous unity of purpose through the overflowing of love... can transform the old into the new and drive out the deadly cancer of sin."[17]   The development of authentic peaceful community will require God-connectedness through the inspiration of the Holy Spirit. As God inspires persons, peace will become the reality that will lead to authentic community.

III. Introspection

One of the keys to authentic community-building and peace-making is for persons to engage in an ongoing process of introspection and self-examination. M. Scott Peck points out that one of the activities that communities engage in is contemplation.[18] Community examines itself. It is self-aware. It knows itself. The fourteenth-century classic on contemplation, *The Cloud of Unknowing,* said, "Meekness in itself is nothing else than a true knowing and feeling of a man's self as he is. Any man who truly sees and feels himself as he is must surely be meek indeed."[19]

The word "contemplation" has a variety of connotations. Most of them center upon awareness. The essential goal of contemplation is increased awareness of the world outside oneself, the world inside oneself, and the relationship between the two. Self-awareness is the key to insight. Plato asserted: "The life which is unexamined is not worth living."[20]

Henri Nouwen pointed out that peacemaking is a work of love, and "in love there can be no fear, but fear is driven out by perfect love." (1 John 4:18) Nothing is more important in peacemaking than that it flow from a deep and undeniable experience of love. Only those who know deeply that they are loved and rejoice in that love can be true peacemakers...Intimate knowledge of being loved sets us free to look beyond the boundaries of death and speak and act fearlessly for peace. Prayer is the way to that experience of love.[21]

In prayer, again and again we discover that the love we are looking for has already been given to us and that we can come to the experience of that love. Prayer is entering into communion with the One who molded our being in our mother's womb with love. There, in the first love, lies our true self, a self not made up of rejections and acceptances of those with whom we live, but solidly rooted in the One who called us into existence. In the house of God we were created. To that house we are called to return. Prayer is the act of returning to God. Prayer is the basis of all peacemaking precisely because in prayer we come to the realization that we do not belong to the world in which conflicts and wars take place, but to him who offers us peace. The paradox of peacemaking is indeed that we can speak of peace in this world only where our sense of who we are is not anchored in the world. We can say, "We are for peace" only when those who are for fighting have no power over us. We can witness for the Prince of Peace only when our trust is in him and him alone…Only by living in the house of peace can we come to know what peacemaking will mean.[22]

> With regard to prayer, Howard Thurman stated that:
> Prayer is a form of communication between God and man and man and God. It is the essence of communication between persons that they shall talk with each other from the same agenda. Wherever this is not done, communication tends to break down. If however, an atmosphere of trust can be maintained, then one learns to wait and be still.[23]

Thurman further stated:
> The experience of prayer… can be nurtured and cultivated. It can create a climate in which a man's life moves and functions. Indeed, it may become a way of living for the individual. It is ever possible that the time may come when a man carries such an atmosphere around him and gives its quality to all that he does and communicates its spirit to all who cross his path.[24]
> The processes of community-building and peacemaking require introspection, self-examination and prayer throughout. As persons are thoughtful about themselves and about God, they become increasingly thoughtful about others. No community can expect to be in perpetually good health. What genuine community does, because it is contemplative, is recognize its ill health when it occurs and quickly take appropriate action to heal itself. Indeed, the longer they exist, the more efficient healthy communities become in this recovery process. Conversely, groups that never learn to be contemplative either do not become community in the first place or else rapidly and permanently disintegrate.[25]

IV. Imagination

Author and professor Eric Law, in *The Wolf Shall Dwell with the Lamb,*" offers a perspective on the notion of the peaceable realm where the wolf and the lamb are able to live together in harmony. (Isaiah 11:6) The vision of the biblical prophet Isaiah is that the wolf and the lamb, although different in disposition and character, through a common spirit would learn to peaceably co-exist because it is in their interests to dwell together. Their life depends on it. Amidst the turmoil, pestilence and virulence that had become a part of Israel's existence, Isaiah imagined a peaceable realm, where persons who differed would live together. It was a vision of God moving persons toward the realization of peaceful community – where "swords would be turned into plowshares, and spears into pruning hooks." (Micah 4:3)

With regard to imagination, Walter Brueggemann, in *The Prophetic Imagination* offers this perspective:

> I understand imagination is no doubt a complex epistemological process, to be the capacity to entertain images of meaning and reality that are beyond the givens of observable experience. That is, imagination is the hosting of the "otherwise" …beyond the evident. Without that we have nothing to say. We must take risks and act daringly to push beyond what is known to that which is hoped for and trusted, but not yet in hand.[26]

Imagination leads us to dream and envision the possibilities of peaceful community among the people of God. The Scriptures offer that "where there is no vision, the people cast off restraint." (Proverbs 29:18) The prophet Joel's eschatological vision imagines the possibilities of God's presence as people look to the future with hope:

> "In the last day, I (God) will pour out my spirit on all flesh, and your sons and daughters shall prophecy, and the old shall dream dreams and the young shall see visions." (Joel 2:28)

Howard Thurman pointed out that we are accustomed to thinking of imagination as a useful tool in the hands of the artist as he reproduces in varied forms that which he sees beyond the rim of fact that encircles him. There are times when the imagination is regarded as a delightful and often whimsical characteristic of what we are pleased to call the "childish mind."[27]

Thurman goes on to speak of the place of imagination in human relationships:

> But the place where imagination shows its greatest powers as the *angelos* of God is in the miracle which it creates when one man, standing in his place, is able, while remaining there, to put himself in another man's place. To send his imagination forth to establish a beachhead in another man's spirit, and from that vantage point so to blend with the other's landscape that what he sees and feels is authentic – this is the great adventure of human relations. But this is not enough. The imagination must report its findings accurately without regard to all prejudgments and private or collective fears. But this is not enough. There must be both a spontaneous and a calculating response to such knowledge which will result in sharing of resources at their deepest level.[28]

The movement toward peaceful community requires the sharing of dreams and visions for building bridges and overcoming the obstacles to unity. Matthew Fox suggests that there is a close connection between imagination and compassion:

> Compassion is not (merely) knowing about the suffering and pain of others. It is, in some way, knowing that pain, entering into it, sharing it and tasting it insofar as that is possible... But how does one know another's feeling and not merely know about it? Imagination is absolutely necessary for such a compassionate learning experience.[29]

Peace, in essence, is unconditional love. And unconditional love involves compassion and the willingness to listen to others. Compassion is the ability to empathetically enter into the suffering of another and experience it from the inside. We can have compassion even for those who do evil; for they suffer from a blindness and a darkness that prevent them from seeing truth. [30]

Howard Thurman asserted that without imagination human love would be impossible of achievement for there can be no love among human beings where there is no power of self-projection.

The mechanism of love is the ability to put oneself in the life of another and to look upon the world through the other's eyes – to enter into the feeling and thinking and reacting of another, even as one remains oneself...Imagination is the creative vehicle that carries one spirit into he dwelling place of another. There could be no sympathy in the world if men had not the gift of imagination. The spirit of man could never take flight in dreams, hopes, or aspirations if there were no wings of imagination given as a part of man's equipment for life.[31]

With Howard Thurman and Martin Luther King, Jr., we need to take an imaginative look toward a fresh and generous ideal of peace for all humanity. There is a need to renew the ancient wisdom of nonviolence as practiced by the likes of Mohandas Gandhi, Thurman and King, and to create new cultures of nonviolence and peace – what King envisaged as the *Beloved Community.*

Langston Hughes wrote imaginatively of a world of peace in a poem:

> I dream a world where man
> No other man will scorn,
> Where love will bless the earth
> And peace its paths adorn.
> I dream a world where all
> Will know sweet freedom's way,
> Where greed no longer saps the soul
> Nor avarice blights the day
> A world I dream where black and white
> Whatever race you be,
> Will share the bounties of the earth
> And every man is free,
> Where wretchedness will hang its head
> And joy, like a pearl
> Attends the needs of all mankind –
> Of such I dream my world![32]

Christian hope and Christian humility are inseparable within the context of peacemaking. The quality of nonviolence is predicated largely on the purity of the Christian hope and imagination behind it. The Christian knows that there are radically sound possibilities in everyone, and believes that love, grace and mercy always have the power to bring out those possibilities at the most unexpected moments. Therefore, if one has hope that God will grant peace to the world, it is because one also trusts that humanity, God's creature, is not basically evil, that there is in us a potentiality for peace and order which can be realized, provided the right conditions are there. Christians will do their part in creating these conditions by preferring love and trust over hate and suspiciousness. Obviously, once again, this "hope in humankind" must not be naïve. But experience itself has shown, in the last few years, how much an attitude of simplicity and openness can do to break down barriers of suspicion that had divided people for centuries.[33]

In the new millennium, it is important to creatively and imaginatively apply the wisdom of nonviolence to politics, economics, and science. For many in the West, increased materialism and unprecedented consumerism have not led to inner peace or happiness. It has resulted in what Cornel West refers to as "nihilism" – an existential state of nothingness, meaninglessness and lovelessness.[34] Although technology has afforded us many benefits, it has not helped us distinguish between what enhances life and humanity, and what destroys life and humanity. As we look to the future, we look imaginatively and hopefully at ways that we might use technology, politics, economics, and science to foster community.

V. Intentionality

Efforts toward building peaceful community have too often entailed placing persons of diverse cultural backgrounds in the same social context (place, institution, school, church, etc.) and expecting them to get along, without facilitating constructive relationship-building, cross-cultural understanding and valuation of the self and other. As a result, the different groups' natural instincts (perceptions and behaviors) eventually take over, and intercultural confusion and conflict ensues.

As long as human beings – each with incumbent fears, insecurities and the instinct to survive - seek to interrelate, conflict will be an inevitable aspect of the movement toward community.

For authentic peaceful community to emerge, there must be the will to act intentionally – sometimes against human instinct – in order to develop the space in which people of different backgrounds can not only tolerate each other, but develop the capacity to understand and appreciate one another even though they may not always agree.

Raleigh Washington and Glen Kehrein note the importance of sincerity in seeking to relate peacefully across cultures. According to Washington and Kehrein, sincerity is a willingness to be vulnerable, including self-disclosure of feelings, attitudes, differences, and perceptions with the goal of resolution and building trust. Additionally, they point out that intentionality is important in building multicultural relationships and community. Intentionality is the purposeful, positive and planned activity that facilitates reconciliation. Sincerity and intentionality are two principles that are closely related.[35]

Mairead Corrigan Maguire suggests that there are several basic and intentional steps that persons can take to create peaceful community in the new millennium.[36] First, we need to teach nonviolence and peace to the children of the world. In the 1980s, twenty-two Noble Peace Prize laureates asked the United Nations to declare the first decade of the new millennium as "a decade for a culture of nonviolence for the children of the world," in the hope that every nation would begin to educate its children in the way of nonviolence, in schools and homes. Second, as individuals, we can exorcise the violence from our own lives. Persons can choose to stop supporting systemic violence, and make a dedication to nonviolent social change and peace-making. Persons can take public stands for disarmament and justice in our communities and around the world. Third, we can urge the media to stop sensationalizing violence and instead to highlight interactions, promote nonviolence, and uphold those who strive for peace in our world. Fourth, we can embrace the wisdom of nonviolence that serves as the foundation of each of the world's religions. Every religion contains the ancient truth of nonviolence. Every religion needs to begin more and more to teach and promote nonviolence, and to worship the God of nonviolence. Mohandas Gandhi said, "If religion does not teach us how to achieve the conquest of evil by overcoming it with goodness, it teaches us nothing." A great deal can be learned from the great religions of the world with regard to peace. Fifth, the church can choose to live in solidarity with the poor among us. Mohandas Gandhi said that poverty is the worst form of violence. Howard Thurman and Martin Luther King, Jr. expressed a profound concern with regard to the church's moral imperative to address poverty, and to engage in ministry to the *disinherited*. Both suggested on many occasions that the way of Christ, is ministry with the dispossessed and the disenfranchised in our society.

Poverty rates in America are highest among those who have borne the brunt of racial prejudice and discrimination – the disinherited. African Americans are about three times more likely to be poor than white Americans. While one of every nine white Americans is poor, one out of every three black Americans lives in poverty.[37]

Martin Luther King, Jr. asserted that poverty results not from a lack of resources, but from an unequal distribution of existing resources. In 1967, Thomas Merton spoke of the need to evaluate the ideal of nonviolence within the context of poverty and the practice of Christianity in contemporary context. A practical difficulty emerges here, according to Merton, in that if the Gospel is preached to the poor; if the Christian message is essentially a message of hope and redemption for the poor, the oppressed, the underprivileged and those who have no power humanly speaking, how are we to reconcile ourselves to the fact that Christians belong, for the most part, to the rich and powerful nations of the world? Seventeen percent of the world's population control eighty percent of the world's wealth, and most of these seventeen are supposedly Christian. Admittedly those Christians who are interested in nonviolence are not ordinarily the wealthy ones. Nevertheless, like it or not, they share in the power and privilege of the most wealthy and mighty society the world has ever known. Even with the best subjective intentions in the world, how can they avoid a certain ambiguity in preaching nonviolence?[38]

Poverty, as prohibitive to the actualization of peace with justice, is to be understood in terms of its common effect upon all of humanity. The apostle Paul offered that members of the Body of Christ are interconnected and interrelated. "If one member suffers, all suffer together with it; if one member is honored, all rejoice together with it." (1 Cor. 12:26) Martin Luther King, Jr. elaborated on the notion of poverty as a common societal concern when he said:

> As long as there is poverty in this world, no [one] can be totally rich even if he [or she] has a billion dollars. As long as diseases are rampant and millions of people cannot expect to live more than twenty or thirty years, no [one] can be totally healthy, even if [she or] he has a clean bill of health from the finest clinic in America. Strangely enough, I can never be what I ought to be until you are what you ought to be. You can never be what you ought to be until I am what I ought to be. This is the way the world is made.[39]

In the sense that all life is interrelated, the agony of the poor impoverishes the rich, and the betterment of the poor enriches the rich. We are inevitably our brother's keeper because we are our brother's brother. Whatever affects one directly, affects all indirectly.[40] It is in the area of economic justice that the church might take the lead in helping to ensure a more equitable and just distribution of the world's resources. Gilbert Caldwell in *Race, Racism and Reconciliation,* poignantly asserts that the church must discover ways to "be in solidarity with the poor" among us. The church must remember to act on what it believes. Caldwell goes on to state:

> We believe God is creator and parent. God is an equal opportunity creator and parent. We are not created by God to be rich or poor, powerful or powerless. We of the church believe that every creature on this earth was created by God, and we thus share the same parent, and we are brothers and sisters. We must see to it that our brothers and sisters do not suffer. When they suffer, we must suffer.[41]

Caldwell points out several specific ways that Christians can be in solidarity with the poor. First, we must acknowledge that too often we represent the problem rather than the solution. Second, we must be honest about who we are, what we do, what is important to us, in terms of our lifestyle. Third, we must be consistent and persevering. Our faith does not give us the right to burn out. Fourth, we must be willing to critique systems. Fifth, we must be positive and hopeful because the gospel of the church is a gospel of hope.[42]

Marjorie Thompson in *Soul Feast: An Invitation to the Christian Spiritual Life,* speaks of intentionality in terms of the need for persons to practice hospitality with one another as a means of community-building:

> Our love for one another is a direct expression of our love for God. "Those who do not love their brother or sister whom they have seen, cannot love God whom they have not seen." (1 John 4:20) One of our more persistent problems is that we do not see each other as sisters or brothers, much less love each other as such.[43]

In the early church, hospitality, fellowship and a sense of community were exemplified in the intentional sharing of social, material and spiritual gifts. Therefore, none within the community had need as long as persons had resources to share. (Acts 2:22-45) When three thousand pilgrims who had been converted on the day of Pentecost remained in Jerusalem to be taught and established in the Christian faith, it was the church that accepted responsibility for them. (Acts 2:42-47) Paul wrote to the Romans, "Be devoted to one another in brotherly love." (Romans 12:10) There is a tremendous need among persons in contemporary society for a sense of community. There is a yearning for a sense of belonging. The willingness of persons to intentionally share diverse religious, social and cultural experiences can serve as the impetus for community that is enriched, empowered and enlightened toward the realization of peace.

Howard Thurman and Martin Luther King, Jr. demonstrated that love, as an active, intentional means of developing peaceful community, carries a huge responsibility. When we love, we look at circumstances and people differently. We don't react negatively to the negative actions of others. When we love, we bear insults, and we tolerate mean temperaments. When we love, we exhibit kindness and gentleness though it may not be returned, we pray for those who have wronged us, we fight against injustice and strive for liberation. When we love, we show and we teach unloving people what it means to know God.

To love our neighbors as ourselves is one of the greatest commandments because it is not easily accomplished. To love in the face of adversity, injustice, and oppression is one of the most difficult requirements of humanity. But if we can achieve it, if we can learn to love despite our circumstances, we can realize our hope for an end to violence and oppression. King and Thurman taught society that love can conquer violence, and that we would not intentionally hurt those whom we love.

VI. Invitation

Developing peaceful community involves a willingness to accept the invitation that Christ extends to us, as well as inviting others – those who may in some way be unlike us – into dialogue and relationship. Community is the reality where persons can be themselves, and have the same value as their neighbor. It is a safe reality, an inclusive reality where peace (*shalom*) prevails.

Reflection on the cultural context and diversity in which Christ sought to create peaceful community is insightful in seeking to arrive at a conceptuality for developing peaceful community in the 21st century. Harold Recinos, in *Jesus Weeps: Global Encounters on our Doorstep,* elaborates on the cultural environment that surrounded the town of Nazareth, and Galilee – the broader region - during the time that Jesus lived:

> Jesus comes from a part of the world rejected by the Jerusalem establishment (Nazareth of Galilee). Within the global and culturally diverse context of Galilee, Jesus directed his ministry toward those persons rejected by organized religion, and neglected by society. Yet, this Galilean carpenter who walked with society's outcasts proceeds from the countryside toward Jerusalem, instructing people along the way about their oppression and turning away from God. Directing attention to the kingdom (realm) of God at hand.[44]

Alienation can be viewed as a barrier to invitation and developing authentic peaceful community. In a 1967 lecture titled, "Youth and Social Action," Martin Luther King, Jr. warned that alienation is one of the dangerous evils in the contemporary world. Alienation is an evil force because it separates and divides persons. All of the forces of good in the world are founded on inter-connnectedness and unity. King states, "Growth requires connection and trust. Alienation is a form of living death. It is the acid of despair that dissolves society."[45] King elaborated on the matter of alienation:

> Gargantuan industry and government, woven into the intricate computerized mechanism, leave a person outside. The sense of participation is lost, the feeling that ordinary individuals influence important decisions vanishes, and man becomes separated and diminished. When an individual is no longer a true participant, when he no longer feels a sense of responsibility to his society, the control of democracy is emptied. When culture is degraded and vulgarity enthroned, when the social system does not build security but induces peril, inexorably the individual is impelled to pull away from a soulless society. This produces alienation – perhaps the most pervasive and insidious development in contemporary society. [46]

Peaceful community is not built on a presupposed division, but on the basic unity of humankind. It is not out for the conversion of the wicked to the ideas of the good, but for healing reconciliation.[47] As Mohandas Gandhi saw it, the full consistent practice of nonviolence and peace demands a solid metaphysical and religious basis both in being and in God. This comes before subjective good intentions and sincerity. For the Hindu this metaphysical basis was provided by the Vedantist doctrine of the Atman, the true transcendent Self which alone is absolutely real, and before which the empirical self of the individual must be effaced in the faithful practice of dharma.[48]

The attempt is to arrive at a comprehension of what Carl Raschke has referred to as a unity-behind-the-diversity approach, which is widely held among scholars and lay people.[49] Professor John Macquarrie of Oxford University offers one clear expression of this perspective. Taking a philosophical approach, Macquarrie sees the riddle of religious pluralism as analogous to the age-old debate about "the one and the many," an argument that goes back at least to the ancient Greeks. "God," for Macquarrie, is the name of the ultimate unity beyond all seeming contradictions and differences. He writes:

> These religions will be living side by side on earth in the foreseeable future. They must seek to draw more closely together and demonstrate by common life and action their fundamental commitment to the One, however that One may be named in each religion... No single faith has yet attained to the understanding of the fullness of the One... Therefore each faith must be respectful and ready to learn from the spiritual insights of others.[50]

Rascke describes this as the "Hindu solution" to the question of pluralism. It claims, in effect, that the variegation in religious traditions is only a secondary quality, that underneath, all the separate rivers and rivulets of faith draw on a single mighty reservoir. All the gods are avatars of the divine reality.[51]

The early Christian community sought to make sense of their cultural diversity and the need for peace in their midst. It has been suggested that the community of faith, as it gathered on the day of Pentecost, essentially comprised the first authentically multicultural Christian congregation. (Acts 2) As persons gathered for worship on that day, they were led to speak in several tongues – their native languages – among themselves.

From the early church's experience of Pentecost, it is evident that peaceful community is indeed possible, and certainly necessary for strengthening the church as a community of faith. Community is evidenced in the concern, among people, for the well-being (the *shalom*) of others who comprise community. In the book of Acts it is recorded, "Now the whole group of those who believed were of one heart and soul, and no one claimed private ownership of any possessions, but everything they owned was held in common." (Acts 4:32)

A subtext of the biblical view of community is the perspective of the "stranger." This emphasizes God's embrace of all nations of people. God speaks to and acts for humanity through those who were considered foreigners or strangers – a Moabite woman becomes the ancestral mother of Jesus; a Syrophoenician woman expands Jesus' vision of his mission; a Roman centurion becomes an example of faithfulness. A list of these surprising agents of God could be lengthy. The paradigmatic embrace of all nations, however, occurred at Pentecost when Jews from all the known nations of the world heard in their own tongues the Galilean disciples praising God. Some years later Paul the apostle would dramatize the "strangeness" of that new experience of community in his description of the relationship of the Jews and Gentiles in the Corinthian congregation as "members of one another."[52]

The apostle Paul was a Jew, Roman citizen, former persecutor of the early Christian community, and one who would encounter Christ, and eventually become a servant-leader of the church. Paul offers a clear annunciation of the nature of the church when he proclaims, "For as many of you who have been baptized into Christ have put on Christ. There is neither Jew nor Greek, there is neither bond nor free, there is neither male nor female; for you are all one in Christ Jesus." (Galatians 3:27-8) Despite the growing diversity among people throughout our world, Christ – "the Church's one foundation" – continues to invite the possibility of unity within the Christian faith community.

The nature the church, the very essence of Christianity, is the movement toward peaceful community. Christ and his ministry modeled what it meant for the church to be universal in its perspective (globality), catholic in its spirit, yet inclusive in its practice of community-building.

Christ is our peace, and the unity that he offers is clearly expressed in the song:

Blest be the tie that binds
our hearts in Christian love;
The fellowship of kindred minds
is like to that above.
Before our Father's throne
we pour our ardent prayers;
Our fears, our hopes, our aims are one,
our comforts and our cares.[53]

All persons are invited to join in the work of building peaceful community. We cannot live or grow without community, for in a world of interdependence, community extends to the farthest shores of our imaginations. In community we learn the both/and lessons of living. In community, we learn that survival does not belong to the "fittest" (understood as being the "most powerful"). Survival is about learning how to fit into our community and how the community fits us. [54]

In the 21st century, it is clearly evident that the human family is multi-ethnic, multicultural, and pluralistic in nature. If society is to survive and develop, it will be necessary that persons learn to live together peacefully. The opportunities for the church and society to become all that God calls us to be lie in our abilities to understand and ultimately value peaceful community. In an increasingly diverse society, peace is to be comprehended and appropriated within the context of various forms and shapes of diversity among us – race, ethnicity, class, gender, and even age, and how we are persistently invited to share and grow in this diversity.

VII. Interaction

Interaction involves the process of making the radical choice to live in community with those who may appear different than we are. It is actively seeking to understand, and to come to value and embrace the lives of those who are the "others" among us. Martin Luther King, Jr., in a sermon, recounted the story of the time in 1958 when he was stabbed in Harlem, and found himself on the brink of death. Doctors worked feverishly and faithfully to save his life, and he was able to escape death. As he lay in the recovery room, one of the physicians came by and talked to King. The physician informed him how very close he was to actually dying. Martin Luther King, Jr. learned that the letter-opener had been lodged in his chest in a way that if he had sneezed, it would have severed his aorta and he would have bled to death. In the aftermath of this experience, King received a letter from a young girl whom he had never met. He discovered that she was a white girl. In her letter, the girl wrote, "Dr. King, I'm writing to tell you how sorry I am that you got stabbed, but I also want you to know that I'm glad that you didn't sneeze."

Martin Luther King, Jr. stated that:

> The most creative turn of events in humanity's long history was when man set down his ax stone and began to cooperate with his neighbor. That seemingly elementary decision set in motion what we know now as civilization. At the heart of all that civilization has meant and developed is 'community,' the mutually cooperative and voluntary venture of man to assume a semblance of responsibility for his brother. The Cross is the eternal expression of the length to which God will go in order to restore broken community. The Resurrection is a symbol of God's triumph over all the forces that seek to block community.[55]

Howard Thurman's life served as an example of the role of interaction in cross-cultural context. According to Alton Pollard, Howard Thurman's approach to interpersonal relations is sensitive and complex: a mix of high vision, quietistic discourse, and practical intimacy.[56] Carlyle Fielding Stewart refers to the Thurman mode as "intuitive," a kind of spiritual-ethical liberation,[57] while Luther Smith notes that Thurman's "convictions are not adopted systems of belief, but convictions which have been shaped, tested, and proved within life experiences.[58] However stated it is manifestly clear that Thurman embraced a compelling, consistent, intersubjective mode of human interaction in the world.

In postmodern context, cultural particularities are especially noteworthy when affirmed within the context of cultural differences. Many persons – to one degree or another – are beginning to see the world through cultural lenses that are somewhat different than their own. In the United States, there are many different peoples from most parts of the world that comprise the nation. This broadening diversity should be viewed as a blessing of the coming together of the unique gifts and graces of different persons. When we see ourselves as we ought, both in terms of our particularities and our commonalities, we are like a mosaic – "a piece of inlaid work composed of bits of stone or glass which form a pattern or a picture.[59] We must come to a point in our history and life together where we celebrate, with enthusiasm, the peculiar and particular cultural gifts each of us offers society.[60]

On an individual level, it is important to understand that persons are affected by the interaction of cultures. A comprehension of what Professor Ewert Cousins (Fordham University) refers to as "a new global consciousness" might be helpful in better understanding and actualizing human interaction, community, and peacemaking, given the degree of human suffering and disintegration experienced among many persons throughout the world.[61]

The understandings of God, culture, humanity, and the positive or negative meanings that are given to the various differences between persons are shaped or constructed within the context of particular webs of "social relationships." They are not fixed in stone, but rather are influenced by and influence these particular relationships. This is the primary assumption from which the subject of multiculturalism is approached, and is formally known as the theory of *social construction*. Joan M. Martin offers that social construction theory allows her to keep her faith rooted in the realities of this world. For her, spiritual realities are rooted in everyday life.[62]

Social construction theory says we not only give meaning to the relationships between us as people... we also structure them, embedding meanings of power in them, thus shaping the way we act in our families, and through religions; economic and social forces; community norms, *mores*, and regulations; political agendas and policies. In theological language, "the freedom we have been given to make the world around us is...so all-consuming, so confidently given to us by God, that we have the freedom to create that which is of ourselves."[63] When we understand that oppressive ideas about race, gender, and class are constructed by people, we realize they can be deconstructed. Social construction theory requires us to seek out, listen to, and act upon the concerns of people from various perspectives of racial, economic, gender, and cultural experience to learn how difference has been used to construct both superior and inferior social positions. Beyond deconstruction of oppression, we are free to construct ideas about appreciating the differences between us as gifts, rather than approaching the reality of our differences as a problem.

The creation of space for the free interchange of thoughts, feelings and beliefs between persons of different views, perspectives and backgrounds is critical in the process of developing peaceful community. Eric H. F. Law in *The Bush Was Burning But Not Consumed,* refers to this process as *dialogue.*[64] Dialogue is the meeting with the other person, the other group, the other people which confirms in its otherness, yet does not deny oneself and the ground on which it stands. The choice is not between oneself and the other, nor is there some objective ground to which one can rise above the facing sides, the conflicting claims. Rather, genuine dialogue is at once a confirmation of otherness and togetherness – the living embodiment of the biblical creation in which persons are really free, yet remain bound in relation with God. In genuine dialogue, each of the partners, even when standing in opposition to the other, heeds, affirms, and confirms the opponent as an existing other.

Raleigh Washington and Glen Kehrein refer to a closely related construct, "*interdependence.*" Interdependence recognizes our difference, but realizes that each person who is a part of a given community offers something that the other person needs, resulting in equality in the relationship. Change strategist, Stephen Covey, points out that interdependence is a higher value than independence.[65] Interaction may begin with dialogue, but it moves us toward action that is based on the personal strengths that we bring to community. We begin to discover the profound ways that we are being led to interact with persons who might be culturally different from us, and the benefit this holds for community.

Charles Foster (Emory University), in *Embracing Diversity,* speaks of interaction in terms of the ways in which we might embrace strangers:

> The challenge of embracing the strangers we meet in our communities and congregations does not occur in the abstract. It emerges from the interactions of people from diverse cultural groups in the daily comings and goings of our life and work together.[66]

Foster goes on to point out how he became personally aware of the challenge of embracing strangers:

> This challenge was underscored for me during a conversation with a pastor serving a congregation of people whose ancestries could be traced back through the European im-

migration and the African Diaspora, and people who had recently come to the United States from thirteen different nations in Africa, Europe, the Caribbean, South America, the South Pacific, and Asia. Although the children and grandchildren of many long-time members visit from time to time, the congregation has only five three-generation families – three with European ancestries and two from Liberia. That is to say that the ties contributing to the ethos in this congregation do not rely on the bonds of kinship.[67]

Cultural assumptions about the meaning of community and the ways that persons are to interact therein are to be identified before persons can begin to affirm the differences among themselves. Tensions often arise among persons who find themselves together, but who come from different social and geographical locations, and have different understandings and experiences of culture. Many of these differences may appear to be negotiable on the surface – affirmation and valuation occurs within the context of interaction, as diverse persons engage in the process of interacting and embracing the cultures of others. And yet interaction is a process that over time requires the appropriation of previously discussed principles like intentionality, introspection, compassion, sincerity, and dialogue in efforts to build relationships and come to a sense of actualized community.

Thomas Merton pointed out that the test of our sincerity in human interaction in the practice of nonviolence and movement toward peaceful community is: *"are we willing to learn something from our adversaries?"*[68]   If a new truth is made known, will we accept it? The dread of being open to the ideas of others generally comes from our hidden insecurity about our own convictions. We fear that we may be "converted" – or perverted – by a pernicious doctrine. On the other hand, if we are mature and objective in our open-mindedness, we may find that in viewing things from a basically different perspective we discover our own truth in a new light and are able to understand our own ideals more realistically.

Merton further observed that "the whole idea of compassion is based on a keen awareness of the interdependence of all living things which are all part of one another and involved in one another."[69]   Compassion is the moral law of interconnectivity, the cosmic law of responding to another's pain and suffering, as well as to another's joy and celebration.

Indian Catholic Raimundo Panikkar, a priest and mystic whose father was a Hindu and whose mother was a Spanish Roman Catholic, points out that most dialogues between religious persons go astray when the participants begin advocating, comparing, defending, conceding – like diplomats negotiating a treaty. What Panikkar yearns for is more respect for silence, more shared awe and ecstasy. (This is a dialogue that draws partners into the "unspoken center" they share). One neither hides the differences nor trumpets the similarities, but allows both to be what they are. One waits and listens. The procedure is a nonviolent one, reminiscent of Gandhi's *ahimsa* [70]

The willingness to take an alternative approach to a problem will perhaps relax the obsessive fixation that others might have in seeking to impose one's particular perspective and viewpoint upon others, thus resulting in ongoing dissension and division. It is the refusal of alternatives – a compulsive state of mind which Merton calls the "ultimatum complex" – which makes wars in order to force unconditional acceptance of one oversimplified interpretation of reality. The mission of Christian humility in social life is not merely to edify, but to keep minds open to many alternatives. The rigidity of a certain type of Christian thought has seriously impaired this capacity, which nonviolence must recover.[71]

Authentic interaction among persons of different cultural groups will ultimately result in the need for reconciliation. Reconciliation is more than the absence of violence. Reconciliation must include recognition of the equal worth of all, and must actively embrace peace and social justice. It was what Dietrich Bonhoeffer called "a costly grace."[72] The heart of the Gospel warrants a profound encounter between persons and among peoples. At the center of Christian faith, Jesus reconciles persons to God. He also reconciles persons to each other. He is the One who "breaks down the dividing wall and makes us one."

212 C. Anthony Hunt

VIII. Innovation

Innovation helps us to draw upon the creative gifts that we have been given by God in the development of peaceful community. What innovative and creative approaches might we take, to building peaceful community? What gifts has God given us (music, dance, poetry, literature, liturgy, prayer, capacity-building, consensus-building) that might make us effective in fostering peaceful community?

Carlyle Fielding Stewart, III. points out that to innovate is to create a different hermeneutic or motif for human existence.[73] Innovation is the power to create something new that either embraces, diverges from, or transcends the normative order or pattern. It means taking what is given and transforming it into something meaningful, useful, and purposeful. Innovation suggests the power to see old things in new ways, to forge and create something viable from that which has lost its vitality.[74]

Innovation brings comprehension to humanity's creation in God's image. Matthew Fox in *Creation Spirituality: Liberating Gifts for Peoples of the Earth,* points out that creation is all things in us. It is us in relationship with things. "All our relations," the Lakota people pray (whenever they gather). "All our relations" implies all beings, all things, the ones we see and the ones we do not...Creation is all space, all time – all things past, present, and future. Of these three ways of conceptualizing time, creation leans the most in the direction of the present, for the most significant of the times is the Now, the "Eternal Now." By the choices we make about what we (create), the past presses into the future. Whether the future presents itself as still more beauty or still more pain depends on our choices as we respond to our role as co-creators in an ever-unfolding creation. In us the past and present come together to create the future.[75] As Meister Eckhart puts it:

God is creating the entire universe fully and
totally in this present now.
Everything God created six thousand years ago –
and even previous to that as God made the world –
God creates now all at once.
Everything which God created millions of years ago

and everything which will be created by God
after millions of years –
if the world endures until then –
God is creating all that in the innermost and
deepest realms of the soul.
Everything of the past and everything of the present
and everything of the future
God creates in the innermost realms of the soul.[76]

Creation, then, at its core, is about relationship. It is the spiraling, dancing, crouching, springing, leaping, surprising act of relatedness, of communing, of responding, of letting go, of being. Being is about relationship. Eckhart says that "relation is the essence of everything that exists" and the "isness is God." Thus, all creation is a trace, a footprint, an offspring of the Godhead. Creation is the passing of divinity in the form of *isness*. It is God's shadow in our midst. It is sacred. All our relationships are sacred...Jesus taught it. (" I am the vine, you are the branches... my father and I are one.") Christians and other believers must learn anew the sacredness of creation.[77]

Innovation is an important aspect of building peaceful community because it encourages and preserves the creativity of the Spirit and invariably ties people to the wellsprings of personal, spiritual and cultural vitality.

Innovation speaks to the freedom and creative powers that persons possess in God. The essence of creative freedom is found in the power and capacity to create idioms of spirituality, life, and culture that encourage people to freely and innovatively live with hope, power, love and human dignity. Innovation is the power to think and create on terms that reinforce personal sanctity, identity, and value of all persons, and ultimately to facilitate the creation of new shapes and forms of community.

IX. Interpretation

The development of peaceful community among persons of diverse cultures insists upon the consistent interpretation of the meanings of the various symbols and practices that become a part of the new cultural reality. Human interpretation is inescapably subjective, and yet therein lies a part of the value of cultural understanding through interpretation. As a result of the subjective nature of interpretation, our understanding only has tentative authority.

This, however, does not diminish the value of interpretation. The process of interpretation helps us to move with hope and joy from those perspectives perhaps long held, and yet too partisan. Walter Brueggemann suggests that we may learn from the rabbis the marvelous rhythm of deep interpretive dispute and profound common yielding in joy and affectionate well-being. The characteristic and sometimes demonic mode of (some) interpretation is not tentativeness and relinquishment, but tentativeness hardening into absoluteness.[78]

Ewert Cousins, in *Christ of the 21st Century,* offers a framework for interpreting religion – particularly Christian faith – within the context of the broadening socio-cultural, postmodern realities of the new millennium. Christ is to be seen within the context of culture, and is to be understood within the fabric of all that comprises human life. Religion has typically reflected and often contributed to what occurs in society. The paradoxical nature of religion is that it is often directly or indirectly complicit in both the good and evil that exists in society.[79]

Religion is to be viewed as a process, and must now be understood in global context. It is no longer an option to confine religious thinking and practice to narrow and particular cultural contexts. In postmodernity, cultures are brought into closer contact by technology.[80] Cousins offers the illustration of an astronaut who travels into space for the first time, and looks down upon the earth. The astronaut is overwhelmed with what he sees, as he now views the earth from a new and broader perspective. Likewise, a new global reality causes us to view the world from a different perspective.[81]

The result is the emergence of a global reality where it is now possible to comprehend diversity in the midst of unity. Cousins refers to this as the whole of "global consciousness."[82]   This global consciousness will significantly impact religion in that there will be a more pronounced and intense meeting of world religions in the years to come. Currently, the impact of this global consciousness on religion can be seen in an increasing secularization of modern culture. In the future this secularization will result in an "emptying of heritage." [83]

According to Cousins, global consciousness is to be understood in historical context. He identifies three periods as paradigmatic in the shaping of the consciousness of the world. The first is referred to as the "pre-axial period," which is the time prior to 200 BCE. The pre-axial period is characterized as "tribal" in the way that persons were typically organized. The period is also characterized by the focus on the collective, the myth (mythos), and the ritualistic.

The second period is identified as the "axial period." The axial period began around 200 BCE and endured until the close of the 20th century. This period brought about a transformation of consciousness from the pre-axial period. The axial period is characterized by its focus on individualism, an attitude and ethic of "know thyself," and an emphasis on logic (logos) over myth (mythos).

The 21st century has ushered in another transformation of consciousness, which is referred to as the "second axial period." The second axial period is characterized by global consciousness, the movement from divergence to convergence in religion and culture, and an intensified level of diversity. The second axial period, according to Cousins, is further characterized by a focus on justice, peace, and well-being in the global context, along with a re-appropriation of the unity of tribal conscience experienced in the pre-axial period.

Pierre Tiellard de Chardin's optimistic view of the universal and the "cosmic Christ" (1955) is helpful in better understanding this era of convergence and full impact of Christ upon the world. With a clearer understanding of the nature of Christ in universal context, there is the possibility of the Christian church facilitating more substantive inter-religious and inter-cultural dialogue. [84]

Within the framework of global conscious, Cousins offers the notion of the "mutational age," noting that different cultures and persons throughout the world are at different stages in the axial/second axial perspective. An appropriation of the second axial period raises the prospect of what the future might look like. There will be an intensification of change – both spiritual and logical.

This will be a period that focuses on dialogical rather than dialectical perspective. Societal structures will become more horizontal than vertical. Religious implications may generally be seen in a more holistic approach to spirituality – where more people have input into what is spiritually relevant and what is not.

X. Integration

Community is integrative.[85]   By its very nature, authentic community includes persons of different races, sexes, ages, religions, cultures, viewpoints, lifestyles, and stages of development by integrating them into a whole that is greater – more actualized and dynamic – than the sum of its parts. Forms of disintegration and disunity are, therefore, to be understood as antithetical to community.

Integration is not a melting process; it does not result in a bland average. Rather, it has been compared to the creation of a salad in which the identity of the individual ingredients is preserved, yet simultaneously transcended.[86]   The development of authentic, peaceful community is a dynamic process in which the various cultural groups maintain their identities while engaging in a constructive dialogue with each other. True community seeks to maintain balance of power, communication, and authenticity among different cultural groups. No group in this dynamic process will dominate, nor will any be made disadvantaged.[87]

The promise of integration is at the heart of Christ's work; in him human beings are sons and daughters of God, and brothers and sisters to one another. The church, the community of those who confess Christ as Lord, is a sign of unity within history. For this reason, the church must help the world to achieve unity, while knowing that unity among human beings is possible only if there is real justice for all. In a divided world the role of the ecclesial community is to struggle against the radical causes of social division. If it does so, it will be an authentic and effective sign of unity under the universal love of God.[88]

Martin Luther King, Jr. offered that "there is an amazing power in unity. Where there is true unity, every effort to disunite only serves to strengthen the unity."[89]   In 1957, King spoke prophetically of the challenges and opportunities that faced the new emerging world. King said:

> We are challenged to rise above the narrow confines of our individualistic concerns to the broader concerns of all humanity. The new world is a world of geographical togetherness. This means that no individual or nation can live alone. We must all learn to live together, or we will be forced to die together. This new world of geographical togetherness has been brought about, to a great extent, by man's scientific and technological genius. Man, through his scientific genius, has been able to dwarf distance and place time in chains; he has been able to carve highways through the stratosphere. Our world is geographically one. Now we are faced with the challenge of making it spiritually one. Through our scientific genius we have made of the world a neighborhood; now through our moral and spiritual genius we must make of it a brotherhood. We are all involved in the single process. Whatever affects one directly affects all indirectly. We are all links in the great chain of humanity.[90]

The principle of integration is related to the notion of synergy. Synergy is about producing a third alternative – *not my way, not your way, but a third way that is better than either of us would come up with individually*. It is the fruit of mutual respect – of understanding and even celebrating one's differences in solving problems, and seizing opportunities. Synergistic (communities) thrive on individual strengths so that the whole becomes greater than the sum of the parts.[91]

Community does not solve the problem of pluralism by obliterating diversity. Instead it seeks out diversity, welcomes other points of view, embraces opposites, desires to see the other side of every issue. It is holisitic. It integrates human beings into a functioning, living mystical body.

The word "integrity" comes from the verb "to integrate." Authentic community is always characterized by integrity. It is no accident that Erik Erikson also labeled the final stage of individual psychosocial development "Integrity."[92] Just as it encourages the highest mystical, holistic form of individual functioning, so the integrity of community characterizes the highest form of group functioning.

Integration is also closely related to interdependence. Martin Luther King, Jr. pointed out the degree to which all persons are interdependent:

> Every nation is an heir of a vast treasury of ideas and labor to which both the living and the dead of all nations have contributed. Whether we realize it or not, each of us lives eternally "in the red." We are everlasting debtors to known and unknown men and women. When we arise in the morning, we go into the bathroom where we reach for a sponge, which is provided for us by a Pacific Islander. We reach for soap that is created for us by a European. Then at the table we drink coffee, which is provided for us by a South American, or tea by a Chinese, or cocoa by a West African. Before we leave for our jobs we are already beholden to more than half the world.[93]

In the final analysis, the reality is that America and the world are rapidly changing. No longer can we simply view ourselves as black and white. Lewis Brown Griggs and Lente-Louise Louw in *Valuing Diversity: New Tools for a New Reality,"* suggest that differences in culture, ethnicity, gender, race, perspectives, personality, style, values and feelings need to be honored and encouraged, not merely tolerated. The real value of diversity is that it produces synergistic interactions across the various forms and shapes of difference. It is this synergy that produces unpredictable consequences in terms of breakthrough and results. [94] It is this synergy that will ultimately result in authentic peaceful community.

Conclusions

In order to bring the contemporary significance of the lives and ministries of Howard Thurman and Martin Luther King, Jr. into perspective, it is necessary to have a clear picture of their respective pastoral-prophetic identities in light of their persistent yearning to appropriate peaceful community. It has been the attempt of this dissertation to demonstrate that the two thinkers' respective approaches to developing community – within the context of the Christian love-ethic - can serve as helpful resources in the explication and application of the principle elements involved in the conception, character, and actualization of peaceful community in contemporary Christian perspective.

Clearly, there is a great similarity and kinship in the thinking of Thurman and King. Both were Christian ministers. They believed in God. Both accepted the Christian account of Jesus as the key to a full and necessary understanding of God, and the meaningful appropriation of peaceful community. Both saw the Kingdom of God as a communal expression of God, which was revealed in the life and mission of Christ. A point of distinction rests in the fact that Thurman – to a greater extent than King - often sought to comprehend this divine love within the context of prophetic expressions outside the norms of traditional Christianity. In these expressions, Thurman saw the hand of God seeking to pull humanity - in all its rich diversity, dreams, hopes and fears - into vital and peaceful harmony.

The ten principles that have been developed as a culmination of this study reflect the common appropriation of Christian spirituality – a spiritual theology - of Thurman and King as a foundation for social transformation. For both Howard Thurman and Martin Luther King, Jr., spirituality found its origins and coherency in the Black church, along with family (nuclear and extended) and community structures of the American South of the first half of the 20th century. Through their dialectical analysis of various strands of theological and socio-political thinking, Thurman and King sought to synthesize and articulate the relationship between love, justice, forgiveness, righteousness and power, with particular focus on the eradication of oppression on the basis of race, class, and other aspects of social location and distinction in American society. Their persistent objective was to raise the consciousness of society and the church, and to move the nation and the world toward the actualization of just and peaceful community. This was ultimately accomplished through King's appropriation of *Beloved Community,* and Thurman's persistent striving toward the actualization of *Multicultural Community* in the search for common ground.

In the final analysis, both Howard Thurman and Martin Luther King, Jr. went to great lengths – indeed they lived and offered their lives - to explicate the quality of whole-hearted, profound Christian love which can and must be the substance uniting all humanity into a common bond of sisters and brothers, showing forth in all human relationships.

NOTES

[1] Francis of Assisi, Italy, 13th Century, see *The United Methodist Hymnal* (Nashville, TN: United Methodist Publishing, 1989), 481. See also *St. Francis and the Foolishness of God* by Marie Dennis, et. al. (Maryknoll, NY: Orbis Books, 1997).

[2] Martin Luther King, Jr. "Loving Your Enemies," *Strength to Love,* 41f.

[3] Martin Luther King, Jr., "Facing the Challenge of a New Age," *Fellowship* (New York: Fellowship of Reconciliation, 1957).

[4] William H. Shannon, *Seeds of Peace,* 129.

[5] John Dear, ed. *Henri Nouwen: The Road to Peace* (Maryknoll, NY: Orbis Books, 1998), 6.

[6] Ibid.

[7] Eric H.F. Law, *The Bush Was Burning But Not Consumed,* 59.

[8] See Milton J. Bennett, "A Developmental Approach to Training for Intercultural Sensitivity," in *Theories and Methods in Cross-Cultural Orientation,* ed. Judith N. Martin, International Journal of Intercultural Relations, Vol. 5, No. 2 (New York: Persimmon Press, 1986), pp. 179-196, and Milton J. Bennett, "Toward Ethnorelativism: A Developmental Model of Intercultural Sensitivity," in *Cross-Cultural Orientation*, ed. R. Michael Paige (Lanham, MD: University Press of America, 1986), pp. 46-69.

[9] Ibid.

[10] See Raleigh Washington and Glen Kehrein, *Breaking*

Down Walls: A Model for Reconciliation in an Age of Racial Strife (Chicago: Moody, 1993), chapter 15, for a complete discussion of Washington and Kehrein's conception of "call."

[11] Thomas Merton, *The Nonviolent Alternative* (New York: Farrar, Straus and Giroux, 1980), 112.

[12] Ibid.

[13] Jon Sobrino, *Spirituality of Liberation: Toward Political Holiness* (Maryknoll, NY: Orbis Books, 1988), 142.

[14] Matthew Fox, *Creation Spirituality: Liberating Gifts for The Peoples of the Earth* (New York: HarperCollins, 1991), 13.

[15] Ibid.

[16] Mairead Corrigan Maguire, "Gandhi and the Ancient Wisdom of Nonviolence," *Fellowship* (New York: Fellowship for Reconciliation, June 1988).

[17] Martin Luther King, Jr., *Strength to Love,* 124.

[18] M. Scott Peck, *The Different Drum,* 65.

[19] Ira Progoff, trans., *The Cloud of Unknowing* (New York: Julian Press, 1969), 92.

[20] J. W. Mackail, ed., *The Greek Anthology* (1906), Vol. IIII, p 38.

[21] John Dear, *Henri Nouwen: The Road to Peace,* 16.

[22] Ibid., 17.

[23] Howard Thurman, *Disciplines of the Spirit,* 272-273.

[24] Ibid, 286.

[25] M. Scott Peck, 67.

[26] Walter Brueggemann, *The Prophetic Imagination* (Minneapolis, MN: Fortress Press, 1978), 80f.

[27] Howard Thurman, *The Mood of Christmas*, 44.

[28] Ibid.

[29] Matthew Fox, *A Spirituality Named Compassion and the Healing of the Global Village, Humpty Dumpty and Us* (Minneapolis: Winston Press, 1979), 21.

[30] William Shannon, 126.

[31] Thurman, *The Mood of Christmas,* 49.

[32] Langston Hughes, "I Dream a World," *The Collected Poems of Langston Hughes,* ed. Arnold Rampersad (New York; Vintage, 1994), 311.

[33] Ibid.

[34] Cornel West, *Race Matters* (Boston: Beacon Press, 1991), 14. West offers further explication of "nihilism" at various points throughout this work.

[35] Raleigh Washington and Glen Kehrein, *Breaking Down Walls,* Washington and Kehrein offer an in-depth analysis of *Intentionality* and *Sincerity* as two important practices in facilitating racial reconciliation at Rock of Our Salvation Church in Chicago, IL.

[36] Mairead Corrigan Maguire, "Gandhi and the Ancient Wisdom of Nonviolence." Using Maguire's thinking as the basis of discussion, I have chosen to make adaptations to her steps for peacemaking.

[37] National Conference of Catholic Bishops, *Economic Justice for All* (Washington, DC: National Conference of Catholic Bishops, 1986), 8.

[38] Merton, "Blessed are the Meek: The Roots of Christian Nonviolence," *Fellowship*
(New York: Fellowship of Reconciliation, May 1967).

[39] Martin Luther King, "The American Dream," *A Testament of Hope,* ed. James Melvin Washington, 210.

[40] Martin Luther King, Jr. *Where Do We Go from Here?,* 181.

[41] Gilbert H. Caldwell, *Race, Racism and Reconciliation* (Philadelphia: Simon Printing and Publishing, Inc., 1989), 32.

[42] Ibid., 34.

[43] Marjorie Thompson, *Soul Feast: An Invitation to the Christian Spiritual Life* (Louisville, KY; Westminster John Knox Press, 1995), 127.

[44] Harold Recinos, *Jesus Weeps* (Nashville: Abingdon, 1992), 45-46.

[45] Martin Luther King, Jr., *The Trumpet of Conscience* (New York: Harper and Row, 1967), 44.

[46] Ibid.

[47] Thomas Merton, "Blessed are the Meek."

[48] Ibid.

[49] See Harvey Cox, *Many Mansions: A Christian's Encounter with Other Faiths* (Boston: Beacon Press, 1988), 166f. Cox discusses Carl Rasche's four typologies as an attempt at arriving at answers to the "truth question" among persons of diverse cultures and religions.

[50] Ibid., 167-168. See also John Macquarrie, *Christian Unity and Christian Diversity* (London: SCM Press, 1975), here Macquarrie offers a complete explication of the unity-diversity issue in religious perspective.

[51] Cox, 168.

[52] Charles Foster, *Embracing Diversity* (Washington, DC: The Alban Institute), 52.

[53] See the *United Methodist Hymnal* Nashville: United Methodist Publishing House, 1989), 557. Written by John Fawcett, 1782.

[54] Matthew Fox, *Creation Spirituality,* 50.

[55] Martin Luther King, Jr., *Stride Toward Freedom,* 105-6.

[56] Alton Pollard, *Mysticism and Social Change,* 95.

[57] Carlyle Fielding Stewart, "Comparative Analysis of Theological-Ontology and Ethical Method in the Theologies of James H. Cone and Howard Thurman," (Ph.D. dissertation, Northwestern University, 1982), pp. 362-75.

[58] Luther Smith, *The Mystic as Prophet,* 117.

[59] Charles Shelby Rooks, *Rainbows and Reality: Selected Writings of the Author* (Atlanta: The ITC Press, 1985), 104.

[60] Michael I. N. Dash, et al., *Hidden Wholeness,* 114.

[61] Ewert Cousins, *Christ of the 21st Century* (New York: Continuum, 1998), 2-3.

[62] Joan M. Martin, presentation at Living Values II Consultation at the Scarritt Center in Nashville, Tennessee, January

1993, 10-11. See also Anne Bathurst Gilson and Barbara A. Weaver, "Barriers Among Us and Within Ourselves: Ethical Issues of Life in a Multicultural Society," *First, We Must Listen: Living in a Multicultural Society* (New York: Friendship Press, 1996), 95.

[63] Ibid.

[64] Eric H.F. Law, *The Bush Was Burning, But Not Consumed*, x.

[65] Stephen Covey, *The Seven Habits of Highly Effective People* (New York: Fireside, 1990), A key concept for actualizing the "Seven Habits" of success, according to Covey is *Interdependence.* Interdependence is closely related to the principle of *synergy.* I suggest that Interdependence and Synergy are critical for developing authentic community in the postmodern perspective.

[66] Foster, 52.

[67] Ibid., 53.

[68] Merton, "Blessed are the Meek."

[69] Ibid.

[70] Cox, 169.

[71] Ibid.

[72] Dietrich Bonhoeffer, *The Cost of Discipleship* (New York: Collier Books, 1949, First published in 1937), Throughout, Bonhoeffer elaborates on the distinction between "cheap grace" and "costly grace" within the context of Christian discipleship.

[73] Stewart, *Soul Survivors,* 73.

[74] Ibid.

[75] Fox, *Creation Spirituality,* 8.

[76] Ibid., 9.

[77] Ibid.

[78] Walter Brueggemann, "Biblical Authority" in *The Christian Century* (Chicago: The Christian Century, January 3-10, 2001), 16.

[79] Ewert Cousins, 2-3.

[80] Ibid., 3.
[81] Ibid.
[82] Ibid.
[83] Ibid.
[84] Ibid., pp. 163-193.
[85] M. Scott Peck, *The Different Drum,* 234.
[86] Ibid.
[87] Eric H.F. Law, *The Bush Was Burning, But Not Consumed,* x.
[88] Gustavo Gutierrez, *A Theology of Liberation,* 161.
[89] Martin Luther King, Jr. *Stride Toward Freedom,* 150.
[90] Martin Luther King, Jr., "Facing the Challenge of A New Age."
[91] Stephen Covey, see *Seven Habits of Highly Effective People.* Synergy is habit number six.
[92] See James Fowler, *Stages of Faith* (New York: HarperCollins, 1981), pp. 42-52. Fowler offers an analysis of Erik Erikson's conception of psychosocial development in relation to faith development. Stage seven of Erikson's model is maturity, which is characterized by integrity.
[93] Martin Luther King, Jr., *Where Do We Go from Here?,* 181.
[94] Lewis Brown Griggs and Lente-Louise Louw, 1-6.

BIBLIOGRAPHY

Achebe, Chinua. *Things Fall Apart.* New York: Anchor Books, 1959.

Adams, Maurine, Warren J. Blumenfield, Rosie Castaneda, Heather W. Hackman, Madeline L. Peters, Ximena Zuniga, eds. *Reading for Diversity and Social Justice: An Anthology of Racism, Antisemitism, Sexism, Heterosexism, Ableism, and Classism.* New York: Routledge, 2000.

Adeney, Bernard T. *Strange Virtues: Ethics in a Multicultural World.* Downers Grove, IL: InterVarsity Press, 1995.

Alport, Gordon W. *The Nature of Prejudice.* Reading, MA; Addison-Wesley Publishing Company, 1979.

Ansbro, John J. *Martin Luther King, Jr.: The Making of a Mind.* Maryknoll, NY: Orbis Books, 1982.

Ansbro, John J. *Martin Luther King, Jr.: Nonviolent Strategies and Tactics for Social Change.* Maryknoll, NY: Orbis Books, 2000.

Archer, Carol M. *Living with Strangers in the U.S.A.: Communicating Beyond Culture.* Englewood Cliff, NJ: Prentice Hall Regents, 1991.

Asante, Molefi Kete. *The Afrocentric Idea.* Philadelphia: Temple University Press, 1987.

Asante, Molefi Kete. *Afrocentricity: The Theory of Social Change in Contemporary Black Thought.* Trenton, NJ: African World Press, 1988.

Asante, Molefi Kete and Kariamu Asante. *African Culture: The Rhythms of Unity.* Trenton, NJ: African World Press, 1990.

Ayres, Alex, ed. *The Wisdom of Martin Luther King, Jr.: An A-to-Z Guide to the Ideas and Ideals of the Great Civil Rights Leader.* New York: Merridian, 1993.

Barnes and Noble Books. *The Encyclopedia of Eastern Philosophy and Religion.* New York: Otto Willhelm-Barth Verlag, 1986.

Baldwin, Lewis V. *There is a Balm in Gilead: The Cultural Roots of Martin Luther King, Jr.* Minneapolis: Fortress Press, 1991.

Balswick, Jack O. and J. Kenneth Moreland. *Social Problems: A Christian Understanding and Response.* Grand Rapids, MI: Baker, 1990.

Barnett, Victoria J., ed. *Shalom Papers: A Journal of Theology and Public Policy, Spring 2000, Vol. 11, No. 2.* Washington, DC: Center for Theology and Public Policy, 2000.

Billingsley, Andrew. *Climbing Jacob's Ladder: The Enduring Legacy of African-American Families.* New York: Simon & Schuster, 1992.

Billingsley, Andrew. *Mighty Like a River: The Black Church and Social Reform.* Oxford, UK Oxford University Press, 1999.

Birch, Bruce C. *Let Justice Roll Down: The Old Testament, Ethics and Christianity.* Louisville, KY: Westminster John Knox Press, 1991.

Birch, Bruce C. *To Love As We Are Loved: The Bible and Relationships.* Nashville, TN: Abingdon, 1992.

Birch, Bruce C. *What Does the Lord Require? The Old Testament Call to Social Witness.* Philadelphia: Westminster Press, 1985.

Birch, Bruce C. and Larry L. Rasmussen. *The Predicament of the Prosperous.* Philadelphia: Westminster Press, 1978.

Bondurant, Joan V. *Conquest of Violence: The Gandhian Philosophy of Conflict.* Princeton, NJ: Princeton University Press, 1958.

Bonhoeffer, Dietrich. *The Cost of Discipleship.* New York: Collier Books, 1949, First published in 1937.

Boyd, Herb and Robert L. Allen, ed. *Brotherman: The Odyssey of Black Men in America – An Anthology.* New York: Ballantine Books, 1995.

Brightman, Edgar S. *Moral Laws.* New York: Abingdon Press, 1933.

Brislin, Richard W. *Improving Intercultural Interactions: Modules of Cross-Cultural Training Programs.* Thousand Oak, CA: Sage Publishers, 1994.

Brueggemann, Walter. *Living Towards a Vision: Biblical Reflections on Shalom.* New York: United Church Press, 1976.

Brueggemann, Walter. *The Prophetic Imagination.* Minneapolis: Fortress Press, 1978.

Bruteau, Beatrice. *What We Can Learn From the East.* New York: Crossroad, 1995.

Budge, E. A. Wallis. *The Egyptian Book of the Dead.* New York: Bell Publishing, 1960.

Caldwell, Gilbert H. *Race, Racism and Reconciliation.* Philadelphia: Simon, 1989.

Carson, Clayborne, ed. *The Papers of Martin Luther King, Jr., Volume I: Called to Serve.* Berkley CA: University of California Press, 1992.

Carson, Clayborne, ed. *The Papers of Martin Luther King, Jr., Volume II: Rediscovering Precious Values.* Berkley, CA: University of California Press, 1994.

Carson, Clayborne, ed. *The Papers of Martin Luther King, Jr., Volume III: Birth of a New Age.* Berkley, CA: University of California Press, 1997.

Carson, Clayborne and Peter Holloran, ed. *A Knock At Midnight: Inspiration from the Great Sermons of Reverend Martin Luther King, Jr.* New York: Warner Books, 2000.

Cauthen, Kenneth. *The Impact of American Religious Liberalism.* New York: Harper & Row, 1962.

Chapman, Mark L. *Christianity on Trial: African-American Religious Thought Before and After Black Power.* Maryknoll, NY: Orbis Books, 1996.

Chopp, Rebecca. *The Praxis of Suffering.* Maryknoll, NY: Orbis Books, 1986.

Condon, John C. and Fathi Yousef. *An Introduction to Intercultural Communication.* New York: Macmillan, 1975.

Cone, Cecil. *The Identity Crisis in Black Theology.* Nashville: AMEC Press, 1975.

Cone, James H. *A Black Theology of Liberation.* New York: J. B. Lippincott Co, 1970.

Cone, James H. *Black Theology and Black Power.* New York: Harper & Row, 1969.

Cone, James H. *For My People: Black Theology and the Black Church.* Maryknoll, NY: Orbis Books, 1984.

Cone, James H. *God of the Oppressed.* New York: Seabury Press, 1975.

Cone, James H. *Martin and Malcolm and America: A Dream or a Nightmare.* Maryknoll: NY: Orbis Books, 1991.

Cone, James H. *My Soul Looks Back.* Maryknoll, NY: Orbis Books, 1995.

Cone, James H. *Speaking the Truth: Ecumenism, Liberation and*

Black Theology. Maryknoll, NY: Orbis, 1986.

Cone, James H. *The Spirituals and the Blues.* Maryknoll, NY: Orbis, 1972.

Cooper-Lewter, Nicholas and Henry Mitchell. *Soul Theology: The Heart of American Black Culture.* Nashville: Abingdon Press, 1986.

Cousins, Ewert H. *Christ of the 21ˢᵗ Century.* New York: Continuum, 1998.

Cox, Harvey. *Many Mansions: A Christian's Encounter with Other Faiths.* Boston: Beacon Press, 1988.

Dalton, Harlan. *Racial Healing: Confronting the Fear Between Blacks and Whites.* New York: Anchor Books, 1995.

Dash, Michael I. N., Jonathan Jackson and Stephen C. Rasor. *Hidden Wholeness: An African American Spirituality for Individuals and Communities.* Cleveland, OH: United Church Press, 1997.

Davies, Susan E. and Sister Paul Teresa Hennessee, S.A. *Ending Racism in the Church.* Cleveland, OH: United Church Press, 1998.

Davis, Cyprian. *The History of Black Catholics in the United States.* New York: Crossroad, 1990.

Davis, Kortright. *Serving with Power: Reviving the Spirit of Christian Ministry.* New York: Paulist Press, 1999.

Dear, John, ed. *Henri Nouwen: The Road to Peace.* Maryknoll, NY: Orbis Books, 1998.

Deats, Richard. *Martin Luther King, Jr.: Spirit-Led Prophet - A Biography.* New York: New York City Press, 2000.

Dennis, Marie, Joseph Nangle, Cynthia Moe-Lobeda and Stuart Taylor. *St. Francis and the Foolishness of God.* New York: Orbis Books, 1993.

DeYoung, Curtis Paul. *Coming Together: The Bible's Message in an Age of Diversity.* Valley Forge, PA: Judson Press, 1995.

DuBois, W. E. B. *The Souls of Black Folk.* Chicago: A. C. McClurg & Co., 1903.

Dungy, Robert E. *Dimensions of Spirituality in the Black Experience.* Nashville: Abingdon, 1992.

Dyson, Michael Eric. *I May Not Get There With You: The True Martin Luther King, Jr.* New York: Free Press, 2000.

Dyson, Michael Eric. *Making Malcolm: The Myth and Meaning of Malcolm X.* Oxford, UK: Oxford University Press, 1995.

Dyson, Michael Eric. *Reflecting Black: African-American Cultural Criticism.* Minneapolis: University of Minnesota Press, 1993.

Egan, Eileen. *Peace Be With You: Justified Warfare or the Way of Nonviolence.* Maryknoll, NY: Orbis, 1999.

Ela, Jean-Marc. *My Faith as an African.* Maryknoll, NY: Orbis Books, 1988.

Ellis, Anne Leo, ed. *First, We Must Listen.* New York: Friendship Press, 1996.

Elmer, Duane. *Cross-Cultural Conflict: Building Relationships for Effective Ministry.* Downers Grove, IL: InterVarsity Press, 1993.

Erikson, Erik H. *Gandhi's Truth: On the Origins of Militant Nonviolence.* New York: .W. Norton, 1969.

Erskine, Noel Leo. *King Among the Theologians.* Cleveland, OH: Pilgrim Press, 1994.

Evans, James H. *We Have Been Believers: An African-American Systematic Theology.* Minneapolis: Fortress Press, 1992.

Featherstone, Mike. *Undoing Culture: Globalization, Postmodernism and Identity.* London, UK: SAGE Publications, 1995.

Felder, Cain Hope. *Troubling Biblical Waters: Race, Class and Family.* Maryknoll, NY: Orbis, 1989.

Fitzgerald, Kelley, ed. *Racism: The Church's Unfinished Agenda – A Journal of the National United Methodist Convocation on Racism.* Washington, DC: The United Methodist Church, General Commission on Religion and Race, 1987.

Fitts, Leroy. *A History of Black Baptists.* Nashville: Boardman Press, 1985.

Fluker, Walter Earl, ed. *The Stones the Builders Rejected: The Development of Ethical Leadership from the Black Church Tradition.* Harrisburg, PA: Trinity Press International, 1998.

Fluker, Walter Earl. *They Looked For a City: A Comparative Analysis of the Ideal of Community in the Thought of Howard Thurman and Martin Luther King, Jr.* New York: University Press of America, 1989.

Fluker, Walter Earl and Catherine Tumber, eds. *A Strange Free-*

dom: The Best of Howard Thurman on Religious Experience and Public Life. Boston: Beacon Books, 1998.

Foster, Charles R. *Embracing Diversity.* Washington, DC: Alban Institute, 1997.

Foster, Charles R. and Theodore Brelsford. *We are the Church Together: Cultural Diversity in Congregational Life.* Valley Forge, PA: Trinity Press International, 1996.

Fong, Bruce W. *Racial Equality in the Church: A Critique of the Homogeneous Unit Principle in Light of a Practical Theology Perspective.* Lanham, MD: University Press of America, 1996.

Fowler, James. *Stages of Faith.* San Francisco: Harper & Row, 1981.

Fox, Matthew. *Creation Spirituality: Liberation Gifts for the Peoples of the Earth.* New York: Harper, 1991.

Fox, Matthew. *Original Blessing.* Santa Fe, NM: Bear and Company, 1983.

Fox, Matthew. *A Spirituality Named Compassion and the Healing of the Global Village, Humpty Dumpty and Us.* Minneapolis: Winston Press, 1979.

Franklin, John Hope and Alfred A. Moss, Jr. *From Slavery to Freedom: A History of African Americans.* New York: McGraw Hill, 1994.

Franklin, Robert M. *Another Day's Journey: Black Church Confronting the American Crisis.* Minneapolis: Fortress Press, 1997.

Franklin, Robert M. *Liberating Visions: Human Fulfillment and Social Justice in African American Thought.* Minneapolis: Fortress Press, 1990.

Frazier, E. Franklin. *The Negro Church in America.* New York: Schocken Books, 1963.

Fulop, Timothy E. and Albert J. Raboteau, eds. *African-American Religion: Interpretive Essays in History and Culture.* New York: Routledge, 1997.

Gandhi, Mohandas K. *The Way to God.* Berkley, CA: Berkley Hills Books, 1999.

Garrow, David J. *Bearing the Cross: Martin Luther King, Jr. and the Southern Christian Leadership Conference.* New York: Quill, 1986.

Gates, Henry Louis and Cornel West. *The African American Century: How Black Americans Have Shaped Our Century.* New York: Free Press, 2000.

Gaustad, Edwin S., ed. *A Documentary History of Religion in America, Since 1865.*

Grand Rapids, MI: Eerdmans Publishing, 1993.

Gillian, James. *Violence: Reflections on a National Epidemic.* New York: Vintage Books, 1996.

Goldberg, David Theo, ed. *Multiculturalism: A Critical Reader.* Oxford, UK: Blackwell, 1994.

Griggs, Lewis Brown and Lente-Louise Louw. *Valuing Diversity: New Tools for a New Reality.* New York: McGraw Hill, 1995.

Gudykunst, William B. and Young Yun Kim. *Communicating with Strangers: An Approach to Intercultural Communication.* Reading, MA: Addison-Wesley Publishing, 1984.

Gutierrez, Gustavo. *On Job: God-Talk and the Suffering of the Innocent.* Maryknoll, NY: Orbis Books, 1985.

Gutierrez, Gustavo. *A Theology of Liberation.* Maryknoll: NY: Orbis Books, 1971.

Gutierrez, Gustavo. *We Drink from Our Own Wells: The Spiritual Journey of a People.* Maryknoll, NY: Orbis Books, 1984.

Hall, Edward T. *Beyond Culture.* New York: Doubleday, 1976.

Hall, Edward T. *The Dance of Life.* New York: Doubleday, 1983.

Hall, Edward T. *The Hidden Dimension.* New York: Doubleday, 1966.

Hall, Edward T. *The Silent Language.* New York: Doubleday, 1973.

Harding, Vincent. *Hope and History: Why We Must Share the Story of the Movement.* Maryknoll: New York: Orbis, 1990.

Haring, Bernard. *The Healing Power of Peace and Non-violence.* New York: Paulist Press, 1986.

Harris, James H. *Pastoral Theology: A Black Church Perspective.* Minneapolis: Fortress Press, 1991.

Hooks, Bell and Cornel West. *Breaking Bread: Insurgent Black Intellectual Life.* Boston, MA: South End Press, 1991.

Hopkins, Dwight N. *Introduction to Black Theology of Liberation.* Maryknoll: NY: Orbis, 1999.

Hopkins, Dwight N. *Shoes That Fit Our Feet: Sources for a Constructive Black Theology.* Maryknoll, NY: Orbis, 1993.

Hunt, C. Anthony. *The Black Family: The Church's Role in the African American Community.* Bristol, IN: Wyndham Hall Press, 2000.

Ivory, Luther D. *Toward a Theology of Radical Involvement: The Theological Legacy of Martin Luther King, Jr.* Nashville, TN: Abingdon, 1997.

Jesudasan, Ignatius. *A Gandhian Theology of Liberation.* Maryknoll, NY: Orbis, 1984.

James, William. *The Varieties of Religious Experience: A Study of Human Nature – Being the Gifford Lectures on Natural Religion Delivered at Edinburgh in 1901-1902.* New York: The Modern Library, 1999.

Johnson, Alonzo. *Good News for the Disinherited: Howard Thurman on Jesus of Nazareth and Human Liberation.* New York: University Press of America, 1997.

Johnson, Charles. *Dreamer: A Novel.* New York: Scribner, 1998.

Johnson, Charles and Bob Adelman. *King: The Photobiography of Martin Luther King, Jr.* New York: Viking Studio/Penguin Group, 2000.

Jones, Cheslyn, Jeffrey Wainwright and Edward Yarnold, eds. *The Study of Spirituality.* Oxford, UK: Oxford University Press, 1986.

Jones, E. Stanley. *Gandhi: Portrayal of a Friend.* Nashville: Abingdon, 1948.

Jordan, Clarence. *Sermon on the Mount.* Valley Forge, PA: Judson Press, 1952.

Kapur, Sudarshan. *Raising Up a Prophet: The African American Encounter with Gandhi.* Boston: Beacon Press, 1992.

King, Bernice A. *Hard Questions: Heart Answers.* New York: Broadway Books, 1997.

King, Coretta Scott, *My Life with Martin Luther King, Jr.* New York: Holt, Reinhart, and Winston, 1969.

King, Martin Luther, Jr. "A Comparison of the Conceptions of God in the Thinking of Paul Tillich and Henry Nelson Wieman." Ph.D. dissertation. Boston, MA: Boston University, 1955.

King, Martin Luther, Jr. *The Measure of a Man.* Philadelphia: Fortress Press, 1988.

King, Martin Luther, Jr. *Strength to Love.* New York: Harper &

Row, 1963.

King, Martin Luther, Jr. *Stride Toward Freedom: The Montgomery Story*. New York: Harper & Row, 1958.

King, Martin Luther, Jr. *The Trumpet of Conscience*. New York: Harper & Row, 1967.

King, Martin Luther, Jr. *Where Do We Go From Here: Chaos or Community?* New York: Harper & Row, 1967.

King, Martin Luther, Jr. *Why We Can't Wait*. New York: HarperCollins, 1963.

Kohls, L. Robert. *Developing Intercultural Awareness*. Yarmouth, ME: Intercultural Press, 1994.

Kunjufu, Jawanzaa. *Hip-Hop vs. MAAT: A Psycho/Social Analysis of Values*. Chicago: African American Images, 1993.

Law, Eric H. F. *The Bush Was Burning, But Not Consumed*. St. Louis, MO: Chalice Press, 1996.

Law, Eric H. F. *Inclusion: Making Room for Grace*. St. Louis, MO: Chalice Press, 2000.

Law, Eric H. F. *The Wolf Shall Dwell with the Lamb: A Spirituality for Leadership in a Multicultural Community*. St. Louis, MO: Chalice Press, 1993.

Lebacqz, Karen. *Justice in an Unjust World*. Minneapolis: Augsburg Publishing House, 1987.

Lerner, Michael and Cornel West. *Jews and Blacks: Let the Healing Begin*. New York: Grosset Putnam, 1995.

Lewis, C. S. *The Four Loves*. San Diego, CA: Harcourt Brace and Company, 1960.

Lincoln, C. Eric. *The Black Church Since Frazier*. New York: Schocken Books, 1974.

Lincoln, C. Eric. *Coming Through the Fire: Surviving Race and Place in America*. Durham, NC: Duke University Press, 1996.

Lincoln, C. Eric. *Martin Luther King: A Profile*. New York: Hill & Wang, 1970.

Lincoln, C. Eric. *Race, Religion and the Continuing American Dilemma*. New York: Hill & Wang, 1984.

Lincoln, C. Eric and Lawrence Mamiya. *The Black Church in the African-American Experience*. Durham, NC: Duke University Press, 1990.

Lingenfelter, Sherwood G. *Ministering Cross-Culturally: An*

Incarnational Model for Personal Relationships. Grand Rapids, MI: Baker Books House, 1986.

Litteral, Robert Lee. *Community Partnership in Communications for Ministry.* Wheaton, IL: Billy Graham Center, Wheaton College, 1988.

Locke, Don C. *Increasing Multicultural Understanding.* Thousand Oaks, CA; Sage Publications, 1992.

Long, Edward, L. *Peace Thinking in a Warring World: An Urgent Call for a New Approach to Peace.* Philadelphia: Westminster Press, 1983.

Lovin, Robin, et al. *Creating a New Community: God's People Overcoming Racism.* Nashville: Graded Press, 1989.

Lyght, Ernest S. *The Religious and Philosophical Foundations in the Thought of Martin Luther King, Jr.* New York: Vantage Press, 1972.

Lynd, Straughton and Alice Lynd, eds. *Nonviolence in America: A Documentary History.* Maryknoll, NY: Orbis, 1995.

Macquarrie, John. *Christian Unity and Christian Diversity.* London: SCM Press, 1975.

Marable, Manning. *Race, Reform, and Rebellion: The Second Reconstruction in Black America: Problems in Race, Political Economy, and Society.* Boston: South End Press, 1983.

Marty, Martin E. *Pilgrims in Their Own Land: 500 Years of Religion in America.* New York: Penguin Books, 1984.

Maas, Robin. *Crucified Love.* Nashville: Abingdon, 1989.

Mathabane, Mark. *Kaffir Boy: The True Story of a Black Youth's Coming of Age in Apartheid South Africa.* New York: Plume, 1986.

Matsuoka, Fumitaka. *The Color of Faith: Building Community in a Multicultural Society.* Cleveland, OH: United Church Press, 1998.

Mbiti, John. *African Religions and Philosophy.* New York: Anchor Books, 1970.

McClain, William B. *Black People in the United Methodist Church: Whither Thou Goest?* Nashville: Abingdon, 1990.

McClain, William B. *Travelling Light.* New York: Friendship Press, 1981.

McClendon, James Wm. *Biography as Theology.* Philadelphia:

Trinity Press International, 1974.

Merton, Thomas. *Contemplation in a World of Action.* Notre Dame, IN: University of Notre Dame Press, 1998.

Merton, Thomas. *Faith and Violence: Christian Teaching and Christian Practice.* Notre Dame, IN: University of Notre Dame Press, 1968.

Merton, Thomas. *The Nonviolent Alternative (*Revised edition of *Thomas Merton on Peace).* New York: Farrar, Straus and Giroux, 1980.

Metzger, Bruce M. and Roland E. Murphy, eds. *The New Oxford Annotated Bible with the Apocryphal/Deuterocanonical Books (New Revised Standard Version).* New York: Oxford University Press, 1991.

Metzger, Bruce M. and Michael D. Coogan, eds. *The Oxford Companion to the Bible.* New York: Oxford University Press, 1993.

Miller, Craig Kennet. *Postmoderns: The Beliefs, Hopes and Fears of Young Americans.* Nashville, TN: Discipleship Resources, 1996.

Mitchell, Mozella Gordon. "The Dynamics of Howard Thurman's Relationship to Literature and Theology." Ph.D. dissertation. Atlanta: Emory University, 1983.

Mitchell, Mozella Gordon. *Spiritual Dynamics of Howard Thurman's Theology.* Bristol, IN: Wyndham Hall Press, 1985.

Moyd, Olin P. *Redemption in Black Theology.* Valley Forge, PA: Judson Press, 1979.

Moyd, Olin P. *The Sacred Art: Preaching and Theology in the African American Tradition.* Valley Forge, PA: Judson Press, 1995.

Niebuhr, H. Richard. *Christ and Culture.* New York: Haprer & Row, 1951.

Niebuhr, Reinhold. *Moral Man and Immoral Society.* New York: Scribner, 1933.

Nouwen, Henri J. M. *The Path of Peace.* New York: Crossroad, 1995.

Nunez, Emilio A., translated by Paul E. Sywulka. *Liberation Theology.* Chicago: Moody Press, 1995.

Oates, Stephen B. *Let the Trumpet Sound: A Life of Martin Luther King, Jr.* New York: HarperPerennial, 1982.

Paige, R. Michael. ed. *Cross-Cultural Orientation: New Conceptualization and Application.* Lanham, MD: University Press of America, 1986.

Panikkar, Raimundo. *The Unknown Christ in Hinduism.* Revised edition. Maryknoll, NY: Orbis Books, 1982.

Park, Andrew Sung. *Racial Conflict and Healing: An Asian-American Theological Perspective.* New York: Orbis, 1996.

Paris, Peter. *Black Religious Leaders: Conflict and Unity.* Louisville: Westminster/John Knox Press, 1991.

Paris, Peter J. *The Social Teaching of the Black Churches.* Philadelphia: Fortress Press, 1985.

Paris, Peter J. *The Spirituality of African Peoples: The Search for a Common Moral Discourse.* Minneapolis: Fortress Press, 1995.

Peck, M. Scott. *The Different Drum: Community Making and Peace: A Spiritual Journey Toward Self-Acceptance, True Belonging and New Hope for the World.* New York: Touchstone Books, 1987.

Peck, M. Scott. *People of the Lie: The Hope for Healing Human Evil.* New York: Simon & Schuster, 1983.

Phillips, Donald T. *Martin Luther King, Jr. on Leadership.* New York: Warner Books, 1998.

Pollard, Alton B., III. *Mysticism and Social Change: The Social Witness of Howard Thurman.* New York: Lang, 1992.

Raboteau, Albert. *Canaan Land: A Religious History of African Americans.* Oxford, UK; Oxford University Press, 2001.

Rauschenbusch, Walter. *Christianity and the Social Crisis.* New York; Harper & Row, 1907.

Recinos, Harold J. *Jesus Weeps: Global Encounters on Our Doorstep.* Nashville: Abingdon, 1992.

Recinos, Harold J. *Who Comes in the Name of the Lord: Jesus at the Margins.* Nashville: Abingdon, 1997.

Reid, Stephen Breck. *Listening In: A Multicultural Reading of the Psalms.* Nashville: Abingdon, 1997.

Roberts, J. Deotis. *Africentric Christianity: A Theological Appraisal for Ministry.* Valley Forge, PA: Judson Press, 2000.

Roberts, J. Deotis. *Liberation and Reconciliation: A Black Theology.* New York: Orbis, 1994.

Roberts, J. Deotis. *The Prophethood of Black Believers: A African*

American Political Theology for Ministry. Louisville, KY: Wesminster John Knox Press, 1994.

Samovar, Larry and Richard Porter, *Communication Between Cultures.* Belmont, CA: Wadsworht Publishing Company, 1991.

Schneier, Marc. *Shared Dreams: Martin Luther King, Jr. and The Jewish Community.* Woodstock, VT: Jewish Lights, 1999.

Sernett, Milton C., ed. *Afro-American Religious History: A Documentary Witness.* Durham, NC: Duke University Press, 1985.

Shannon, William H. *Seeds of Peace: Contemplation and Non-Violence.* New York: Crossroad Publishing, 1996.

Smith, Elise C. and Louise Fiber Luce. *Toward Internationalism: Readings in Cross-Cultural Communication.* Rowley, MA: Newbury House publishers, 1979.

Smith, Huston, *The Religions of Man.* New York: Harper & Row, 1986.

Smith, Kenneth L. and Ira Zepp, Jr.. *Search for the Beloved Community: The Thinking of Martin Luther King, Jr.* Valley Forge, PA: Judson Press, 1974, 1998.

Smith, Luther E., Jr. *Howard Thurman: The Mystic as Prophet.* Richmond, Indiana: Friends United Press, 1991.

Sobrino, Jon. *Spirituality of Liberation: Toward Political Holiness.* Maryknoll: Orbis Books, 1988.

Solle, Dorothy. *Suffering.* Philadelphia: Fortress Press, 1975.

Solle, Dorothee. *Thinking About God: An Introduction to Theology.* Philadelphia: Trinity Press, 1990.

Sonnenschein, William. *The Diversity Toolkit: How You Can Build and Benefit from a Diverse Workplace.* Chicago: Contemporary Books, 1997.

Sowell, Thomas S. *Race and Culture: A World View.* New York: Basic Books, 1994.

Spencer, Jon Michael. *Protest and Praise: Sacred Music of Black Religion.* Minneapolis: Fortress Press, 1990.

Steele, Shelby. *The Content of Our Character: A New Vision for Race in America.* New York: HarperPerennial, 1990.

Stewart, Carlyle Fielding, III. *African-American Church Growth: 12 Principles for Prophetic Ministry.* Nashville: Abingdon, 1994.

Stewart, Carlyle Fielding, III. "A Comparative Analysis of Theological-Ontological and Ethical Method in the Theologies of James H. Cone and Howard Thurman." Ph.D. dissertation. Evanston, IL: Northwestern University, 1982.

Stewart, Carlyle Fielding, III. *God, Being and Liberation: A Comparative Analysis of the Theologies of James Cone and Howard Thurman.* Lanham, MD: University Press, 1989.

Stewart, Carlyle Fielding, III. *Soul Survivors: An African American Spirituality.* Louisville, KY: Westminster John Knox, 1997.

Stewart, Edward C. and Milton J. Bennett. *American Cultural Patterns: A Cross-Cultural Persepective.* Yarmouth, ME, Intercultural Press, 1991.

Storti, Craig. *Cross-Cultural Dialogues.* Yarmouth, ME: Intercultural Press, 1994.

Storti, Craig. *The Art of Crossing Cultures.* Yarmouth, ME: Intercultural Press, 1989.

Stott, John R. W. *The Message of the Sermon on the Mount (Matthew 5-7) – Christian Counter-Culture.* Downers Grove, IL: InterVarsity Press, 1978.

Thomas, James S. *Methodism's Racial Dilemma: The Story of the Central Jurisdiction.* Nashville: Abingdon, 1992.

Thompson, Marjorie. *Soul Feast: An Invitation to the Christian Spiritual Life.* Louisville, KY: Westminster John Knox Press, 1995.

Thurman, Howard. *Apostles of Sensitiveness.* Boston: American Unitarian Association, 1956.

Thurman, Howard. *The Centering Moment.* Richmond, IN: Friends United Press, 1969.

Thurman, Howard. *The Creative Encounter: An Interpretation of Religion and The Social Witness.* Richmond, IN: Friends United Press, 1954.

Thurman, Howard. *Deep is the Hunger: Meditations for Apostles of Sensitiveness.* New York: Harper and Brothers, 1951.

Thurman, Howard. *Deep River: An Interpretation of Negro Spirituals.* Mills College, CA: Eucalyptus Press, 1945.

Thurman, Howard. *Deep River and the Negro Spiritual Speaks of Life and Death.* Richmond, IN: Friends United Press, 1975.

Thurman, Howard. *Disciplines of the Spirit.* Richmond, IN: Friends United Press, 1963.

Thurman, Howard, ed. *The First Footprints – The Dawn of the Idea of the Church for the Fellowship of All Peoples: Letters Between Alfred Fisk and Howard Thurman.* San Francisco: Lawton and Alfred Kennedy, 1975.

Thurman, Howard. *Footprints of a Dream: The Story of the Church for the Fellowship of All Peoples.* New York: Harper & Row, 1959.

Thurman, Howard. *For the Inward Journey: The Writings of Howard Thurman.* Richmond, IN: Friends United Press, 1984.

Thurman, Howard. *The Greatest of These.* Mills College, CA: Eucalyptus Press, 1944.

Thurman, Howard. *The Growing Edge.* Richmond, IN: Friends United Press, 1956.

Thurman, Howard. *The Inward Journey.* New York: Harper & Row, 1961, Richmond, IN: Friends United Press, 1971.

Thurman, Howard. *Jesus and the Disinherited.* Richmond, IN: Friends United Press, 1969.

Thurman, Howard. *The Luminous Darkness.* Richmond, IN: Friends United Press, 1965.

Thurman, Howard. *Meditations for Apostles of Sensitiveness.* Mills College, CA: Eucalyptus Press, 1947.

Thurman, Howard. *Meditations of the Heart.* Richmond, IN: Friends United Press, 1953.

Thurman, Howard. *The Mood of Christmas.* Richmond, IN: Friends United Press, 1969.

Thurman, Howard. *Mysticism and the Experience of Love.* Wallingford, PA: Pendle Hill, 1961.

Thurman, Howard. *The Negro Spiritual Speaks of Life and Death.* New York: Harper & Row, 1947.

Thurman, Howard. *The Search for Common Ground: An Inquiry into the Basis of Man's Experience of Community.* Richmond, Indiana: Friends United Press, 1971.

Thurman, Howard. *Temptations of Jesus: Five Sermons.* Richmond, Indiana: Friends United Press, 1962.

Thurman, Howard, ed. *A Track to the Water's Edge: The Olive Schreiner Reader.* New York: Harper & Row, 1973.

Thurman, Howard. *With Head and Heart: The Autobigraphy of Howard Thurman.* New York: Harcourt, Brace and Jovanovich,

1979.

Tillich, Paul. *Love, Power, and Justice.* London: Oxford University Press, 1954.

Tillich, Paul. *Theology of Peace.* Louisville: Westminster/John Knox, 1990.

Townes, Emily M., ed. *A Troubling in My Soul: Womanist Perspectives on Evil and Suffering.* New York: Orbis, 1993.

Townes, Emily M., ed. *Embracing the Spirit: Womanist Perspectives on Hope, Salvation and Transformation.* New York: Orbis, 1997.

Townes, Emily M. *In a Blaze of Glory: Womanist Spirituality As Social Witness.* Abingdon, 1995.

Tutu, Desmond. *No Future Without Forgiveness.* New York: Doubleday, 1999.

Volf, Miroslav. *Exclusion or Embrace: A Theological Exploration of Identity, Otherness, and Reconciliation.* Nashville: Abingdon, 1996.

Walker, Wyatt T. *Somebody's Calling My Name: Black Sacred Music and Social Change.* Valley Forge, PA: Judson Press, 1992.

Wallis, Jim. *The Soul of Politics: Beyond the "Religious Right" and "Secular Left."* San Diego, CA: Harcourt Brace and Company, 1994.

Ward, Graham, ed. *The Postmodern God: A Theological Reader.* Oxford, UK: Blackwell Publishers, 1997.

Washington, James Melvin. *Frustrated Fellowships: The Black Baptist Quest for Social Power.* Macon: Mercer University Press, 1986.

Washington, James Melvin, ed. *A Testament of Hope: The Essential Writings and Speeches of Martin Luther King, Jr.* New York: Harper Collins, 1986.

Washington, Raleigh and Glen Kehrein. *Breaking Down Walls: A Model for Reconciliation in an Age of Racial Strife.* Chicago: Moody Press, 1993.

Watley, William D. *Roots of Resistance.* Valley Forge, PA: Judson Press, 1985.

West, Cornel. *Keeping Faith: Philosophy and Race in America.* New York: Routledge, 1993.

West, Cornel. *Prophesy Deliverance! An Afro-American Revolu-

tionary Christianity. Philadelphia: Westminster Press, 1982.

West, Cornel. *Prophetic Fragments: Illuminations of the Crisis in American Religion and Culture*. Grand Rapids, MI: Eerdmans, 1988.

West, Cornel. *Prophetic Reflections: Notes on Race and Power in America*. Philadelphia: Westminster Press, 1982.

West, Cornel. *Race Matters*. Boston: Beacon Press, 1991.

West, Russell W. "That His People May be One: An Interpretive Analysis of the Pentecostal Leadership's Quest of Racial Unity." Ph.D. dissertation. Virginia Beach, VA: Regent University, 1998.

Wilkerson, Barabra. *Multicultural Religious Education*. Birmingham, AL: Religious Education Press, 1997.

Williams, Patricia J. *The Alchemy of Race and Rights: Diary of a Law Professor*. Cambridge MA: Harvard University Press, 1991.

Wilmore, Gayraud. *Black Religion and Black Radicalism*. Marynoll, NY: Orbis Books, 1989.

Wilson, William Julius. *The Bridge Over the Racial Divide: Rising Inequality and Coalition Politics*. Berkley, CA: University of California Press, 1999.

Wilson, William Julius. *The Declining Significance of Race: Blacks and Changing American Institutions*. Chicago: University of Chicago Press, 1978.

Wilson, William Julius. *Power, Racism and Privilege: Race Relations in Theoretical and Sociological Perspectives*. New York: The Free Press, 1973.

Wimberly, Anne Streaty and Edward Wimberly. *Language of Hospitality: Intercultural Relations in the Household of God*. Nashville: Cokesbury, 1989.

Wink, Walter, ed. *Peace is the Way: Writings on Nonvioence from the Fellowship of Reconciliation*. New York: Orbis Books, 2000.

Wiseman, Richard L. and Jolene Koester. *Intercultural Communication Competence*. Newbury Park, CA: Sage, 1993.

Wogaman, J. Philip. *Christian Moral Judgment*. Louisville: Westminster/John Knox Press, 1989.

Wogaman, J. Philip. *Christian Perspectives on Politics*. Philadelphia: Fortress Press, 1988.

Wolterstorff, Nicholas. *Until Justice and Peace Embrace.* Grand Rapids, MI: Eerdmans, 1983.

Yates, Elizabeth. *Howard Thurman: Portrait of a Practical Dreamer.* New York: John Day, 1964.

Young, Josiah U. *Black and African Theologies: Siblings or Distant Cousins.* Maryknoll, NY: Orbis Books, 1990.

244 C. Anthony Hunt

ARTICLES

Bennett, Lerone, Jr. "Eulogy of Howard Thurman: Tributes to Genius," *The African American Pulpit.* Valley Forge, PA: Judson, Winter 2001.

Booth, Newell S. "An Approach to African Religion," *African Religions: A Symposium.* ed. Newell S. Booth. New York: NOK Publishers, 1977.

Carson, Clayborne, "Martin Luther King, Jr., and the African American Social Gospel," *African-American Religion: Interpretive Essays in History and Culture.* Timothy eds. Fulop and Albert Raboteau. New York: HarperPerennial, 1997.

Dear, John. "The Experiments of Gandhi," *Fellowship.* New York: The Fellowship of Reconciliation, January/February, 1988.

Denard, Carolyn C. "Retrieving and Reappropriating the Values of the Black Church Tradition Through Written Narratives," *The Stones that the Builders Rejected.* Ed. Walter E. Fluker. Harrisburg, PA: Trinity Press International, 1998.

Furnish, Victor P. "War and Peace in the New Testament," *Military Chaplains' Review.* Washington, DC: U.S. Army Chaplaincy Services Support Agency, Summer 1988.

Forester, Werner. "Eirene," *Theological Dictionary of the New Testament,* ed. Gerhard Kittel, translated by Geoffrey W. Bromiley. Grand Rapids: Eerdmans, 1964.

Galilea, Segundo. "Liberation as an Encounter with Politics and Contemplation," *The Mystical Dimension of the Christian Faith.* eds. Claude Gaffre and Gustavo Gutierrez. New York: Herder & Herder, 1974.

Gandhi, Mohandas K. "Nonviolence – The Greatest Force," *The World Tomorrow,* October, 1926.

Goodwin, Mary E. "Racial Roots and Religion: An Interview with Howard Thurman," *The Christian Century.* Chicago: The Christian Century, 9 May 1973.

Harding, Vincent. "We Must Keep Going: Martin Luther King, Jr. and the Future of America," *Fellowship.* New York: The Fellowship of Reconciliation, January/February, 1987.

Karenga, Maulana. "Toward a Sociology of Maatian Ethics: Literature and Context," *Egypt Revisited,* ed. Ivan Van Sertima. New Brunswick, NJ: Transaction, 1989.

King, Martin Luther, Jr. "Facing the Challenge of a New Age," *Fellowship*. New York: The Fellowship of Reconciliation, February, 1957.

King, Martin Luther, Jr. "My Pilgrimage to Nonviolence," *Fellowship*. New York: The Fellowship of Reconciliation, September, 1958.

King, Martin Luther, Jr. "Suffering and Faith," *The Christian Century*. Chicago, IL: The Christian Century, April 1960.

King, Martin Luther Jr. "The Unchristian Christian," *Ebony* 20. Chicago: Johnson Publishing, August 1965.

Maguire, Mairead Corrigan. "Gandhi and the Ancient Wisdom of Nonviolence," *Fellowship*. New York: The Fellowship of Reconciliation, June 1988.

Merton, Thomas. "Blessed are the Meek," *Fellowship*. New York: The Fellowship of Reconciliation, May 1967.

Sharp, Gene. "Disregarded History," *Fellowship*. New York: The Fellowship of Reconciliation, March 1976.

Thurman, Howard. "Mysticism and Social Change," *Eden Theological Seminary Bulletin IV.* (Spring, 1939).

Thurman, Howard. "The Will to Segregate," *Fellowship*. New York: The Fellowship of Reconciliation, August, 1943.

Williams, Robert C. "Worship and Anti-Structure in Thurman's Vision of the Sacred," *The Journal of the Interdenominational Theological Center,* eds. Melva Wilson Costen and Darius Leander Swann, Atlanta, GA, Vol. XIV, Fall 1986/Spring 1987, nos. 1 & 2.

ABOUT THE AUTHOR

C. ANTHONY HUNT

A native of Washington, DC, C. Anthony Hunt is a United Methodist Church minister currently serving as the Superintendent of the Baltimore Harford District in Maryland. He was previously the Executive Director of the Multi-Ethnic Center for Ministry of the United Methodist Church in Columbia, MD. Additionally, he is professor of Practical Theology at St. Mary's Seminary and University in Baltimore, MD, and is on the adjunct faculty at Wesley Theological Seminary in Washington, DC. Dr. Hunt is a graduate of the University of Maryland, and holds advanced degrees from Troy State University, Wesley Theological Seminary, and the Graduate Theological Foundation in affiliation with Oxford University (UK). Additionally, he has completed post-doctoral studies at St. Mary's Seminary in Baltimore, MD, and the Center of Theological Inquiry at Princeton University. He is the author of *Upon the Rock: Model for Ministry with Black Families*, and is the co-author of *Building Hope: New Church Development in the African-American Community.*

www.ingramcontent.com/pod-product-compliance
Lightning Source LLC
Chambersburg PA
CBHW030822090426
42737CB00009B/841